The History of the Prince
of Wales's Theatre,
London, 1771–1903

'The Regency Theatre' by W.H. Brooke, 1817. By permission of the London Metropolitan Archive

The History of the Prince of Wales's Theatre, London, 1771–1903

Richard L. Lorenzen

University of Hertfordshire Press

The Society for Theatre Research

First published in Great Britain in 2014 by
University of Hertfordshire Press
College Lane
Hatfield
Hertfordshire
AL10 9AB
UK

British Library Cataloguing in Publication Data
A catalogue record for this book is available from the British Library

ISBN 978-1-909291-21-8 hardback
ISBN 978-1-909291-22-5 paperback

Design by Arthouse Publishing Solutions Ltd
Printed in Great Britain by Henry Ling Ltd, Dorchester, DT1 1HD

The Society for Theatre Research

Contents

Plates

Illustrations

Acknowledgements

Research in a number of archives, beginning with the Ohio State University's Jerome Lawrence and Robert E. Lee Research Institute and progressing to the Heal Collection held by the Borough of Camden at the Highgate Library, provided me with a formidable mass of information, illustrations and reviews. Without the rich resources of the Victoria and Albert Museum Theatre and Performance Collection, the British Library, the British Newspaper Archives, Harvard University Libraries, the New York Public Library and the University of Washington Libraries, I would not have been able to complete the history of the playhouse; the *Oxford Dictionary of National Biography* online with its thorough and current information enabled me to humanise the story.

Many people contributed their expertise and guidance in the research and writing process. John McDowell, George Nash, Sybil Rosenfeld, George Speaight and George Rowell offered perspectives and insights which would have been impossible to ferret out in a timely manner. Over the years, Colin Ford contributed both resources and advice.

Editing the lengthy first draft, with the tireless Michael Gaunt offering suggestions and helping establish clear focus, was a very significant part of the final shaping of the manuscript. Dr Marion O'Connor's patience and clear editorial vision proved invaluable as the manuscript took shape. Dr O'Connor's contributions to the work are considerable, and I am grateful for her direction. Jane Housham at the University of Hertfordshire Press was indefatigable in the final process of editing, and her thoughtful questions and suggestions genuinely improved the manuscript. I would also like to thank Sarah Elvins for her many useful and important recommendations along the way. Finally, Tracey Lorenzen has provided keen editorial guidance for the manuscript as well as my life.

For all of the people who provided assistance, I owe a deep debt of gratitude.

Introduction

As the population of the city of London grew to nearly one million at the turn of the nineteenth century, so did the public appetite for entertainment. The area north of Oxford Street and west of Tottenham Court Road was the site of the Tottenham Fair in the middle of the eighteenth century, and in 1771 Francis Pasquali chose this part of the city to build a concert room. While there were other popular halls nearby, Pasquali concluded that there was sufficient demand for an additional venue for musical entertainments. The structure was modest when compared with the more ornate Pantheon, but it served him and his fashionable audiences well.

Once converted to a theatre, the playhouse became an integral part of the cultural life of the neighbourhood and the city. The Prince of Wales's Theatre, as it was known after 1865, was an unusually intimate playhouse when compared with most London theatres of the time. The earliest drawing of the interior of the playhouse, in Robert Wilkinson's *Londina Illustrata* published in 1817 (Fig. 7), provides a glimpse of a night at the theatre. In 1826, Edward Brayley reported in his *Historical and Descriptive Accounts of the Theatres of London* that the proscenium measured only 21 feet at the opening and that the distance from the front of the stage to the back wall of the house was a mere 36 feet.

From 1775, when the building was first opened, until it was closed in 1882, hundreds of artists pursued their aspirations at the theatre in Tottenham Street and thousands of theatregoers from the neighbourhood, as well as from greater London, sought an evening's entertainment at the little playhouse. This book is the story of the people who managed, performed at and attended the Prince of Wales's for nearly one hundred years.

In order to contextualise the evenings and events at the theatre in Tottenham Street, I have gathered contemporary critical reviews from newspapers and journals of the day. The British Library Newspapers and the British Newspaper Archive were essential for this effort. The reviews and commentaries help illuminate the events of those distant evenings.

The foundation for this book is the rich and diverse Heal Collection held by the Borough of Camden in Highgate Library, London. Created by Ambrose Heal of Heal's of Tottenham Court Road, the collection consists of hundreds of playbills, clippings and illustrations which document the activity at the theatre from the earliest days until it was razed in 1903. The Victoria and Albert Museum Theatre and Performance Collection possesses additional materials, in particular playbills and illustrations, which enabled the telling of a more complete story. The British Library, the National Portrait Gallery, the New York Public Library and the Harvard University Theatre Collection also contain invaluable resources for this work.

Throughout the history of the Prince of Wales's, management changes occurred with considerable frequency. To the casual observer, the theatre appeared to be under new management more often than not. A writer in the 17 April 1865 edition of *The Times* maintained that writing the history of the playhouse was a daunting task:

> The historian who would attempt to write the chronicles of the theatre in Tottenham-street should first try his hand at the Spanish American Republics. If he cannot grapple with the Presidents and ex-Presidents of the latter, assuredly he will not be able to tackle the rapidly changing managers of the former. The principles illustrated in both cases are simple enough, but the details are tremendous.

Heeding this cautionary advice, I have striven to produce a readable history of the theatrical activity at the Prince of Wales's from the beginning in 1771 to its demise in 1903. This history of diverse entertainments, the colourful artists and the audiences who frequented this playhouse is a mirror of the vital and intense theatrical activity which dominated London theatres throughout the nineteenth century. The dynamics of the popular theatre, driven by the tastes of its patrons, convey much about the tenor of the times.

Chapter One

Tottenham Court Fair, New Rooms in Tottenham Street, Concerts of Ancient Music and the Pic-Nic Society, 1717–1809

The population of London increased from 630,000 in 1715 to 1,000,000 by the turn of the nineteenth century.[1] During this period, the boundaries of London were extended beyond the old walls, and the open fields were randomly claimed for houses, shops and places of entertainment. The region north of Oxford Street and west of Tottenham Court Road, depicted on John Rocque's 1746 map (Fig. 1), was transformed from a grassy expanse of unoccupied land to a densely populated urban settlement in the second half of the eighteenth century.[2]

Newcomers to the city, showing little interest in or regard for city planning or aesthetics, built new neighbourhoods on the land flanking Tottenham Court Road. Local arbiters of taste considered this area crude and dangerous, and their worst fears were substantiated when entertainers and pugilists gathered there for the Tottenham Court Fair. However unsavoury the neighbourhood, the general populace ignored the threat of thieves, dishonest shopkeepers and entertainers to partake of the amusements.[3] The Tottenham Court Fair was a major event for that region of the city, though the exact date of the first Fair is uncertain. A 'Mr Leigh and Jubilee Dickey Norris' (identified on their advertisements 'as from the Theatre Royal') operated a theatrical booth at the Fair from 5 to 13 August in 1717.

The *Daily Courant* of 22 July 1727 reported that unlawful games and plays encouraged boisterous crowds and an epidemic of crime in the area. The local magistrates exerted their authority to protect the morals of apprentices by attempting to disperse the rogues and vagabonds performing plays. Demand for the entertainments prevailed, and the populace applauded the resumption of the Fair for the remainder of the summer season. In the following autumn and winter, the

---

1   Clive Emsley, Tim Hitchcock and Robert Shoemaker, 'London History – A Population History of London', *Old Bailey Proceedings Online* <http://www.oldbaileyonline.org>, version 7.0, accessed 27 November 2013.

2   For an engaging history of the vicinity, see E. Beresford Chancellor, *London's Old Latin Quarter* (London, 1930).

3   Sybil Rosenfeld, *The Theatre of the London Fairs in the 18th Century* (Cambridge, 1960), 121.

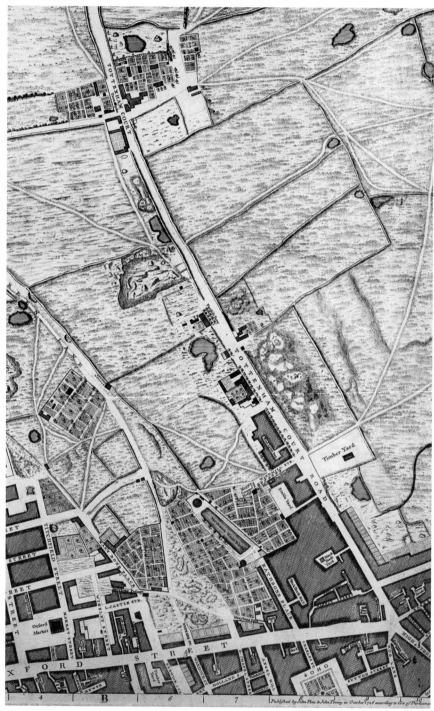

1 Rocque's Map of London, 1746. Motco Enterprises Limited, ref: http://www.motco.com

watchdogs of morality attacked the 'disgraceful behaviour and disturbances' created by the Fair, but their opposition did not prevent an anonymous dancing master from applying for a Fair patent in 1728. The request included booths for drolls, music and plays. Reporters estimated the man's potential profits at £3,000, but no Fair was held that year.[4] In 1729, a Mr Reynolds advertised his theatrical booth:

> during the time of the Fair, will be presented a Comical, Tragical, Farcical Droll, called the *Rum Duke and the Queer Duke; or, a Medley of Mirth and Sorrow*. To which will be added a celebrated operatical Puppet-show, called *Punch's Oratory, or, the Pleasures of the Town*; containing several diverting passages, particularly a very elegant dispute between Punch and another great Orator; Punch's Family Lecture, or Joan's Chimes on her tongue to some tune. No Wires – all alive! With entertainments of dancing by Monsieur St Luce, and others.[5]

By 1731, a number of booths were erected for the Tottenham Court Fair, including a 'new theatre' in Tottenham Road under the management of J. Petty offering continuous performances for two weeks in August from 10am to 9pm. In subsequent years, other booths were constructed in the area. Messrs Fielding and Hallam[6] were located close to present-day Euston Road and Tottenham Court Road; Messrs Lee, Harper and Petit also operated a booth in the same general area. Five years later in 1736, people planning excursions to the green fields and fresh air of Tottenham Court were invited to visit an 'Amphitheatrical Booth' on Easter Monday. Mr French, the manager of the establishment, informed his prospective audiences that he planned a wide variety of entertainments with generous prizes to be awarded to the victorious participants in cudgelling, wrestling, boxing and jigging. The admission was pit 2s, first gallery 1s and upper gallery 6d.[7]

All performances were regulated by law: 'the terms of the Licensing Act of 21 June 1737 prohibited the acting of legitimate drama at any place not sanctioned by a Royal patent ... creating a situation in light of which all productions of the minor theatres must be considered'.[8] Under these constraints, the various fair-theatre operators

---

4   Emmett L. Avery, *The London Stage, 1700–1729*, in Emmett L. Avery, Arthur H. Scouten, Charles Beecher Hogan, George Winchester Stone, Jr and William Van Lennep (eds), *The London Stage, 1660–1800*, 11 vols (Carbondale, IL, 1960–8), Part 2, xxvii.

5   Chancellor, *London's Old Latin Quarter*, 32.

6   Arthur Scouten (ed.), *The London Stage, 1729–1747*, in Avery et al. (eds), *London Stage, 1660–1800*, Part 3, xl. See also Jared Brown, 'Hallam, William (1712?–1758?)', *Oxford Dictionary of National Biography* (ODNB) online (Oxford, 2004) <http://www.oxforddnb.com>, accessed 18 November 2013. The Hallam family was involved in theatricals and appeared at both the fair booths and licensed theatres. It would seem likely that the Hallam involved in the venture near Tottenham Court Road was either Adam, who regularly maintained a booth at Bartholomew Fair, or possibly one of his sons, William (c.1712–58) or Lewis (1714–55). In 1751 William, after a disastrous season at Goodman's Fields Theatre, sent Lewis to Williamsburg, Virginia where he and members of the company began performing in September 1752.

7   Scouten (ed.), *London Stage, 1729–1747*, xlii–xliii.

8   *Ibid.*, li.

found little opportunity to fulfil their aspirations. Sometimes they were prosecuted and closed down, on other occasions they were allowed to present their performances without interruption. By 1744 the fairs were very active and there were 'two booths at the Tottenham Court Fair, five at Bartholomew Fair, and two at Southwark Fair, with one troupe acting sporadically on into the winter season and four in Mayfair'.[9]

In May 1744, 'the *Daily Advertiser* printed another presentment of the Middlesex Grand Jury, wherein booths at Tottenham Court Fair were singled out for mention and the constables told to apprehend the players'.[10] On 18 April 1748 'a court order was promulgated to prohibit acting at the fairs. This time Tottenham Court Fair, the Shepherd's Bush Fair, the Welsh Fair, the Mile-End Fair, Bow Fair and Mayfair were all cited. This order was more closely enforced than were previous edicts, and the gradually increasing number of performances was again reduced, if not stopped entirely.'[11]

In the vicinity of the Tottenham Court Fair site, there were several 'nurseries' or schools of self-defence operated by well-known pugilists. James Figg's nursery was near Tottenham Court and Euston Roads, and Messrs Smallwood and Taylor are known to have built an amphitheatre for boxing as early as 1720. In John Street (later named Whitfield Street[12]) Abraham Saunders opened a riding academy called the School of Bucephalus.[13] But it was not until the latter part of the eighteenth century, as the vicinity became more inhabited and less threatening to outsiders, that a permanent building for music and dramatic performances was built.

New Rooms in Tottenham Street

Francis Pasquali financed the laying of the foundations and construction of the rooms that became the New Rooms in Tottenham Street.[14] A lease dated 18 February 1771 bears the signature of Francis Pasquali (*fl.* 1743–94), a double bass player and music publisher,[15] for a plot of land described as 'all that piece or parcel of ground situate lying and being in a certain new street, new in building, intended

---

9   *Ibid.*, liv.

10 *Ibid.*, lv.

11 *Ibid.*, lix.

12 John Street was renamed Whitfield Street after the evangelist George Whitfield whose Tabernacle was built in 1756 on the west side of Tottenham Court Road between Tottenham Street and Howland Street.

13 Chancellor, *London's Old Latin Quarter*, 32ff. See also J.R. Howard Roberts and Walter H. Godfrey (gen. eds), *Survey of London*, vol. 21: *Tottenham Court Road and Neighbourhood* (London, 1949).

14 Robert Elkin, *The Old Concert Rooms of London* (London, 1955), 82–91. Elkin notes that Pasquali played in the Handel Commemoration Concerts in 1784.

15 'Pasquali, Francis', in Philip H. Highfill, Jr, Kalmin A. Burnim and Edward A. Langhans (eds), *A Biographical Dictionary of Actors, Actresses, Musicians, Dancers, Managers and Other Stage Personnel in London, 1660–1800*, 16 vols (Carbondale, IL, 1973–93), vol. 11, 230–1. Francis Pasquali was the younger brother of Niccolò Pasquali (1717–57), a musician and composer. They arrived in London from Italy in 1743. In 1745 Francis performed at the Haymarket. From 1760, Francis published music from an address in Poland Street. In 1780, he was associated with King's Theatre. Pasquali's daughter Regina married Michael Novosielski. See also *The John Marsh Journals: Life and Times of a Gentleman Composer: 1752–1828*, ed. Brian Robins (Stuyvesant, NY, 1998); and David J. Golby, 'Pasquali, Francis (1743–1795)', *ODNB*, accessed 18 November 2013.

to be called Tottenham Street in the parish of Saint Pancras and in the county of Middlesex'.[16] The size of the tract was 139 feet from north to south and 34 feet from east to west. The annual rent, exclusive of taxes, was established at £12 and the tenure of the lease was fifty-six and one-half years.[17]

Francis Pasquali supervised the design and construction of the building on the site, and while the identity of the architect is not certain, Pasquali's son-in-law was the Polish architect Michael Novosielski (1750–95), who was in London to work as assistant to James Wyatt in the building of the Pantheon from 1770 to 1772.[18] When the New Rooms, Tottenham Street were completed in late 1775, Pasquali and Novosielski were identified in the tax records as partners in the management of the building.[19] Thus, it is safe to assume that Novosielski was at the very least consulted about the design of the building, if in fact he was not the architect. In 1790–1, Novosielski rebuilt the Opera House in the Haymarket.[20]

The New Rooms were dedicated to vocal and instrumental music under the direction of Pasquali. In February of 1776, Pasquali advertised a four-night subscription season with admission of 2 guineas for three tickets (to be used by a gentleman and two ladies). Tickets were available from the New Rooms and would be delivered.[21] Vigorous competition existed among the several London concert rooms, including the Dean Street Rooms, Carlisle House, Pantheon and Willis's Rooms, for the fashionable patrons of music. The Tottenham Street Rooms, an alternative name for the building used by Pasquali, became the headquarters of the Concert of Ancient Music, established by the Earl of Sandwich and others in 1776. The organisation had a board of directors who drew up the programme.[22] Artists advertised a subscription season of no more than ten nights, to comply with licensing restrictions, and ticket sales were not permitted at the box office. Often, concerts were advertised as a benefit for the artists, who either sold the tickets themselves or entrusted them to nearby shopkeepers.

Mrs Stuart's subscription season in 1777 is representative of the musical evenings at the New Rooms under Pasquali's management. In January, she advertised in the newspaper:

> Mrs Stuart presumes to acquaint those noble subscribers who have already honoured her with their patronage and protection, as well as the nobility and Gentry in general, that her New Rooms, in Tottenham Street, near Charlotte-street, is intended to be opened on the

---

16   Original lease in Guildhall Library, London.

17   *Ibid.*

18   H.M. Colvin, *A Biographical Dictionary of English Architects, 1660–1840* (London, 1954), 121.

19   Pasquali and Novosielski are listed in the St Pancras Rate and Poor Tax records for 1776. The records are located in Holborn Public Library: Camden Local Studies and Archives Centre: St Pancras Rate Books.

20   Daniel Nalbach, *The King's Theatre, 1704–1867* (London, 1972), 28–32, 52–3.

21   *Morning Chronicle*, 20 February 1776.

22   Elkin, *Old Concert Rooms*, 83–4.

For the Benefit of Mr. Jones. a Concert of Music.
On Wednesday 21. of April.
New Rooms, Tottenham Street
Ticket.. 10.. 6

2 Benefit ticket for Mr Jones, 21 April 1779. Heal Collection,
Camden Local Studies and Archives Centre, London

last Thursday in this month, where her Winter Concert will commence. After the concert will be a ball. And Cards for those who may not choose to dance.[23]

Signor Giordani directed the musical entertainments and Mr Lamotte conducted the band. Mrs Stuart featured two other artists (adopting fashionable Italianate names to capitalise on the popularity of Italian opera in the city), Signor Savoy and Signora Cecilia Davies, from the King's Theatre, on 20 February. The major musical selection for the evening was *Acis e Galatea*, described as a new Italian cantata for three voices, to be performed by Signor Savoy, Signora Davies and Signor Hawke. The admission was five guineas for the ten-night season, and the number of subscribers was limited to four hundred.[24]

Several different artists appeared at the rooms during the next two years. Mr Jones (1752–1824) booked the New Rooms for two benefit performances beginning 21 April 1779. He was probably the noted harpist, Edward Jones, who was active in London music circles at this time.[25] Tickets for his benefit (10s 6d) could be obtained from Mr Jones at 127 New Bond Street, at Mr Welcher's Music Shop in the Haymarket and Mr Napier's Music Shop, corner of Lancaster Court in the Strand (Fig. 2). These shops were located in more fashionable areas of the city and were regularly employed by artists who appeared at the New Rooms.

Concerts of Ancient Music

In 1783 the Ancient Concerts, an organisation devoted to music at least twenty years old, signed a lease for the New Rooms.[26] The leaders of this group engaged a favourite of King George III, James Wyatt, a court architect, to build a gallery on the model of the one constructed in Westminster Abbey for Handel's Commemoration.[27] The King visited the Ancient Concerts often, and on 26 April 1784 he was accompanied by the Princess Royal, Prince Edward and the Princesses Augusta and Elizabeth. One observer noted that the Ancient Concert subscription was the only one ever honoured by the King.[28] The *Morning Chronicle* observed, 'The patronage of the KING has induced the Directors of this concert to enlarge the room, and fit it up with suitable decorations. A superb gallery is erected for the

---

23   *Morning Chronicle*, 11 January 1777.

24   Elkin, *Old Concert Rooms*, 90.

25   'Jones, Edward', in Highfill et al. (eds), *Biographical Dictionary*, vol. 8, 23–31. He was born in Wales and may have first appeared in London in 1776. By 1778 he was recommended for membership in the Royal Society of Musicians. In 1783 he was appointed bard to the Prince of Wales.

26   Programmes for the *Concerts of Antient* [sic] *Music* from 1783–94 were published with the words of the songs and choruses and the names of the artists performing each selection. They were printed for W. Lee by Henry Reynell. University of Washington Library, Eighteenth Century collections online.

27   Jocelyn Perkins, *Westminster Abbey* (London, 1937), 186.

28   *Morning Chronicle*, April 1784. The newspaper also reported that the Ancient Concerts orchestra had been supplemented by twelve German musicians brought to England for the Queen's band.

Majesties and the Royal Family, at the east end of the room.'[29] The King's attendance at the New Rooms became a regular fixture in the royal calendar. In 1785, the Ancient Concerts received the patronage of King George III. Accordingly, 'all the etiquettes, then invariably attendant on the presence of royalty, were strictly observed. His Majesty's private band and the boys of the Chapel Royal attended in their full dress liveries, and the royal family occupied a state box, to which they were regularly ushered by the director of the night and from which alone applause or encore might proceed.'[30]

The membership of the Ancient Concerts obtained free access to the rooms adjoining the central hall that were normally used for serving refreshments. In addition, a second entrance to the hall was constructed (through a house in Pitt Street that paralleled Tottenham Street, most likely number 4).[31] The new entrance, intended to facilitate a quieter entrance of the King and his entourage, mollified those who had been annoyed by the noisy arrival of the royal party through the main entrance on previous occasions. An obsequious writer in the *Morning Chronicle* suggested that the royal party should use the principal entrance and that the subscribers might use the less convenient Pitt Street passage.[32]

The Ancient Concerts (it was renamed the Concert of Ancient Music in 1786) were so successful that the directors negotiated a longer lease with Pasquali and Novosielski. The signatories of the lease were men of rank and power: Brownlow Earl of Exeter; John Earl of Sandwich; Henry Earl of Uxbridge; John Viscount Dudley and Ward; Richard Viscount Fitzwilliam of the kingdom of Ireland; Francis Lord Osborne, Marquis of Carmarthen; Thomas Lord Grey de Wilton; Sir Watkins Williams-Wynn, Baronet; and Sir Richard Jebb, Baronet.

In the late 1770s, according to the St Pancras Rate and Poor Tax records, rents were estimated at £40; by 1786, the figure had increased to £60.[33] The Ancient Concert lease provided for twelve Monday evening concerts between the first day of February and the first day of June. Twelve nights of rehearsal were stipulated in the 26 April 1786 lease and cost an additional £210. Provision was made for renegotiating the lease after seven, eleven, fourteen or seventeen years.[34]

In addition to the rent, the lessees assumed responsibility for operating expenses, including candles, charwomen, refreshments, constables, soldiers for each night and servants to ensure the comfort of guests. A schedule attached to the lease included £265 in costs for supplies and services to be paid for by the lessees:

29   *Ibid.*
30   Elkin, *Old Concert Rooms*, 84.
31   Roberts and Godfrey (eds), *Tottenham Court Road*, 33–7. Pitt Street was renamed Scala Street, presumably when the Scala Theatre opened in 1904 on the site previously occupied by the Prince of Wales's Theatre.
32   *Morning Chronicle*, 19 February 1785.
33   Holborn Public Library: Camden Local Studies and Archives Centre: St Pancras Rates Book: St Pancras Rate and Poor Tax, 1786. All subsequent references to rates and taxes are from the St Pancras Rate and Poor Tax records.
34   *St Pancras Notes and Queries*, no. 232, 180A.

candles per night £5.5s	£63.0.0
coal for nine fires	£19.14.6
8 waiters and attendants for Performances	£12.8.0
Constables	£14.8.0
2 charwomen four times a week	£ 9.12.0
pint of porter for company and servants at £3 per night	£36.0.0
refreshments for the company at £5.5s. a night	£63.0.0
4 women attending the tea-room	£ 4.16.0
King's servants	£25.4.0
soldiers 14s.6d. each night	£ 8.14.0
stabling horses for Guards	£ 4.1.6

The building was fitted with an organ, music stands, sofas, seats and benches, four large lustres in the Great Room, stoves, carpets, chairs and furniture of every sort in and about the premises. The busts of Handel and Purcell, furniture in the King's Box, two large lustres in the Great Room and four pictures of Handel, Geminiani, Purcell and Corelli belonged to the lessees.[35]

The royal family attended an early concert arranged by Sir Richard Jebb.[36] The selection of airs, choruses and full pieces focused on the works of Handel, with Pergolesi, Martini, Geminiani and Gluck also on the programme. Samuel Harrison (1760–1812) sang Gluck's 'Rasserena il mesto ciglio' from *Artamene*. He was one of the leading singers for the Ancient Concerts until 1789 when he was replaced by Michael Kelly.[37] Madame Mara presented with inimitable grace and feeling 'Ah! mio cor' from *Alcina* and an English piece, 'Heart, the Seat of Soft Delight', which was less appreciated. The high point of the evening was the popular 'Hallelujah Chorus', enthusiastically repeated at the demand of the audience. Handel's appeal to audiences had increased, as the result of growing familiarity and in deference to the King. Because the King was partial to Handel, the Concert of Ancient Music evenings regularly featured his work.

During its first few seasons, the Concert of Ancient Music presented several notable performers: Madame Gertrud Elisabeth Mara (1749–1833), Mr Parke, Mr Harrison, Mr Knyvett (1752–1822) and Wilhelm Cramer (1746–99) whom many, including the King, thought the best conductor in England.[38] In 1784, shortly

---

35   *Ibid.*

36   Programme for *Concert of Antient [sic] Music*, 22 March 1784.

37   Highfill et al. (eds), *Biographical Dictionary*, vol. 7, 143–5. See also *The Harmonicon* (London, 1830), I, 181; and L.M. Middleton, 'Harrison, Samuel (1760–1812)', rev. Anne Pimlott Baker, *ODNB*, accessed 18 November 2013. He was born in Belper, near Duffield, in Derbyshire. He was a leading performer in oratorios at several London theatres.

38   'Cramer, Wilhelm', in Highfill et al. (eds), *Biographical Dictionary*, vol. 4, 27–30. See also Nicolas Slonimsky (ed.), *Baker's Biographical Dictionary of Musicians* (New York, 1958). Cramer was born in Mannheim and was a violinist. He came to London in 1772 and was successful as a concert performer and conductor.

3 Madame Mara as Armida, 1794. Courtesy of the New York Public Library

after Madame Mara arrived in London, she became associated with the Ancient Concerts. According to her contemporaries, she performed Handel's compositions with natural grandeur and effect.[39] Madame Mara (Fig. 3) possessed a clear and distinct voice well suited to Handel's works, and her contributions to the Tottenham Street evenings earned her favourable comparison with Signora Storace, a leading artist of the day.

---

39   'Mara, Mrs Gertrud Elisabeth', in Highfill et al. (eds), *Biographical Dictionary*, vol. 10, 77–87; Michael Burden, 'Mara, Gertrud Elisabeth (1749–1833)', *ODNB*, accessed 18 November 2013; and Theodore Baker, *Biographical Dictionary of Musicians* (New York, 1900). She was born in Germany and her family name was Schmelling. As a child she studied the violin, but in later years she was trained as a singer. Madame Mara sang at Dresden Opera, 1766–71, and received a life appointment at the Berlin Court Opera. From 1784 to 1802, Madame Mara resided in London.

Charles Knyvett was a court favourite and an accomplished organist.[40] He became musical conductor of the Ancient Concerts around 1784, succeeding Messrs Bates and Cramer. His artistic contribution to the Concerts was the direction of a series of oratorios on the six Fridays in Lent, from 1786 to 1788. These performances were mounted at the request of His Majesty, and they were offered as a supplement to the regular Concert season. The 1786 season of oratorios was: *Messiah*, *Samson*, *Saul*, *Israel in Egypt*, *Joshua* and *Jephtha*.[41] Tickets were 3 guineas for six tickets in the first season. By 1788, tickets were 3 guineas for each performance.[42] These special evenings enhanced Knyvett's reputation, and he was ultimately appointed Gentleman of His Majesty's Chapel Royal in 1786. The Lenten concerts moved to Covent Garden in 1789.

The King's musical tastes were ridiculed by some, and when he participated in the evenings' entertainments in Tottenham Street he was further derided by his critics. It was reported that His Royal Highness encouraged Cramer, as conductor, to look to the royal box for the royal Hand marking the proper time for Handel. Such involvement in the musical evenings prompted Peter Pindar (Rev. J. Wolcott, MD) to observe:

> Monarchs who with Rapture wild,
> Hear their own Praise with Mouths of gaping wonder,
> And Catch each Crotchet of the Birth-Day Thunder.
> Discord, who makes a King delight in Ode,
> Slight Square of Hanover for Tottenham Road;
> Where with the taste sublime of Goth and Vandal,
> He orders the worst works of heavy Handel;
> Encores himself till all the audience gape,
> And suffers not a quaver to escape.[43]

James Gillray, the caricaturist, found the excesses of the evenings worthy of record: 'Antient [*sic*] Music', published 10 May 1787 (Plate 1). At the left in the illustration is King George, Sir Watkin Williams-Wynn is the sleeping goat-like creature and Madame Mara is depicted as an owl. Sir J. Mawbery holds a pig and the Chancellor (Thurlow) is shown whipping two children.[44]

40   'Knyvett, Charles', in Highfill et al. (eds), *Biographical Dictionary*, vol. 9, 72–3; and Olive Baldwin and Thelma Wilson, 'Knyvett, Charles (1752–1822)', *ODNB*, accessed 18 November 2013.

41   The 1787 season was *Athalia*, *Judas Maccabaeus*, *Deborah*, *L'Allegro* with Dryden's *Ode*, *Theodora* and *The Messiah*. The 1788 season was *Solomon*, *Alexander's Feast* with *The Choice of Heracles*, *Joseph*, *Acis e Galatea* with Dryden's *Ode*, *Esther* and *The Messiah*.

42   *The Times*, 1 January 1788.

43   Peter Pindar [Dr John Wolcott], *The Works of Peter Pindar, Esq.*, 3 vols (London, 1794), vol. 1, 417.

44   For a detailed explication of the caricature, see Thomas Wright and R.H. Evans, *Historical and Descriptive Account of the Caricature of James Gillray* (London, 1851), 20.

From 1786 through 1791, the *Daily Universal Register* and *The Times* published notices for concerts and benefits at the rooms in Tottenham Street. The artists were familiar to patrons of the rooms: Madame Mara, Mr Samuel Harrison, Miss Harwood, Mademoiselle Denis and Nancy Storace, all of whom appeared in either 1787 or 1788. Madame Gautherot, a celebrated violinist from Paris, also performed in March of 1789 under the auspices of the Concert of Ancient Music.

Michael Kelly (1762–1816) was an Irish singer and composer who studied and performed in Italy and Vienna, where he was engaged for four years. He appeared in London at Drury Lane in 1787. He composed music for sixty-two stage pieces, kept a music shop and was a wine merchant.[45] In his *Reminiscences*, Kelly recalled his debut at the Concert of Ancient Music in 1790 under the direction of the Earl of Uxbridge. The songs assigned to him were 'Jephtha's Rash Vow' and the laughing song from Handel's *L'Allegro*, 'Haste thee, Nymph, and Bring with thee'. Kelly recalled the considerable talents of his fellow performer Samuel Harrison at the Tottenham Street concerts: 'No Divine from the pulpit, though gifted with the greatest eloquence, could have inspired his auditors with a more perfect sense of duty to their Maker than Harrison did by his melodious tones and chaste style.' But Kelly expressed reservations about the singer's limitations when performing more animated songs: 'I heard him sing the laughing song, without moving a muscle; and determined, though it was a great risk, to sing it my own way, and the effect it produced justified the experiment.' Kelly recalled his interpretation: 'instead of singing it [the laughing song] with the serious tameness of Harrison, I laughed all through it, as I conceived it ought to be sung, and as must have been the intention of its composer: the infection ran; and their Majesties, and the whole audience, as well as the orchestra, were in a roar of laughter.' The signal of approval came from the royal box, and Kelly repeated the song with even greater effect.[46] He performed at the Concert of Ancient Music throughout the season.

The 1790 Concert of Ancient Music season began on 26 January. The artists were favoured by the presence of their Majesties and the three elder Princesses. Miss Anna Selina (Nancy) Storace (1765–1817)[47] and Miss Poole sang Italian arias. One reviewer found these selections to be 'a very pretty relief to the grave music of Handel'.[48]

Royal patronage of the Concert of Ancient Music required the King's entourage to venture out in the night. Although critics did not always share the royal interest

45   'Kelly, Michael', in Highfill et al. (eds), *Biographical Dictionary*, vol. 8, 291–300; and Baker, *Biographical Dictionary*, 390.

46   Michael Kelly, *The Reminiscences of Michael Kelly*, 2 vols (London, 1826), vol. 2, 320–1.

47   'Storace, Nancy', in Highfill et al. (eds), *Biographical Dictionary*, vol. 14, 294–305; and Baker, *Biographical Dictionary*. She was born in London of Italian parents, studied voice with Rauzzini and Sacchini in Venice, and sang in Florence, Milan and Parma. In 1784 she appeared at the Vienna Opera and returned to London in the same year.

48   *The Times*, 27 January 1790.

in George Frederick Handel, the *au courant* of the court dutifully gathered to demonstrate their support for royal taste. The evenings in Tottenham Street were attended by the fashionable and the aspiring. As they entered the neighbourhood, a mixture of rogues and thieves formed a reception party looking for anything of value that could be stolen swiftly in the dark confusion. On one occasion a lady had a pearl-encrusted cap snatched from her head, and later a group of boys dazzled a man with a torch while others took his money. Such incidents were not uncommon, and the press regularly cautioned patrons to beware of the potential dangers in the Tottenham Street area.[49] A 1791 account contrasts the glitter inside the concert hall with the harsh reality outside:

> It is stated that the King's Concert Rooms were crowded to suffocation, chiefly with the 'nobs' and their ladies, rich in gorgeous attire, sparkling with jewels, and graced with feathers and flaunting fans. Rapturous applause greeted the performers from first to last, and many a dainty bouquet was flung from the boxes to the stage. Outside the concert rooms the light-fingered gentlemen were assembled in full force, to ease the crowd of their purses and valuables as they tripped lightly over the gravel path that led from the house and into the several carriages awaiting them. We may mention that amongst the vehicles were some of the best-known and most magnificent equipages in London.[50]

In 1794 the Concert of Ancient Music abandoned their long-term lease and the New Rooms and moved to the more commodious King's Theatre, Haymarket. Francis Pasquali, the landlord of the New Rooms, died in this same year. A note in the St Pancras Rate and Poor Tax records for 1795 indicates that 'because of a loss in revenues' the taxes were unpaid.

The Pic-Nic Society
In 1800 John Hyde, a trumpeter, leased the New Rooms. He had performed at Drury Lane and the Haymarket in the 1790s. For his early concerts, the leader of the band was Mr Cramer; performers were Nancy Storace and Mr Braham. Tickets were 10s 6d each, to be had of Mr Hyde at the Rooms. No money was to be taken at the door. Hyde planned to offer a series of subscription seasons for vocal and instrumental performers. He called the building either the Tottenham Street Rooms or Hyde's Rooms.[51] Hyde remained the lessee of record until early 1807. He sublet the rooms in 1801 to the Pic-Nic Society, a confederation of wealthy amateurs, who negotiated a lease for a series of private subscription entertainments.

---

49   As quoted in *St Pancras Notes and Queries*, March 1899.
50   HC: clipping, 1791.
51   'Hyde, John', in Highfill et al. (eds), *Biographical Dictionary*, vol. 8, 67; and Elkin, *Old Concert Rooms*, 91.

The Pic-Nic Society staged performances of instrumental music, singing and plays, usually followed by lavish post-performance suppers. Lady Albina Buckinghamshire, whose love of banquets and entertainments encouraged her to form the Society, had organised soirées at the home of Monsieur Le Texier, a well-known bon vivant, whose talents included dazzling society with his eloquent recitations from the works of Racine and Molière.[52] The popularity of the Le Texier evenings and Lady Buckinghamshire's interest in creating a season of plays, balls and suppers led her and the Pic-Nic Society to the New Rooms in Tottenham Street.[53] The membership was required to recruit the musicians for the orchestra as well as the actors (or act themselves). They were also to supply all the food and drink for the dinners to be enjoyed after the entertainments. Few of the dilettante societies in London at the turn of the nineteenth century boasted such a distinguished list of participants. Initially, three hundred invitations were circulated, with provision for an additional one hundred. The organising committee, in addition to Lady Buckinghamshire, consisted of the Prince of Wales, Lords Cholmondeley, Valletort, Carlisle, Spooner, Kirkcudbright and Derby, the Duke of Queensberry, Lady Salisbury, Lady Jersey and Mrs Fitzherbert.[54]

Colonel Henry Francis Greville (1760–1816) was to be the Pic-Nic Society's director, spokesman, producer, leading performer and arbiter of taste. He was to receive £1,500 for his appointment. His splendid manners, tact and dedication to amateur entertainment earned him comparison with the legendary Beau Nash. Although little is known about Greville's theatrical experience prior to his appointment, he was educated at court and served as a page to the King. He later became a commissioned officer in the Guards and rode in the Enniskillen dragoons.[55] Greville was the organiser of the subscription evenings for the Pic-Nic Society and he circulated details about the forthcoming dramatic performances at the Tottenham Street Rooms on 20 February 1802. Greville and the Pic-Nic Society secretary, R. Bullock, published a prospectus which outlined the goals of the Society. They also invited the public at large to seek membership:

Tottenham-Street

Rules and Regulations for the Society

The Number of Members shall be limited to 300, among which shall be

Twelve Lady Patronesses

One Director

Six Managers and One Subdirector

The Evening amusements shall commence at Half past Eight;

52   *St Pancras Notes and Queries*, 18 April 1891, 309–10.
53   Gillian Russell, *The Theatres of War, 1793–1815* (Oxford, 1995), 126–35.
54   V&A: summary of documents found in the Prince of Wales's Theatre files.
55   Henry Angelo, *The Reminiscences of Henry Angelo*, 2 vols (New York and London, 1969), vol. 1, 228.

after the Plays, or Proverbs, the Theatre will be converted
into a Ball-room, and Apartments made ready for such of the
Company as chuse Cards; at Half past Twelve there shall be
a Pic-Nic Supper, succeeded by Catches and Glees.
The First Representation to be on Monday, March 1, and to be
continued once in every alternate Week, until further notice.

PATRONESSES

Her Grace Duchess of Devonshire	Viscountess Melbourne
Her Grace Duchess of Gordon	Viscountess Dungannon
Rt. Hon. Marchioness of Salisbury	Lady Templetown
Rt. Hon. Countess Cholmondeley	Lady Campbell
Rt. Hon. Countess Buckinghamshire	Hon. Mrs Damer
Rt. Hon. Countess Mount Edgecumbe	Mrs Crewe

MANAGERS

The Earl of Cholmondeley	William Spenser, Esq.
The Earl of Mount Edgecumbe	T. Sheridan, Esq.
Hon. P. Lamb	William Maddocks, Esq.

Director of the whole ESTABLISHMENT
Henry Francis Greville[56]

The subscription price was to be 6 guineas and the prospective members were advised that cards were transferable, gentlemen to gentlemen and ladies to ladies. No one could be admitted at the Tottenham Street evenings without an invitation card.

The planning and rumours surrounding the Pic-Nic membership did not escape the close scrutiny of theatrical, religious and political leaders. When the Pic-Nic Society's plans became known, the managers of the patent theatres (Richard Brinsley Sheridan at Drury Lane and Joseph Richardson at Covent Garden) invoked their exclusive prerogatives as holders of the royal patents for the presentation of plays. The patent theatre managers asserted that the proposed Pic-Nic productions violated the existing laws. Since the patent theatres were struggling nightly to attract audiences, they viewed the Pic-Nic performances as unwelcome and unlawful competition for theatre patronage. The patent theatre managers were determined to enforce the historic licensing laws strictly.[57]

Upon receiving the complaints from the patentees, Greville outmanoeuvred his adversaries by 'trying the issue' in the public press. His letters to the patentees (printed in the newspapers) characterised the patents as unfair and the patentees as lacking the authority to prevent the Pic-Nic evenings. The patent holders responded

---

56   *Morning Post*, 20 February 1802.
57   Letters dated 15 March 1802 were printed in the *Morning Post*, 18 March 1802.

to Greville's challenge and sternly reminded him, also in the public press, that they did have authority and precedent on their side. The patentees further stated that if the Pic-Nic Society expected to present any theatrical entertainments, they must adhere to conditions set by the patentees. Greville agreed to postpone the opening from 1 March to 15 March in an effort to negotiate a more favourable agreement, but his hopes were dashed when the patentees' conditions were delivered to him on 14 March. The document was explicit: performances must be limited to ten during the season; no performers could be paid; members of the society would be required to act all the roles in the plays they presented (whether in French or English); and, finally, the invitation cards should bear the inscription 'dramatic entertainments will be performed with the consent of proprietors of Established Winter Theatres'.

Greville had one day to review and accept the terms. He signed the document to signify compliance, but immediately sent off another letter to the newspapers in which he complained that he had already acquiesced to the point of humiliation by postponing the original opening night. Greville castigated Sheridan for mistreating him, and he questioned the motives of both Sheridan and Richardson. He stated that he had agreed to the dictates under pressure, that his signature was merely an expedient to ensure the first performance on the 15th and that he had no intention of following the arbitrary limitations prescribed in the 'terms' unless the Society decided to accept them. Greville restated the proposed objectives and intentions of the Society and denied any competition with the Winter Theatres. Finally, he noted that threats against the Society represented an infringement upon the right to entertainment that belonged to every Englishman as long as he kept within the law and morality. Greville received no immediate outpouring of support in the press, but his questions did provoke enough public and political concern to put Sheridan and Richardson on the defensive for being overly aggressive. Many observers, including those with power and authority, believed the existing licensing laws were antiquated, but no one called for a review or revision of the long-standing laws. In the interest of avoiding public censure, the patent managers accepted a moratorium on any action, and the Pic-Nics were given permission to launch their first season as planned.[58]

Those supporting the existing law soon restated their opposition to the Pic-Nic evenings on the grounds of propriety. Was English morality threatened by the Pic-Nic Society evenings? The critics of the Pic-Nics and their plans suggested that the Society was founded on highly questionable practices, possibly of French origin. The attacks on the Pic-Nic Society intensified. The gossips resurrected anti-French sentiments and asserted that the Pic-Nics would not only produce French plays, but also engage French gentlemen, dressed in women's costumes, to perform.[59] One indignant critic observed that even the tasteless and indiscreet Italians had

---

58   *The Theatrical Repertory; or, Weekly Rosciad*, No. XXVI, 16 March 1802, 300–5.
59   *Morning Post*, 17 March 1802.

forbidden private theatricals. In anticipation of the supposed threat to peace and public morality, local authorities as well as Bow Street officers were summoned to maintain order. The opening night passed without disturbance.[60]

Greville greeted an elegant audience of two hundred with an original prologue describing the goals of the Society. Following the prologue, two French proverbs and an act of the *Gentleman Author; or, Bedlamites*, adapted from the original French, were presented. An epilogue soliciting new subscribers completed the entertainments, and for this first evening the Pic-Nic supper, thought to be less than successful, was provided by a nearby tavern. Some in the audience were offended by the appearance of three Frenchmen dressed as women, performing comic antics and proving the gossips right.[61] The first evening attracted wide attention in the public press, and James Gillray's caricature commemorated the night (Plate 2). 'Blowing up the Pic-Nics; or, Harlequin Quixote Attacking the Puppets; Vide Tottenham Street Pantomime', dated 2 April 1802, depicts an amateur production in progress with the angry protestors threatening the stage:

King Pic-Noc [*sic*] a compound Sovereign, is represented by Lord Cholmondeley, who is throwing up his arms in consternation; the figure next to him is said to be General Grenville; little Lord Valletort is clad in armour as 'Tom Thumb.' Lady Buckinghamshire (whose figure is treated somewhat freely), and Lady Salisbury, are horror-struck at the exposure of their revels to the light of publicity. Kemble, recoiling in tragic horror, is supporting his proprietor; Mrs Siddons, grasping the dramatic dagger, is looking with deadly aversion to the revellers ... The shade of Garrick has burst the stage-boards in his amazement at the degeneracy of the age which has succeeded him ...[62]

Subscriptions increased, but Greville had difficulty coaxing full participation from his membership. The Pic-Nics proceeded, undaunted by adverse publicity, and focused their energies on preparing new pieces. On the first of May, Garrick's *Lethe; or, Aesop in the Shades* and *La Soirée orageuse* by Nicolas Dalayrac (1753–1809) were performed with Henry Angelo (1756–1835)[63] and General Arabin in the leading roles. Angelo's participation in the Society's performances resulted from his parallel involvement in a second series of productions christened the Dilettanti Theatricals by the press. Greville had formed a second company, possibly to circumvent the lease provisions accepted by the Pic-Nics and to provide additional

---

60   *Ibid.*, 18 March 1802.

61   *Ibid.*

62   Thomas Wright, *The Works of James Gillray, the Caricaturist with the Story of His Life and Times* (London, 1873), 228.

63   Malcolm Fare, 'Angelo, Domenico [formerly Dominico Angelo Malevolti Tremamondo] (1717–1802)', *ODNB*, accessed 18 November 2013. He was the father of Henry Angelo (1776–1802), a fencing master. Domenico came to London in the company of Peg Woffington and opened a fencing academy. Henry became the head of the school around 1785.

dramatic entertainment for the Society. The Dilettanti Theatre evenings mirrored the Pic-Nic's format by offering varied entertainments and a picnic supper. On 4 May 1802 Greville engaged two ladies, Mrs Wisely and Mrs Gardiner, who were students of Mr Girous, to dance reels with their distinguished partners, Lord Charles Bentinck and the Hon. Mr Cornwall. Henry Angelo recalled the theatre pieces for the evening as the entire *Gentleman Author; or, the Bedlamites*, followed by the French proverb, *Le Cadet*. By late April the audience numbered 350. Angelo notes that audiences were sizeable in May and into June for both Dilettanti and Pic-Nic evenings.[64]

Greville prepared *La Soirée orageuse* and *The Liar* for a mid-May Dilettanti evening. For the evening of 17 May members of the Guards, including Captains Caulfield and Brialt, took the principal roles. Colonel Greville and Messrs Snowden and Carlton joined them. Miss Norton also made her debut on this date. She was the niece of Margaret Thornton Martyr, a popular singing actress in the late eighteenth century.[65] In July, Miss Norton was given a benefit by the Pic-Nic Society in appreciation of her performances. She received £25.[66] The evening's audience was a vision of elegance and fashion, led by the loyal patroness, the Duchess of Devonshire, and a number of 'foreign ladies'. In his *Reminiscences*, Henry Angelo described how members were assigned the responsibility for provision of food and drink for the supper following the dramatic part of the evening. The number found on the membership ticket was matched with lots drawn from a silken bag. Angelo described the system:

Nothing could exceed the amusement, which this lottery gastronomic produced. Those who had the least to spare were the first to draw the most expensive lots; and those, on the contrary, to whom money was of little import, drew the cheapest. Some luckless fair, whose beauty was her sole dowry, drew a perigord pie, value three guineas at least, whilst her rich neighbour drew a pound cake, value half a crown. Then some needy sprig of fashion, a younger brother, drew his lot of misery in a ticket for a dozen of champagne; and a wealthy nabob, another for half a dozen China oranges. Many a rich, grudging visage was woefully elongated, on drawing a dish, the mere cooking of which would amount to more than the board wages of their starving establishments for a month. Then the laugh was long and loud.[67]

---

64   *Reminiscences of Henry Angelo*, vol. 1, 228–9.

65   'Norton, Miss J', in Highfill et al. (eds), *Biographical Dictionary*, vol. 11, 62–3. There were two Norton daughters, J. Norton, who appeared at the Haymarket in 1800, and S. Norton, who is recorded as appearing in Edinburgh in 1810. They were active at this time. See also *The Thespian Dictionary; or Dramatic Biography of the Present Age*, 2nd edn (London, 1805). According to *The Times*, 29 June 1802, Miss Norton (probably S. Norton) made her first appearance at the Haymarket on 28 June 1802 in *Lovers' Vow*.

66   *Morning Post*, 27 July 1802.

67   *Reminiscences of Henry Angelo*, vol. 1, 226.

Members were required to supply their own liquid refreshment and to dispatch six bottles each of red and white wine to Tottenham Street. When these arrangements became known, the protectors of public morality were outraged. The critics were suspicious that the Pic-Nics were organising a grand orgiastic fête. What happened to the food and drink that remained after the evening's festivities? Did the carousing continue until the wine and food were totally consumed? What was the intention of these 'private' meetings? Fear arose that excesses of food and drink might lead to further temptation and that the play would become secondary. Indeed, the moralists predicted that the membership might forego performing and employ actors, a flagrant violation of existing laws. Henry Angelo defended the Pic-Nics against such public speculation and judged the accusations unwarranted, for 'no public assembly in high life could enjoy more rational, not to say intellectual, pleasure, at less expense than under the directors of the Pic-Nic'.[68]

In early June, Greville scheduled a Dilettanti production of Rossini's *Il barbiere di Siviglia*, which was to be followed by a scene from *Wags of Windsor*. A few nights later Greville arranged for the Marquis de Choiseul to hold a theatrical soirée at the Tottenham Street Rooms. The highlights of the evening were performances of *L'esprit de contradiction* and an opera entitled *Camille; ou, Le Souterrain* with the Countess de la Belinaye in the title role. The Pic-Nics attended in large numbers and the whole evening 'went off with a great éclat'. On 20 June, the Dilettanti performances at the playhouse concluded with a repeat of *La Soirée orageuse*, and Greville in his closing address said he hoped that, like the phoenix, the Pic-Nic Society would rise from its ashes with redoubled splendour. The grand finale of the season was a water festival at Ranelagh, during which Mr Garnerin, with Greville at his side, ascended in a balloon. Music, fireworks displays and a dinner for two thousand people celebrated both the Peace of 1802 and the conclusion of the amateur-theatrical season.[69]

Greville's open letter to subscribers and the press recalled the successes of the first season, praised the demeanour of the Pic-Nics, stressed the moral integrity of the Society and asserted the organisation's compliance with the law. In response to allegations that the group was creating a French theatre, Greville assured the public that he had no such intent, nor did the membership plan to challenge other theatres by presenting French plays. His conciliatory statement reiterated his hope that reason would prevail in the conflict between the patent Theatres and the Pic-Nic Society.

Colonel Greville and Mr Hyde placed a notice in the *Morning Post* advertising the 1803 Pic-Nic season. The second season would begin in February with the evenings to be scheduled on alternate Thursdays from February to June. Every fourth

---

68   *Ibid.*, 228.
69   *Morning Chronicle*, 29 June 1802.

week a dinner would be offered, and one dress ball and one masquerade would complement the meetings of the Society. Tickets would be limited to five hundred, and dramatic performances were to consist of two French and two English plays with one farce to be played nine times in the course of the season. In addition, six concerts were to be scheduled under the direction of Mr Saloman at the Hanover Rooms, leased by the Pic-Nics for a concert season. The subscription costs were to be: Gentlemen £9 9s, Catch and Glee Singers £2 2s and Ladies 7 guineas. Dinner would be catered and served, unlike the previous year, at a cost of £1 5s per person. Response was less than expected at the early February subscription meeting. To stimulate interest, Greville circulated the names of those who made early commitments to the Society: the Marquesses of Abercorn, Headford and Lorne; Lords Holland, Harrington, Stanhope, Cowper, Langford, Limerick, Borington, Stair, Graves, C. Bentinck, Mountnorris, Conyngham; Sirs H. Hambert, J. Shelly, C. Asgill and General Taylor.[70]

In November, prior to the beginning of the second Pic-Nic season, Captain Caulfield and other members of the Foot Guards staged an amateur production of Shakespeare's *Henry IV*. Several of the actors had previously performed as part of the Pic-Nic and Dilettanti companies. The Foot Guards officers offered a second performance of *Henry IV* in late November. An audience of nearly four hundred filled the theatre to see Captain Caulfield as Hotspur, Captain Hicks as King Henry, J. Maddocks as Falstaff and Miss Norton as Lady Percy. The reviewers avoided 'critical severity' when attending the Foot Guards productions and focused instead on those in attendance and the ambience of the theatre. Attention was directed to the inscription that appeared over the stage: 'On fait ce qu'on peut, Et non ce qu'on veut.' *Othello* was presented in December to an audience of four hundred.

Without warning, the Pic-Nic Society cancelled their second season. A sale bill dated 16 March 1803 notified the public that Colonel Greville's health and financial losses forced the Pic-Nic Society to cease all activity in Tottenham Street. Greville had recovered sufficiently by 1804 to lead a crusade for an English Opera at the Pantheon. His efforts to establish a third winter theatre continued over the next several years. Later, in 1809, after Drury Lane was destroyed by fire, he joined with S.J. Arnold, the proprietor of the Lyceum, to obtain a licence from the Lord Chamberlain.[71]

Greville may or may not have suffered a debilitating illness. Membership interest had declined from the previous year and the patent managers remained reluctant to grant any permission for an additional subscription season. Greville had few, if any, options. The Pic-Nics, especially with the expanded offerings of the Dilettanti theatricals, had violated both the letter and the spirit of the earlier agreements. By

---

70   *Morning Post*, 26 July 1802.

71   Watson Nicholson, *The Struggle for a Free Stage in London* (London, 1906), 161ff.

doubling the number of performances at the theatre, hiring performers from outside the Society membership and engaging French actors, the Pic-Nics had provoked the patentees to rule any previous agreement annulled. It was a tenuous arrangement at best, and the Pic-Nic Society had not earned the trust or confidence of the patentees. The silence of Greville in this matter would imply that the Pic-Nic Society was threatened with legal action and/or had lost sufficient public support to continue. By the middle of March, the Pic-Nic Society was defunct and its obituary published:

Died

Last Week, at his lodgings in Tottenham Street
To the infinite regret of his numerous friends and dependants,
In the 400th year of his age, according to Hindoo chronology,
and in the 14th month, according to our mode of reckoning,
ORIGINAL PIC NIC, Esq.
He was a Gentleman of Extraordinary merit,
And his short life was devoted to useful purposes.
As usual however with men of great worth,
His value will not be properly appreciated but by Posterity.
Though naturalized in England,
He was of foreign extraction, and his ancestry is lost in
The highest antiquity.
A celebrated as well as witty biographer, Mr Jack Bannister,
Informed a very curious and gratified audience last year,
That savages of America were of the Pic Nic family, and held
Frequent Pic Nics in the wood.
From this and other circumstances,
We are led to believe that the founder of the family was
NEBUCHADNEZZAR.
Higher than him we modestly confess we cannot trace it, and are bound to
Own we do not claim kindred with
NOAH
As he undoubtedly stocked the whole Ark himself.
Mr PIC NIC
Has by will appointed us his sole heirs and executors;
And among other obligations,
Has imposed upon us the sacred one of rescuing
His posthumous fame from obloquy and unmerited accusation.
We shall fulfil his dying injunctions;
And we announce to the world our intention of
Publishing
In the course of next month,

The Life and Adventures of Original Pic Nic, Esq.
Together with a selection of those beautiful passages in
THE MORNING POST,
Which have justly entitled that celebrated work to the patronage of
Panegyrized Fashion.
As also those original Letters and Documents,
Written to him from the kingdom of
Rugdignag,
Claiming him as a subject.
Which claim he successfully refilled,
And in order the more effectually to aid and enrich this Collection,
We intend to annex to it
Twelve of our most invaluable Numbers,
As well as out of respect to our late Relative,
As in consequence of the change which the following
Flattering distinction
Conferred upon us necessarily obliges us to adopt,
And which we herewith impart to our Readers.
N.B. Mr PIC NIC
Is to be interred on the 31st of the present month in
The family Vault
And the chief Mourners are to be
ALL THE FASHION.[72]

Notice for a March 1803 sale appeared. To be sold by private contract were the stage scenery and trestled tables with benches lately used by the Pic-Nic Society. Prospective buyers were to view the property by appointment with John Hyde prior to the 20th of the month and all was to be removed by 22 March.[73]

After the Pic-Nic Society
John Hyde resumed the management of entertainments and renamed the building Hyde's Rooms. He offered a series of benefits, and some of the Pic-Nic Society membership attended an evening for Hyde, either in a display of goodwill or to compensate him for an early termination of the lease. Nancy Storace, famous for having performed Susanna in the premiere production of Mozart's *Le nozze di Figaro*, was a featured artist. She was the companion of John Braham (1777–1856),[74]

---

72 HC: printed flyer, 19 March 1803.
73 *Morning Post*, 11 March 1803; and HC: sale notice, 16 March 1803.
74 'Braham, John', in Highfill et al. (eds), *Biographical Dictionary*, vol. 2, 291–304; and George Biddlecombe, 'Braham, John (1777?–1856)', *ODNB*, accessed 18 November 2013. John Braham made his debut at the Royalty Theatre in Wellclose Square in 1787. He was performing at Bath in 1794 and gave voice lessons to Lady Nelson in 1795. He travelled with Nancy Storace, his companion for twenty years, to Italy in 1797. They performed in

who also appeared often at Hyde's Rooms (Plate 3). Other artists on the occasion were Miss Mortimer, Miss Myrty, Wilhelm Cramer (leader of the band) and John Hyde (trumpet). In the weeks that followed, the rooms were used infrequently for benefits and local charities.

In 1804, officers of the Second Regiment of Life Guards notified the public that they would perform *The Revenge* by Edward Young on a Monday evening in mid-March. Captain Chad, who would play the character of Don Manuel, humbly delivered an original prologue, cautioning the audience that the company could not boast 'Kemble's Art' and that they should remember:

> Whoever expects a faultless piece to see
> Thinks what ne'er was, nor is, nor e'er shall be
> In ev'ry work regard the writer's end,
> Since none can compass more than they intend;
> And, if the means be just, the conduct true,
> Applause, in spite of trivial faults, is due.

The critics were charitable in their consideration of the actors, but they singled out the band's performance between the acts as the most successful part of the evening. A supper, reminiscent of the days of the Pic-Nic Society, followed the presentation of the play, and general festivities continued until four o'clock in the morning, when a breakfast concluded the entertainment. The *Morning Post* noted that the Margravine of Anspach with her 'usual party' was in attendance.[75] The success of the March evening encouraged the amateurs to schedule another performance of the play for April.

Near the end of 1808, after offering seasons of occasional musical entertainments, John Hyde leased the New Rooms to Abraham Saunders, junior. He was the son of Abraham Saunders who, in the latter part of the previous century, owned the riding academy in nearby John Street called the School of Bucephalus. Having learned the staging of equestrian entertainments from his father, the younger Saunders had honed his riding skills at the Royal Circus and Astley's Amphitheatre.[76] An advertisement in *The Times* for 7 January 1808 notified the public that Abraham Saunders, junior, under the patronage of the Duke and Duchess of York, had taken the Tottenham Street Rooms. The playbill circulated in the neighbourhood

---

Florence and Braham sang at La Scala from 1798–9. He built the St James's Theatre in 1835 and opened the Coliseum the same year. By 1824, he received 25 guineas per performance at Drury Lane. See also Frederic Boase, *Modern English Biography*, 6 vols (Truro, 1897).

75   *Morning Post*, 22 March 1804.

76   'Saunders, Master', in Highfill et al. (eds), *Biographical Dictionary*, vol. 13, 212. The junior Saunders was at the Royal Circus in 1800. He was sometimes called the 'Infant Equestrian Phenomenon'. One of his special acts was 'leaping through two balloons at full speed on a horse and leaping through four garters and over platforms and pyramids of light'. See also M. Willson Disher, *Greatest Show on Earth* (London, 1937), 71–2 where a brief biography appears.

reported that the theatre building had been converted into a new and beautiful amphitheatre, and it would be known as the New Royal Riding Rooms.[77] The theatre opened to the public on 27 January 1808 with an equestrian entertainment. The first production was entitled *The Spring Meeting; or Ploughboy's Stake.* Advertisements encouraged prospective audiences to observe 'the stage and circle joined to recreate the course at Newmarket'.[78] In addition to equestrian exercises, the manager offered slack-wire performers, mock battles, pantomime and dramatic pieces altered to accommodate the quadruped stars. Prices of admission were similar to traditional playhouses: boxes 4s, pit 2s and gallery 1s. The evening began at seven and half-price commenced at half-past eight.[79] The comfort of the audience was an important consideration during the winter months, and on his playbills Saunders assured his audience that the theatre would be thoroughly warmed by patent stoves.[80]

Saunders's management of the Tottenham Street playhouse was ill-fated from the outset. He had a reputation for being eccentric, and his behaviour produced adverse publicity almost immediately.[81] According to a newspaper report, a stage-struck young man, successful in amateur theatricals and impressed with his own talents, sought an engagement with Saunders, but the manager rejected him. The young man persisted in disrupting the morning rehearsal. Saunders finally halted the rehearsal and invited the young man to mount a fiery dragon as part of auditioning for a role. With a flourish, the dragon and the young man were flown to the ceiling of the house. The manager and his company proceeded to douse both creatures with pails of water. Once back on the ground, the young man was directed by Saunders to cross the stage and as he did so a trap door was opened and the would-be thespian tumbled into the cellar. The assault charges filed against Saunders resulted in a modest fine.[82] By mid-year, Saunders had left the theatre, and a note in the rate books revealed that taxes were more than £42 in arrears.[83] For the remainder of 1808 and nearly all of 1809, the theatre appears to have been closed.

---

77 *The Times*, 7 January 1808.

78 *Ibid.*, 27 January 1808.

79 Michael Booth, *Theatre in the Victorian Age* (Cambridge, 1991), 39–40. The tradition of half-price in the eighteenth century was an effort to attract audiences with fewer resources to the theatre. That practice continued in the nineteenth century when audiences at half-price were primarily those seeking less expensive admission to the pit and gallery. Half-price was principally directed at shop clerks and assistants and others who did not complete their work day until 7, 8 or 9pm. Young men about town who were not interested in a full evening at the theatre, which could commence at 6.30 or 7pm, also purchased half-price tickets. For the most part, half-price theatregoers were lower middle-class.

80 *The Times*, 27 January 1808.

81 Obituary, *The Times*, 31 July 1839.

82 *Morning Chronicle*, 11 March 1808.

83 Holborn Public Library: Camden Local Studies and Archives Centre: St Pancras Rates Book: St Pancras Rate and Poor Tax, 1808.

Chapter Two

The Beverly management and Les Soirées françaises, 1810–1828

The growing number of minor playhouses operating with the permission of local magistrates continued to challenge the exclusiveness of the patent theatre monopoly. In 1809 at Covent Garden, the unfashionable theatregoers, the butchers and barbers, protested against the patent theatre management practices. The new manager at Covent Garden, John Philip Kemble, converted the third tier of the playhouse to boxes for the fashionable and raised ticket prices in the pit from 3s 6d to 4s. The public protested these changes for sixty-seven nights and forced Kemble to accede to their demands and to apologise. The authority and relevance of the patents was challenged successfully.[1] The city's expansion and the growing public demand for entertainment encouraged leaders to reassess the restrictions imposed by the patent theatre monopoly. The offices of the Attorney-General, the Solicitor-General and the Privy Council attempted to resolve the conflicts, but they encountered a general reluctance to make change. In the early years of the nineteenth century the minor theatres, so called because they did not hold one of the royal patents, experienced little difficulty obtaining burletta licences from Lord Dartmouth, the Lord Chamberlain, or local magistrates. The licence defined the burletta as a musical entertainment. Managers often defied the law, feigning compliance by having an occasional, nearly inaudible chord struck on a piano during the performance of a play. Prosecution of violators was infrequent and soon the emboldened managers abandoned all pretence of complying with the law. Ultimately, even the occasional sound of the piano disappeared. The authority of the patent theatres was eroding, but the patentees persisted over the next two decades to uphold their prerogatives and to protect themselves from the increasing boldness of the minors.[2]

John Paul obtained a burletta licence, signed a lease for the rooms (adopting the name 'the King's Ancient Concert Rooms, Tottenham Street') and commenced a

---

1   George Rowell, *The Victorian Theatre, 1792–1914: A Survey*, 2nd edn (Cambridge, 1978), 3–4.
2   Ernest Bradlee Watson, *Sheridan to Robertson: A Study of the Nineteenth-Century London Stage*, 2nd edn (New York, 1963), 20–57. See also Jane Moody, *Illegitimate Theatre in London, 1770–1840*, Cambridge, 2000.

KING's   ANCIENT

CONCERT   ROOMS,

TOTTENHAM STREET.

(LICENCED BY ACT OF PARLIAMENT.)

THIS PRESENT TUESDAY Aprl. 24, 1810.

With a New Pastoral Burletta called

The Village Fête,

Founded on the Plot, Incidents, and Diction of *LOVE IN A VILLAGE:*

THE CHARACTERS BY

Mr. SCRIVEN.   Mr. LEE.   Mr. COGLAN.
Mr. LEWIS.   Mr. J. JONES.   Mr. FITZ-WILLIAM.
Mr. T. BLANCHARD.   Mr. WALDRON.   Mr. MALE.
Mrs. PAUL.   Miss DAVIES   Mrs. PARKINSON.
Miss WALDRON, and Mrs. HERBERT.

Previous to the Burletta

An occasional Address by Mr. REES

In the Course of the Evening, a Comic Song, called

" The Cosmetic Doctor," by Mr. HERRING.

After which will be presented a new Pantomime, called

Harlequin at Helicon,

OR,

PANTOMIME RENOVATED.

The Music entirely New by Mr. GLADSTAINES.

THE VOCAL PARTS BY

Mr. J. JONES.   Mr. LEE.   Mr. LEWIS.
Mrs. PAUL.   Miss DAVIES.   Miss DENT.   Mrs. PYNE.
Miss DANTON.   Miss WALDRON.   Miss LETTEN.
Mrs. HERBERT, &c. &c.

PANTOMIMIC CHARACTERS BY

Mr. HOLLINGSWORTH.   Mr. T. BLANCHARD.   Mr. HERRING.
Mr. MALE.   Mr. BOULANGER.   Mr. RICHARDS.

Master LAURENT, and Mr. LAURENT.

Mrs. PARKINSON. Miss PHILLIPS, &c. &c. &c.

WITH APPROPRIATE DANCES.

BOXES 4s. Second Price 2s. PIT 2s. Second Price 1s. GALLERY 1s. Second Price at
Half-past 8 o'Clock.——The Doors to be opened at Half-past 5 o'Clock, and the Performance
to commence at Half-past 6.—Places for the Boxes to be taken at the Theatre, from 10 till 4.
The Decorations of the Theatre, and the whole of the Scenery are designed by
Mr. GREENWOOD, and Executed by him,
And under his immediate direction, by a variety of Able Assistants.

✝✝✝ The above performances were received with universal
applause and will be repeated every Evening till further notice

Lowndes and Builder, Printers, Marquis Court, Drury Lane.

season on 23 April 1810. Paul was a pawnbroker, and he owned a shop on the High Street, Marylebone, and a second in the Strand. Paul paid the taxes, including those in arrears, on the property, assessed with a valuation of £100 rent.[3] He added a portico to the exterior of the building on the Pitt Street side that continued to be a prominent feature of the theatre's architecture for the next several decades. Paul's wife was to be the star attraction under his management. While little was said about the interior of the house, a writer in *The Times* of 24 April 1810 compared it to another London playhouse: 'the theatre, in its form and size, approximates to that of Sadler's Wells; is painted a pale flesh colour, with emblematical devices; and is lighted by a number of elegant cut glass chandeliers.'[4] Another first-night reviewer noted that improvements to the interior and exterior made the little theatre neat, tasteful and commodious – generally worthy of the city. By comparison, the Lyceum was a 'pig-sty'. Admission prices were set at the prevailing levels in most theatres: 4s and 2s and 1s.

The first-night playbill (Fig. 4) advertised a pastoral burletta, *The Village Fete* (19).[5] According to reporters, the original dialogue was retained and spoken, accompanied by the pianoforte, 'but so *piano pianissimo* that the music was a secret to the audience'. The evening concluded with a pantomime, *Harlequin at Helicon, or, Pantomime Renovated* (62). The scenery, designed by Thomas Greenwood, junior, was superior, but the acting was a disappointment. Mrs Paul lacked the elegance and style needed to impress a London audience and the company suffered generally from a lack of adequate rehearsal.[6]

Audiences showed interest in the new venture. The newspapers reported that Lords Dillon and Somerville as well as Sir William Clayton were seen at the playhouse in the midst of a large assemblage of society ladies. Paul was unable to sustain public interest in his venture and by the end of June he was forced to abandon his lease. By August he was bankrupt.[7]

During the late summer playbill and newspaper notices alerted the public to the reopening of the playhouse as the New Theatre, Tottenham Street for a winter season. *The Times* of 20 September 1810 identified the managers: 'Mr Penley, the Actor and two others have taken the Tottenham Court-road Theatre for the ensuing winter.'

---

3   Holborn Public Library: Camden Local Studies and Archives Centre: St Pancras Rate Books: St Pancras Rate and Poor Tax, 1810.

4   *The Times*, 24 April 1810.

5   The number in parenthesis following play titles in the text is an indication of the number of performances of that play in a season. It is the total number of performances, not necessarily consecutive nights on the bills. Because sources are not complete for every season, the number must be viewed as approximate. I have chosen to include this number to identify the most popular productions with audiences. I have assumed that managers were in business to sell tickets and fill the seats. It is possible that once a manager engaged actors and mounted a production, he or she might well have repeated a play to simply fill the bills and/or to recover some part of the initial investment.

6   *Morning Post*, 24 April 1810.

7   *Morning Post*, 11 August 1810.

5 *Ali Baba and the Forty Thieves*, pub. by Mrs M. Hebberd, April 1811. Author's collection

Samson Penley (who had acted previously at Drury Lane), Mr Brierly (a businessman and investor) and Thomas Cobham (a provincial actor who had previously appeared in London at the Surrey and the Royalty[8]) launched the 1810–11 season on 8 October. Initial responses to the new management were positive, and in November the 'new grand melodramatic romance' entitled *Marmion; or, The Battle of Flodden Field* (22), based on Walter Scott's poem, proved popular. This script, written by W.H. Oxberry, featured Cobham. John Poole's *Hamlet Travestie* (13), premiering on 1 January 1811, was an immediate success. It was performed often at many London theatres over the next several decades. The comedian Richard L. Jones, known as 'Gentleman Jones' for his portrayals of the eccentric man, the dashing beau and the hero of madcap farce,[9] appeared as Osrick with Thomas Cobham as Hamlet. Pantomime dominated the bills in the early months of 1811. *Hottentot Venus; or, Harlequin in Africa* (16) featured a grand 'Negro Dance' with Miss Hart and Mr Wollacott leaping through a tambourine six feet high. On 1 April 1811 a production of *Ali Baba and the Forty Thieves* (9), by an anonymous author, featured elaborate settings, according to the playbill:

> The piece opens with a view of the Silver Lake, procession and dance of Fairies, Nymphs, Sylphs, &c. The Fairy of the Lake enters in a Grand Car drawn by Swans. She waves her Wand, and a Transparency is seen with the Figures of Ali Baba and his Son …

Mrs M. Hebberd of Upper Charlton Street, Marylebone, published toy theatre plates of the production on 17 April 1811. The New Theatre, Tottenham Street actors appear in the illustrations with their characters' names (Fig. 5). The season ended in early June when Penley, Brierly and Cobham concluded their management. On Whit Monday, 3 June 1811, members of the Royalty Company performed the first of a series of benefits which continued until the end of July.

The first signs of renewed activity occurred in October when notices were posted bearing the name Regency Theatre for the playhouse. Throughout the remainder of the year and into the next, transient artists and groups performed there until performances ceased in mid-June 1812. In July, the 'wardrobe of dresses, capital scenery by Greenwood &c, and machinery' were offered for sale. Prospective purchasers were invited to assume the lease for a term of fifteen years from the previous Christmas. The annual rental of the property had risen to £177.[10]

In late 1812, Robert Fairbrother circulated bills in the neighbourhoods of St Pancras and Marylebone announcing his 1812–13 winter season of fifty-six nights

---

8   Joseph Knight, 'Cobham, Thomas (1779/1786–1842)', rev. Katharine Cockin, *ODNB*, accessed 18 November 2013. In 1816, he played in *Richard III* at Covent Garden and then worked in Ireland. He later played Iago, Edgar, and the Ghost in *Hamlet* with Kean in Richmond in 1822.

9   Joseph Knight, 'Jones, Richard (1779–1851)', rev. Klaus Stierstorfer, *ODNB*, accessed 18 November 2013. He was born in Birmingham and appeared at Lichfield, Newcastle and Bolton in his early career. In 1799, he was at the Crow Street Theatre, Dublin. His first London engagement was in 1807 at Covent Garden.

10 HC: sale bill.

beginning in December and ending on Shrove Tuesday, 2 March 1813. On his first bill, Fairbrother called the playhouse the Royal Mary-Le-Bone Theatre, Tottenham Street, but the next day his playbill bore the name Regency Theatre. Fairbrother outlined his scheme for raising operating capital in his advertisement:

> Free admissions will be sold for the season to the Boxes and Pit, at half-price of the nightly admission, transferable by Tickets, which will be given to the purchasers for the number of nights intended to perform the different seasons, leaving blanks for their own signatures; and Admission shares of £100 each (not exceeding ten shares) will be disposed of, entitling the holder of each share to free admissions to the boxes or pit, by tickets of their own signature, and the shares bearing interest of five percent, for the time granted, payable quarterly, at the Bankers, Messrs. Marsh Sebbald, and Co. No. 6 Berner's Street, Oxford-Street, or Treasury of the Theatre.

Fairbrother found sufficient shareholder support to start the season, but he soon suffered from poor box office revenues. In May 1813 the *Theatrical Inquisitor's* critic observed that the performers at the theatre presented their plays reasonably well, but that 'It is decidedly a very unprofitable concern; in vain may you produce novelty on novelty; the utmost exertions of manager, authors, performers, composers, &c. are fruitless. We seriously recommend it to the proprietors to convert it into a Methodist meeting. If it does not succeed, *The Devil's In It*.' [11] The house became largely a venue for actors staging benefits.

The Beverly family

In 1814, William Roxby Beverly, senior (1774–1845)[12] acquired the Tottenham Street property at auction with George Robins serving as the disposing agent. Beverly's bid of 310 guineas was accepted. Conditions of the sale allowed the manager to offer continuous performances throughout the year under a previously negotiated magistrate's licence. The total value of the lease was determined at £4,000 upon a term of thirteen years from Christmas of 1813. The exact rental price was £177 per year; the purchase price of the lease (310 guineas) was to be paid in three months. Movable property was valued at £300 and the weekly rental for persons letting the theatre was £20.[13]

For nearly fifteen seasons, from 1814 to 1828, William Roxby Beverly would be the leaseholder and manager of the theatre in Tottenham Street. He retained Regency Theatre as the name for the playhouse. Having learned the intricacies of

---

11 *Theatrical Inquisitor*, May 1813.

12 W.J. Lawrence, 'Beverly, William Roxby (1810?–1889)', rev. C.D. Watkinson, *ODNB*, accessed 18 November 2013. For family history, see also 'William Roxby Beverly', *Walker's Quarterly*, no. 2, January, 1921, 3–27. Note that the Beverly family sometimes spelt their name 'Beverley'.

13 E.L. Blanchard, 'The History of the Prince of Wales's Theatre', *The Era Almanack* (London, 1874), 2.

the theatrical profession from his father, he gained further experience as a North Country actor and later became the leaseholder and manager of the Scarborough and Filey theatres. Beverly was also the manager of the Richmond Theatre in Surrey at this time. He brought with him several members of his family, including his wife and his sons Harry (1796–1863)[14], Robert Roxby (c.1809–66)[15], Samuel (n.d.) and William Roxby Beverly (1810/11–89),[16] who became an admired scenic artist and painter. The *Theatrical Inquisitor* offered Beverly and his family support early in the first season by praising the management and noting that with a tolerable company Beverly would have little difficulty attracting audiences from the parish of Marylebone.[17] With the Beverly family serving as the actors, stage managers and scenic artists, expenses could be maintained at the lowest levels.

W.R. Beverly's 1814–15 season commenced on 26 December 1814. The offerings for the first night were *Barnaby Brittle*, *Woodman of the Alps*, a comic ballet; the song 'Bartlemy Fair' sung by Mr Beverly; and *Sleepwalker; or, Who Is the Lady?* Performances began at half-past six. Admission prices were 4s, 2s and 1s. Half-price began at half-past eight. In March of 1815, *Hero of Switzerland; or, Helvetian Liberty* (10), based on the popular story of William Tell, was mounted. The production was the inspiration for J.H. Jameson's toy theatre plates (Fig. 6). While the Beverly management mounted plays proficiently, the limitations imposed by the small stage and the inexperience of the company were evident. The *Theatrical Inquisitor* observed: 'If the larger houses burn a forest, Beverly burns a tree; if they puff a Miss O'Neill, he displays the talent of Miss Sidney.'[18]

Prior to the 1815–16 season, Beverly added six new private boxes, a handsome new coffee room and a saloon to the playhouse. On 11 December 1815, the season

---

14   Joseph Knight, 'Beverley [or Beverly], Henry [or Harry] Roxby (1796–1863)', rev. Nilanjana Banerji, *ODNB*, accessed 18 November 2013. He sometimes appeared as Henry on the bills. Harry Beverly made his London acting debut at the Regency in 1814. Two years later, at the age of 20, he was the acting manager. In his career, he was associated with the Royalty, the Coburg and the Surrey, and he managed several theatres in the provinces. He was considered a competent actor, especially in low comedy roles. At the Regency, he also supervised the scenic department in the early days and collaborated on the writing of a number of the plays with John Kerr.

15   Joseph Knight, 'Roxby [or Beverly], Robert (c.1809–1866)', rev. Nilanjana Banerji, *ODNB*, accessed 18 November 2013. See also *The Life and Reminiscences of E.L. Blanchard*, ed. Clement Scott and Cecil Howard, 2 vols (London, 1891), vol. 1, 275, 324, 325. Robert Roxby Beverly acted primarily in the provinces. He became a member of the Lyceum and Drury Lane companies after 1839 and served as the stage manager at both the Princess's and Drury Lane. He was stage manager at Drury Lane for eleven years.

16   'Beverly, William Roxby', in Blanchard, *Life and Reminiscences*, vol. 2, 638–9. See also W.J. Lawrence, 'Beverly, William Roxby (1810?–1889)', rev. C.D. Watkinson, *ODNB*, accessed 18 November 2013; and playbills in HC. William Roxby Beverly was born either 1810 or 1811 in Richmond, Surrey. He began his London career as a scenic artist and as an actor in minor roles at the Regency. William's name first appeared on the 1823 bills. In March of 1824 the responsibility for the scenery was attributed to 'A Celebrated Artist and W. Beverly'. The bills confirm that his first production as scenic artist was in April 1824, at the age of thirteen or fourteen. The play was *Haroun Alraschid; or, Orcano, the Fire Fiend* (13). He was the principal scenic artist by the September 1824 Regency production of *Der Freischütz*. Beverly subsequently became the principal scenic artist at the T.R. Manchester (1842–6). He moved to the Princess's with J.M. Maddox (1846–50) and next painted the scenery for J.R. Planché's extravaganzas at the Lyceum from 1847–55. He also exhibited his paintings at the Royal Academy.

17   *Theatrical Inquisitor*, December 1814.

18   *Ibid.*, May 1815.

6 *Hero of Switzerland; or, Helvetian Liberty*, pub. by J.H. Jameson, April 1815. Author's collection

INTERIOR OF THE REGENCY THEATRE, TOTTENHAM STREET, TOTTENHAM COURT ROAD.
BUILT ON THE SITE OF THE KINGS CONCERT ROOMS.

EXTERIOR OF THE ABOVE THEATRE.

London, Published 11 October 1817, by Robert Wilkinson, 125, Fenchurch Street.

7 Regency Theatre, 1817, interior and exterior, engraved by Cook from drawing by Schnebbelie.
Pub. in Robert Wilkinson's *Londina Illustrata*. © Trustees of the British Museum

8 *The Casket of Gloriana; or, The Geni and the Black Enchanter*, pub. by William
West, 15 February 1819 (reissued 1826). Author's collection

opened with Dennis Lawler's *Ways and Means*. The Christmas pantomime was *Carismian Princess or Harlequin & the Beauty* (22) arranged by Harry Beverly, who was identified as responsible for all ballets and pantomimes. It played well into the month of February. In January, a 'burlesque' version of *Tom Thumb* (12) with Samuel Beverly as Tom Thumb, his mother as Dollallolla, and Harry Beverly as Lord Grizzle was offered. The Beverly management concluded their season in August of 1815.

Records for the 1816–17 season are incomplete. The indefatigable Beverly, as the press affectionately described the manager, drew upon his dedicated family, his sense of showmanship, his business experience and sheer perseverance in an effort to keep the Regency doors open. In an effort to build patronage, Beverly resorted to variety entertainments. In the 'Grand Masquerade' a balloon floated from the stage and over the pit where it opened and showered upon the patrons a variety of small balloons, parachutes and forty tickets for the next evening's performance. Singing and dancing followed, and the evening concluded with the singing of 'God Save the King'. Very few playbills or newspaper accounts are available for the 1817–18 season. The economic uncertainties of the day made it a difficult time for most London theatres and it is possible the Regency was dark for extended periods during the year.

Robert Wilkinson published *Londina Illustrata* in 1819. The exterior and interior of the Regency Theatre (Fig. 7) are depicted in engravings which are attributed to Mr Cook, who based his work on the drawings of Robert Blemell Schnebbelie (*fl.* 1803–49). Beyond the lanterns and the portico over the Pitt Street entrance to the theatre, the exterior of the theatre had few distinctive features. The pilasters on the main part of the building repeat the motif of the portico and form a continuation of the basic line. The windows above the entrance were part of the saloon. The interior design featured a unicorn over the proscenium. Chandeliers mounted on both the circle and gallery levels provided illumination, and stage lighting was candlelight and/or oil lamps. The engraving of the theatre interior shows a performance under way on the stage before a traditional wing and border setting. Because the male character appears to be black and in Eastern costume, the play in progress has been presumed to be *Othello*. It is possible that the Wilkinson illustrations may show *The Casket of Gloriana* in performance instead of *Othello*. Toy theatre plates were published by William West for *The Casket of Gloriana* in 1819 (Fig. 8). These illustrations (for which some plates were reissued in 1826) were based on the Regency Theatre 1818 production, and the Beverly family members are identified in them.

The 8 February 1819 playbills bore news of a special benefit arranged for Mr Grove, late manager of the Theatres Royal at Brighton and Windsor. According to the bills, a Mr Roach would appear in *Richard III* as the Duke of Gloucester to settle a 110 guinea wager between two notable theatrical celebrities. Was Mr

9 *Dervise of Bagdad*, pub. by William West, January 1820. Author's collection

Roach's talent equal to that of Charles Kean? The audience was to serve as the jury. The management added a special novelty, Master Richardson, a child actor, reciting from *Douglas, Henry V, Richard III, Julius Caesar* and *The Apprentice*. No reviews appeared. The *Theatrical Inquisitor* bemoaned the general state of the theatre:

> in London, the fashionable can visit no other theatre but Covent Garden or Drury Lane, unless they treat their children with a visit to Astley's. The managers of the minor theatres are certainly indebted to themselves for a considerable portion of the feeling; for in how very few instances are their performances addressed to the rational faculties of the audience, or at all tolerable to a person of any refinement. What but a determination to lounge away an evening somewhere, could entice a person at all above the *canaille* … The Regency is pretty nearly deserted.[19]

The Regency was thought to be a deplorable home for lowly entertainments, with no future or place among the minors for the Beverly management.[20] However, Beverly's efforts were judged as 'thoughtfully put together' by a writer in the February 1819 edition of the *British Stage and Literary Cabinet*. Beverly was, in the writer's opinion, wise to avoid competing with the larger houses in sensational melodrama or spectacular display.[21]

The 1819–20 season, beginning in late August and early September, consisted of revivals. In December a new pantomime entitled *Dervise of Bagdad; or, Harlequin Prince of Persia* (6) was the subject of toy theatre plates by William West, 14 January 1820 (Fig. 9). Master William Beverly made an appearance in the role of the Geni.[22] A young actor from the provinces appeared in two productions during the season, *Forty Thieves* and *Dervise of Bagdad*. Having worked with the Beverly family at Croydon, Benjamin Webster (1798–1882) made his debut and performed at the Regency for several months during this season. His first night was likely 10 December in *Forty Thieves*. His success earned him recognition and the more important double role of Prince and Harlequin in *Dervise of Bagdad*.[23]

In September of the abbreviated 1820 season, Harry Beverly, in collaboration with John Kerr, wrote *The Abbott of Mary, Queen of Scots* (21), a play based on Sir Walter Scott's novel. A translation by John Kerr of *Three Vampires! or, The Light of the Moon* (11) was performed in October. The Beverly management closed the Regency on 14 December and sublet the playhouse for the next thirteen months.

---

19   *Theatrical Inquisitor*, January 1819.

20   *Ibid.*

21   *British Stage and Literary Cabinet*, February 1819.

22   HC: playbill, 27 December 1819.

23   Blanchard, *Life and Reminiscences*, vol. 2, 535. See also Joseph Knight, 'Webster, Benjamin (1798–1882)', rev. Jan McDonald, *ODNB*, accessed 18 November 2013. He was born in Bath, performed at many London theatres and was lessee of the Haymarket from 1837 to 1853. In 1844 he leased the Adelphi with Madame Céleste; he held the lease for twenty years. He last appeared at the Crystal Palace in 1875.

Many London theatres had suffered financially following the conclusion of the Napoleonic War in 1815.[24] The price of food increased substantially and wages declined. The supply of labour exceeded demand, and the agricultural and industrial depression prompted disorder and riots. An atmosphere of fear gripped the nation as the government pursued repressive policies to cope with the volatility of the times.[25] Theatregoing was not the highest priority for Londoners. Beverly tried diligently to present entertainments that would attract audiences, but the prevailing economic conditions were difficult to overcome. In order to honour his commitment to his thirteen-year lease and to sustain his family, he returned to the provinces where he was known and had experienced greater financial security. The income from letting the Regency would be applied to the ongoing cost of his lease.

In late December, playbills were circulated informing the public that the playhouse had been cleaned and decorated. J.H. Amherst (1776–1851), who had taken a short-term lease from William Beverly for the 1820–1 season, was the new manager.[26] Amherst assured the public that his largely provincial company was of the highest quality. He renamed the playhouse the Royal West London Theatre but initiated few changes in the nature of entertainment at the theatre. Opening night featured a melodramatic spectacle called *The Royal Slave*, based on *Oroonoco* (by an anonymous author), which included a grand 'Negro Ballet and War Dance' and closed with a two-act 'tale of enchantment' entitled *Cinderella; or, The Little Glass Slipper*. The Lyceum theatre favourite W.S. Chatterley (1787–1822)[27] appeared on 1 January 1821. His reputation enticed newspaper critics to visit the theatre.

Beginning in January 1821, the bills of fare continued to reflect the prevailing preference for diversity: *My Wife and Freehold; or, Right of Common, Adriane & Louisa; or Love's Stratagem, Midnight Meeting; or, Three Pair of Lovers, Midas* and *Don Giovanni in Ireland; or, He's At It Again*, a 'musical national drama'. Amherst attempted to make his playbills amusing. A playbill for *Don Giovanni; or, Spectre on Horseback* advised readers that the music was 'composed expressly for this piece by Dibdin, Gluck, Handel, Locke, Purcell, Zebrine' and twenty-two others. The scenery 'having most of it appeared before, has been (of course) already received with unbounded acclamations of applause, and will be repeated as often as the manager can write pieces to introduce it'. The costumes and dress 'are as good as the proprietor can possibly afford' and the properties 'are of very little use to any but the owner'. Reviewers and audiences appreciated Amherst's efforts, and several

---

24   Booth, *Theatre in the Victorian Age*, 27.

25   Arthur D. Innes, *A History of the British Nation* (London, 1912), 778–9.

26   William G. Knight, *A Major London 'Minor': The Surrey Theatre, 1805–1865* (London, 1997), 49.

27   Joseph Knight, 'Chatterley, William Simmonds (1787–1822)', rev. Nilanjana Banerji, *ODNB*, accessed 18 November 2013. He appeared at Drury Lane as a child in the 1790s. After performing in Cheltenham and Bath, he returned to London in 1816 at the Lyceum. He appeared at the Adelphi, Olympic, Surrey and other theatres.

productions were performed frequently during his first season. Lady Caroline Lamb attended the first night of *Therese; or the Orphan of Geneva* and permitted her name to appear on the bills as 'The Patroness' of the evening.

Amherst's efforts did not go unnoticed in the *British Stage and Literary Cabinet*: 'New life appears to have been imported to the entertainments at this house by the change which has taken place in the management, and they are now as spirited and varied as those of any other minor theatre ... The principal serious characters are played by Miss Campbell, who appeared at Drury Lane early in the season of 1817–1818. She is somewhat improved since that period but will never be a great actress.'[28]

Les Soirées françaises

From 1821 to 1828, a company of French actors annually appeared at the playhouse in Tottenham Street for multiple-week seasons, sometimes two or more in one year, and on a few occasions near the end of Beverly's leasehold, they performed alternate nights with the Beverly Company. The performances, known eventually as the *Les Soirées françaises*, were presented without a licence, as Pierre (or Peter, as the English press preferred) F. Laporte,[29] a member of the company and partner in the venture, testified before the 1832 Select Committee studying the laws regulating theatres and dramatic literature.[30] To comply with the law, the French performances were designated as 'subscription' nights. The seasons were usually fourteen nights, but they varied considerably, and in two years, 1825 and 1826, the seasons were extended to fifty nights. M. Cloup was initially the manager of the troupe, but Pierre Laporte and M. Pelissié, who were also actors in the company, soon shared management responsibilities. Laporte became the most famous of the trio in London, and for a time he was the manager of both the Haymarket and Covent Garden.

The audiences for the evenings devoted to French drama came from well beyond the immediate neighbourhood. For the people of Europe, including Sweden, Austria, Italy, Spain, Russia, Germany and England, the language of politics and culture was French. They were inspired by the Enlightenment and viewed Paris as the centre of sophistication, fine art and idyllic life. Aristocracy and people of wealth frequently pursued these ideals in their homes and country houses.[31] *Les Soirées françaises* in Tottenham Street offered them a special opportunity to attend professional productions of the drama they admired.

---

28 *British Stage and Literary Cabinet*, April 1821.

29 P.F. Laporte held the lease for Covent Garden in 1832 with an annual rental of £10,000. He left after one year. He was also manager for fourteen years of the King's Theatre (or Italian Opera House) 1828–42. See F.H.W. Sheppard (gen. ed.), *Survey of London*, vol. 35: *Theatre Royal, Drury Lane and The Royal Opera House, Covent Garden* (London, 1970), 79–80; and Nalbach, *King's Theatre*, 100–04.

30 House of Commons, *Report from the Select Committee on Dramatic Literature, with The Minutes of Evidence* (London, 1832), 124–8.

31 Marc Fumaroli, *When the World Spoke French*, tr. Richard Howard (New York, 2001), xv–xxxi, 177–215.

A surviving bill for 2 June 1821 lists what entertainments would be a typical of an evening at the West London Theatre, the name *Les Soirées françaises* adopted.[32] The evening performance commenced at seven with *Guerre ouverte; ou, Ruse contre ruse*, a comedy in three acts by Antoine Jean Dumaniant (the pseudonym of Antoine-Jean Bourlin, 1752–1828). The second piece performed was *Gaspard l'avisé* written by Yves-Pierre Barré (1749–1832), Jean Baptiste Radet (1752–1830) and Françoise-George Desfontaines (1733–1825). The closing one-act vaudeville was *Les Bonnes d'enfants; ou, Une soirée aux boulevards-neufs* by Nicolas Brazier (1783–1838) and Théophile Dumersan (1780–1849). The patronesses for the evening were Princess Esterhazy and Lady Caroline Lamb. The company consisted of ten actors.[33]

In the autumn of 1821, J.H. Amherst opened his second season and, as was the custom, he notified the public on his playbills that he had made extensive improvements to the playhouse, including a new Grecian act curtain, a gothic drop, a new saloon and improved lighting. The reviewers found the changes not entirely successful: 'some dingy slips of faded velvet and tarnished gold lace, which disfigure one or two of the most conspicuous private boxes and detract somewhat from the gay appearance of the theatre, which is in other respects extremely pleasing.'[34] The new ceiling 'has been painted in panels, having a rosette in each, and all converging towards the centre of a large circle. In the centre was an Apollo's head in *alto rilievo*, surrounded with rays of glory, superbly gilt.'[35] Several new actors joined the company: Francis Huntley (1787–1831)[36] from the Surrey; Mr Payne from the Theatre Royal, Haymarket; Mr Montague from Astley's; and Charles Incledon (*c*.1763–1826).[37] Ladies added to the company included Mrs Julia Glover (1782–1850)[38] and Miss Coulston from the King's Theatre.

Amherst announced his plans to offer *Oedipus Tyrannus* (20) on 29 October 1821. This notice aroused the curiosity of London theatregoers and critics. The

---

32   V&A: playbill.

33   Gentlemen: Messrs Cloup, Pelissié, Auguste, Laporte, Joly. Ladies: Mlles Mailhot and Delarte, Mmes Bethéas, Ottonia Nargeo and Adèle Lamoine.

34   *British Stage and Literary Cabinet*, November 1821.

35   *Ibid.*

36   Joseph Knight, 'Huntley, Francis (*c*.1783–1831)', rev. Katharine Cockin, *ODNB*, accessed 18 November 2013. See also *Mirror of the Stage*, 9 September 1822. He first appeared at Brecknock in Wales. He later became a member of the Richmond Theatre under William Beverly's management. For several years he performed at the Surrey for Elliston.

37   John Rosselli, 'Incledon, Charles (*bap*. 1763, *d*. 1826)', *ODNB*, accessed 18 November 2013. He was a Cornish singer who first appeared at Covent Garden in 1790. He was regarded as a leading tenor and ballad singer of the day.

38   Joseph Knight, 'Glover [née Betterton], Julia (1779/1781–1850)', rev. J. Gilliland, *ODNB*, accessed 18 November 2013. See also *Theatrical Times*, 19 December 1846. At five, she appeared as the Page in a production of Otway's *The Orphan* in York under Tate Wilkinson's management. She first performed in London in 1797 at Covent Garden. In 1802, she acted with John Kemble at Covent Garden. After 1818, she became a long-time member of the Haymarket Company. She often portrayed old women in comedy, and she also handled with finesse such characters as Hamlet and Falstaff.

script was compiled from translations by Dryden, Lee, Corneille and T. Maurice. The title of the play (Fig. 10) was set in Greek on the playbill. A lengthy explanation of the plot was included, and Amherst made a promise to 'harmonize the subject matter with popular taste'. He advised theatregoers that real horses would appear as part of the production. *The Times* offered a different perspective on the first night:

> A sizeable audience was attracted this evening by as barefaced an imposition as was ever practiced on a public audience, since the days of the bottle conjuror. It has been ostentatiously announced in the bills, for the last two months, and also in some of the public prints, that the OEDIPUS TYRANNUS OF SOPHOCLES would be acted at this theatre, 'being its first appearance these 2440 years.' Of course many persons, attracted by the accurate chronological knowledge of the supposed translator, went, in the expectation of seeing the ancient tragedy … they were most miserably disappointed; for instead of listening to the simple, yet majestic strains of Sophocles, they were indulged with a cut-down edition of the bombastic, though powerful, tragedy of Lee and Dryden, upon the same subject.[39]

According to the reviewer, Huntley violently shouted his lines, and he was accused of 'tearing the ears' of the audience. Mrs Glover, a respected actress and resident of the neighbourhood, was more kindly received as Jocasta. The remainder of the company was dismissed as the 'stamp usually met with in minor theatres'.[40] Despite a cool reception in the press, Amherst's production played through November.

Amherst next offered a more traditional production of *Macbeth* with Mrs Glover as Lady Macbeth and himself in the title role. The critics found Mrs Glover's performance superior, but believed she deserved a more talented partner.[41] Amherst's management concluded without fanfare. In an effort to recover some of his investment, Amherst offered all his theatrical property for sale. But misfortune followed him to the end: 'just as Mr Algar, the auctioneer, had commenced selling the property, the stage gave way with a tremendous crash, and precipitated several persons below; but … no serious accident occurred'.[42]

Shortly after the beginning of 1822, the Beverly family returned to London for a brief season. They had been absent for thirteen months. After making repairs to the theatre, they mounted revivals of previous productions. In early spring, *Les Soirées françaises* presented a series of vaudevilles. A list of May attendees appeared in *The Times*. Among the fashionable people were the Ladies Jersey, Londonderry,

---

39   *The Times*, 2 November 1821.

40   *Ibid.*

41   HC: clipping, 1821.

42   *Morning Post*, 25 January 1822. A newspaper advertisement in *The Times* for 21 January 1822 provided a brief description of the inventory for the sale: 'The Wardrobe consists of rich spangled suits, an Oedipus dress and armour, Bertram's ditto, cut velvet dresses, shapes, flies, tunics, harlequin's dresses and swords, vases, helmets, breastplates &c. May be viewed tomorrow and morning of sale; and catalogues had at 27 Surrey-street, Strand; at the theatre and of Mr Algar, auctioneer and appraiser, 9-Kingstreet, Holborn.'

10 Playbill for ΟΕΔΙΠΥΣ [*Oedipus Tyrannus*], 8 November 1821. Heal Collection, Camden Local Studies and Archives Centre, London

11 Elizabeth Yates (née Brunton) by James Hopwood, Jr. Pub. 1
November 1817. © National Portrait Gallery, London

Glengall, Lothian and Home; Countesses D'Aglie and Munster; Baronesses Sternjeldt and Werther; Lords Ellenborough, Lowther, Fife, Palmerston and Jersey.[43] A performance in late July was marred when 'In the middle of a comedy performance, an ornamental figure of the sun under the stage box fell on the stage and covered it with plaster. Laporte calmly looked to the place where the sun had shone and restored calm to the house by exclaiming, 'Ce n'est rien qu'une éclipse, Messieurs.'[44] On 9 August 1822, *Les Maris ont tort,* a one-act *comédie vaudeville* by Achille d'Artois (1791–1868), and *Michel et Christine*, a *comédie vaudeville* in one act by Eugène Scribe (1791–1861) and Jean H. Dupin (1791–1887), were offered. Messrs Cloup, Pelissié and Laporte were the principal actors. The ladies in the company were all new: Mlles Josephine, Adline and Constance.[45] As the French troupe ended their season, another new manager arrived in Tottenham Street.

John Brunton

The daunting challenges of the managerial profession, the reputation of the playhouse and the advice of friends and colleagues did not deter John Brunton from signing a sub-lease for the playhouse in the autumn of 1822.[46] The lease-holding Beverly family would not return to Tottenham Street until March of 1823. Brunton chose the name West London Theatre, adopted by *Les Soirées françaises*, for the playhouse. His daughter Elizabeth was highly regarded throughout her dramatic career (Fig. 11). She was to be the principal actress at the West London.[47]

The press lauded John Brunton's managerial plans, and they reported what was thought to be a novel addition on the first night of the season: 'the curtain is of scarlet cloth, and possesses the attraction of novelty, for unlike all others that we have been accustomed to see it is divided into two parts, which, when it is necessary to disclose the scene, are drawn up on each side of the stage'.[48] In addition to Elizabeth Brunton, the acting company comprised Mr Hooper (who later became a leading comedian in Liverpool), Mr Loveday, Mr Lane, Miss Holdaway and Miss Norton.

The first night's bill, on 9 September 1822, included *The Widow Bewitched; or, She Must Be Married*, *What We Must All Come To* and the melodrama *Paul and*

---

43   *The Times*, 20 May 1822.

44   *Ibid.*, 3 August 1822.

45   V&A: playbills, 1822.

46   'Brunton, John', in William Oxberry, *Oxberry's Dramatic Biography and Historic Anecdotes* (London, 1826), 56. See also Moira Field, 'Brunton, John (1741–1822)', *ODNB*, accessed 18 November 2013. John Brunton, who had appeared at Covent Garden as early as 1774, was acting manager for R.W. Elliston at both Birmingham and King's Lynn. He was a well-known manager of the Norwich circuit, and he also managed Brighton for a time.

47   Joseph Knight, 'Yates [née Brunton], Elizabeth (1799–1860)', rev. J. Gilliland, *ODNB*, accessed 10 December 2013. She was born in Norwich on 21 January 1799. She made her debut as Desdemona to Charles Kemble's Othello on 15 March 1815. Her father believed she was more suited to comedy, and she prepared the role of Letitia Hardy in *The Belle's Stratagem*, performing it at King's Lynn and later with Elliston at Birmingham. She next appeared in Worcester, Shrewsbury and Leicester. Her London debut in the role of Letitia Hardy was at Covent Garden, 12 September 1817.

48   'West London Theatre', *The Drama; or, Theatrical Pocket Magazine*, 1822.

Justin. The opening piece on the bill was representative of what Brunton planned to present. The play included lovers, a drunken servant and clever chambermaids who, with the aid of a secret door, created farcical situations. The concluding melodrama *Paul and Justin* was noteworthy, according to one critic, because it lacked sensational effects and introduced Miss Brunton, who appeared in the breeches role of Paul. Samuel Beverly played the half-witted clown. The press was polite but not effusive.[49]

Brunton's commitment to the comic muse was abandoned by early October, when he mounted the sensational melodrama *Anaconda; or, the Terrific Serpent of Ceylon.* The play was inspired by M.G. Lewis's 1808 story 'The Anaconda' published in his *Romantic Tales.* The playbills provided important information for prospective theatregoers: 'The Anaconda is, among serpents, what the Elephant and Lion are among quadrupeds; like the Elephant, they surpass the rest of the serpent race by their size; and like the Lion, excel them in their address, their courage, and their force.' With an enormous snake as the villain of the piece, the play was certain to appeal to neighbourhood audiences. The audiences were enthusiastic. The anaconda, with lifelike movements, lunged repeatedly in its attempt to attack the hero and his son. *Anaconda*, which ran for twenty performances, was presented in the half-price part of the evening.

Elizabeth Brunton aspired to be an actress in comedy, but the audiences at the West London were partial to melodrama and spectacle. She left the theatre in November for provincial engagements. There was no disguising the fact that the Brunton management had not found the right vehicle or an audience for Elizabeth. After appearing in provincial theatres, she married Frederick Yates in 1824, and they accepted engagements at the Adelphi.

The remainder of 1822 reflected the general uncertainty of management at the West London. Brunton presented *The Forest of Bondy; or the Dog of Montargis*, and Miss Brunton made an appearance in the production as Florio. The star attraction for these evenings, Carlo, the Dog of Intelligence, was able, according to the playbills, to convey signals to his master, seize a cup of poison, open a chest in which a traitorous Indian was concealed, pursue the savages and rescue the wife and son of his master. Simpson's trained bear shared the bill (Fig. 12). John Brunton revived *Anaconda* and Elizabeth Brunton performed in a series of benefits beginning in November.

In early March of 1823, the Beverly family returned to the playhouse. They performed a brief joint season with the French troupe headed by M. Cloup. The Beverly Company performed on Tuesday-Thursday-Saturday, while *Les Soirées françaises* played Monday and Friday, with benefits on Wednesday. The high point of this season was the production of Pierre Carlet de Marivaux's *Le Jeu de l'amour*

---

49 *Morning Post*, 11 September 1822.

☞ Engagement of Mr. HECTOR SIMPSON, and his wonderful QUADRUPEDS, who have been the admiration of the most splendid audiences in this Metropolis and on the Continent.

ROYAL
WEST LONDON THEATRE.

WEDNESDAY, NOVEMBER 27, & DURING THE WEEK,
The Performance will commence with, for the First time, the FOREST SCENE taken from

VALENTINE & ORSON;
Or, the Wild Man of the Wood.
IN WHICH WILL BE INTRODUCED
THE REAL BEAR,
Whose Performance is of the most astonishing nature, and is so docile and well trained, that the most timid will feel the utmost confidence in his presence, whilst his strength and agility interest and delight the Audience, at once pleasing, surprising and astonishing.
Valentine, Mr. KIRK, Hugo, (Page to Valentine) Mr. S. BEVERLY,
Orson, (the Wild Man) Mr. H. SIMPSON, under whose direction the Pantomime is produced—under whose training the BEAR performs.

After which, the admired Burletta, called
Laugh When You Can.

Gontanzer, Mr. HOOPER, Bonus, Mr. LOVEDAY, Mortimer, Mr. CORDELL,
Sambo, Mr. DOBBS, Delville, Mr. KIRK, Charles, Master KERR, Costly, Mr. GARDNER,
Gregory, Mr. S. BEVERLY, Waiter, Mr. PARR.
Mrs. Mortimer, Miss NORTON, Emily, Miss MARINUS, Dorothy, Mrs. TURNOUR, Miss Gloomy, Mrs. WATKINSON.

A SKIPPING ROPE PAS DE QUATRE,
From DIDELOT'S Ballet of ZEPHYR.
By Miss BARNETT, Miss HIBBERT, Miss VINE, (Their Third Appearance) and Miss ROMER.
A FAVOURITE SONG, BY MISS HOLDAWAY.

To conclude with a Melo-dramatic Romance, written and produced by Mr. H. Saxrear, to exhibit the combined performances of his REAL BEAR and SAGACIOUS DOG, called The
BritishCaptain
AND
THE INDIAN CHIEF!
ENGLISH.
Captain Moreton, Mr. GARDNER, Jack Ratlin, (With a Song) Mr. DOBBS, Charles, Son to the Captain, Master KERR.
Bertha, the Captain's Wife, Miss MARINUS.
INDIANS.
Teriboo, (a ferocious Chieftain) Mr. H. SIMPSON, Torrembo, a Warrior of the same tribe, Mr. KIRK,
Madinbo, Mr. S. BEVERLY,
In the course of the Piece, a Characteristic Dance.
Amongst the wonderful Feats of that astonishing Animal,
Carlo, the DOG of Intelligence,
He will convey signals to his Master in the hour of distress—seizes a cup of poison whilst treacherously presenting it to his Master—breaks open a Chest in which the traitorous Indian is concealed—pursues the Savages, and rescues the Wife and Son of his Master.
W. Oxberry, Printer, White-Hart Yard, Drury Lane.

12 Playbill for *Valentine and Orson*, 27 November 1822. Heal Collection, Camden Local Studies and Archives Centre, London

et du hasard on 6 June 1823. Subscribers responded with delight when two grand balls were staged by M. Cloup, with the able assistance of M.B. Barnett, described as a Professor of Dance attached to the Opera.[50] Subscription entertainments were restricted to fourteen nights, but the managers, responding to demand, offered two additional seasons immediately following the first in 1823.[51]

The Beverlys reopened the house on 15 September for the 1823–4 season. They adopted the name West London Theatre (used by *Les Soirées françaises*) and retained it until the conclusion of their management. The playbills reassured the public that 'a respectable company' had been engaged, new scenery prepared and the house generally improved with eight boxes being added to the upper circle. The manager 'hopes to cater for the amusement of the families residing in the neighbourhood of the theatre'.[52]

Local taste for sentimental stories, along with generous portions of mystery and intrigue and the requisite triumph of justice, encouraged the Beverlys to produce *The Wizard of the Moor! or, The Fisherman of Glencairn*, adapted from a popular novel. The piece ran for twenty-nine performances. It was an auspicious beginning to the new season. *Guy Fawkes* (28) was also on the bill. *Frankenstein! or, The Danger of Presumption* (18) was presented on 5 November.[53] A short passage from Mary Shelley's novel was quoted on the bill warning the public that the fiction was founded on an event that Dr Darwin and some of the 'physiological writers' of Germany considered possible.[54] Another popular melodrama was Joseph Ebsworth's *Prisoner of Lyons* (24).

The 1824 season of *Les Soirées françaises* began in February and by March and April the Beverly Company briefly shared the bills. The Beverlys played fewer nights this year, only performing on Tuesdays and Saturdays. The French appeared on Mondays and Fridays. The Beverly season was not memorable beyond the fact that Master W.R. Beverly was identified on the playbills as being in charge of the scenery for *Haroun Alraschid; or, Orcano, the Fire Fiend* (13) in April of 1824.

Les Soirées françaises advertised a subscription season of fourteen nights for 1824. Subscriptions were available at the box office of the theatre from 10 to 4 each day, and to ensure compliance with the orders of the local magistrates, the name of each subscriber was to appear on the ticket. The prices of admission illustrate the differences between audiences for the French performances and the Beverly

---

50   Thompson Cooper, 'Barnett, Morris (1800–1856)', rev. John Wells, *ODNB*, accessed 18 November 2013. Barnett was probably Morris Barnett (1810–56), who spent much of his early life in France and was a musical conductor and a playwright. Following his work at the West London with the French actors, he was at the Adelphi in 1829 and Drury Lane in 1833. He became the music critic for the *Morning Post* and *The Era* for nearly seven years.

51   V&A: playbills.

52   HC: playbill, 15 September 1823.

53   Richard Brinsley Peake's adaptation of *Presumption; or, The Fate of Frankenstein* was offered at the English Opera House on 27 July 1823 and H.M. Milner's *Frankenstein; or, the Demon of Switzerland* was at the Coburg on 18 August 1823.

54   HC: playbill, 5 November 1823.

productions. The general subscription was £10 10s for the *Soirées françaises* season. For the more desirable sections of the house, the prices were substantially higher: parterre £15 6s, proscenium boxes £31 10s and dress circle or gallery boxes £21. Single evening admissions were 6s and the parterre was 3s 6d.[55] By comparison the Beverly admission prices were the traditional 4s, 2s and 1s. Half-price admission was available at half-past eight.

The *Soirées françaises* offerings on 29 March consisted of *Le Solliciteur; ou, L'Art d'obtenir des places*, a *chant* featuring M. Laporte, followed by *Les Projets de mariage; ou, Les Deux militaires*, a comedy in one act by Alexandre Duval (1762–1842). The evening concluded with the vaudeville *Les Bonnes d'enfants*. Other plays performed in the season were Scribe's *La Maîtresse au logis*; Duval's *Le Menuisier de Livonie; ou, Les Illustres voyageurs*; and *Ricco; ou, Le Marquis sans le vouloir* by Dumaniant. In *Ricco*, Adrien Perlet (1795–1850) displayed his talents: 'he is a booby clown who puts on the uniform of an officer and is then made against his comprehension and will by the tricks of a valet to play the part of a Marquis and involved in ludicrous distress as a supposed assassin'.[56]

Henry Crabb Robinson (1775–1867), the diarist, was in the West London Theatre audience for the French performances on seven different occasions: four nights in May and three nights in June. While Robinson expressed reservations about the plays and the productions, he was appreciative of some actors in the company. A particular favourite was Adrien Perlet, who joined the company for the second 1824 subscription season (Plate 4). Perlet's comic transformations in *L'Artiste*, written by Eugène Scribe and Perlet himself, required several disguises, and he was described by Robinson as having: 'a grace and humour quite delightful – he resembles [William] Farren but is infinitely beyond him'. Perlet, in Robinson's opinion, played low clowns exceptionally well and provided artistic leadership for the company. Robinson was amused by Messrs Laporte and Cloup when they portrayed English ladies, in *Les Anglaises pour rire; ou, la Table et le logement* by Charles-Augustin Sewrin (1771–1853) and Théophile Dumersan. The production was 'broad burlesque and tolerable fun, but the piece itself is nothing'.[57] Laporte's portrayal of a judge in Racine's *Les Plaideurs* was thought by Robinson to be 'too good – his imbecility – no legitimate subject of comedy – was painfully faithful'.[58] Robinson believed the actors to be more than competent, but he considered the plays to be unsophisticated. He curtly dismissed *Le Bourgeois gentilhomme*: 'the piece not a comedy after all, but mere farce – has not stuff enough for a regular

---

55   V&A: playbill.

56   *The London Theatre, 1811–1866: Selections from the Diary of Henry Crabb Robinson*, ed. Eluned Brown (London, 1966), 106. Reviews are for the 1824 season. See also Vincent Newey, 'Robinson, Henry Crabb (1775–1867)', *ODNB*, accessed 18 November 2013.

57   Robinson, *Diary*, 105–7, 112.

58   *Ibid.*, 105.

full length drama'.[59] Yet, with reservations, he appears to have been amused by the majority of the comedies: 'All French comedy is delicate compared with the parallel characters on the English Stage.'[60] On 2 June he wrote that he was sorry to be in a thinly populated theatre, but later in the month the patronage increased for the better known *Figaro* and *Le Bourgeois gentilhomme*.[61]

The Beverly family opened the 1824–5 season on 23 August. In this season there were at least eight different productions, as well as a travesty version, of Carl Maria von Weber's *Der Freischütz* performed at London theatres. Not to be outdone by their metropolitan competitors, the Beverlys mounted their own production of Weber's opera in September. The adaptation, prepared for the Beverly management by John Kerr, a playwright, adapter and sometimes actor, was an immediate success. *Der Freischütz; or Zamiel, the Spirit of the Forest and the Seventh Bullet* (96) was described on the bills as a 'grand melo-dramatic romance'. It was the most popular production of the Beverly management, and it was offered for 130 performances during the 1824, 1825 and 1826 seasons. The music, according to the playbills, was largely by Weber. New scenery, dresses, decorations and properties were advertised, and several children playing attendants supplemented the cast of thirty. William Roxby Beverly, approximately fourteen years of age, was credited with preparing the thirteen scenes, ranging from a tranquil forest to the 'Wolf's Glen by Moonlight'. The pyrotechnics of the incantation scene and the presence of Zamiel on a black charger, encircled by flames, were highlights of the evening. Beverly was dedicated to keeping his audiences amused. In October of 1824, *Dog of Montargis; or Forest of Bondy* (9) was back on the stage. In the same month, *Life of an Actor; or, the Adventures of Peregrine Proteus* (50), a burletta adapted from the popular work by Pierce Egan, began a long run at the theatre. *Wizard of the Moor* (6) from 1823 was revived in November.

During a brief closure prior to the Christmas holiday, the Beverlys carried out renovations to the playhouse and listed the improvements on their playbills: 'boxes were newly fitted up, the pit made more comfortable, velvet canopies with silk and the most costly ornaments had been added'. The final addition was a new curtain, necessitated by the enlarged proscenium opening required by *Der Freischütz*.[62] After the first of the year, the Beverly Company discontinued performances on Wednesdays, and in the middle of January Beverly announced that the company would not perform on either Mondays or Thursdays to allow for the return of Messrs Cloup, Laporte and Pelissié. From mid-January 1825, *Les Soirées françaises* performed a total of fifty nights.

---

59   *Ibid.*, 108.
60   *Ibid.*, 109.
61   *Ibid.*, 107–8.
62   HC: playbill, 17 December 1824.

The Beverly 1825–6 season was devoted to variety. W.L. Rede (1802–47)[63] appeared as Faustus in *The Devil and Dr Faustus* and Mr Warren, who was also in charge of the scenery, played the wondrous simian in *Jacko! or, The Ape of Brazil*.

Les Soirées françaises commenced the 1826 season in February and performed at the West London until September. Support for the company was strong and contemporary observers expressed surprise that French actors were able to attract English audiences. A writer for the *Everynight Book for 1826* assessed the 1826–7 *Soirées françaises* acting company. He began with M. Cloup:

> you are a respectable, but by no means a brilliant actor; your business on the stage is heavy and arduous – your cast of characters dull – such as afforded the performer few opportunities of eliciting applause, and yet if not played with propriety became wearisome and annoying to the spectator. Your level of declamation is good; in characters of a quiet and unobtrusive humour.[64]

Generous praise was given to M. Pelissié:

> your voice is good, your features rather handsome and sufficiently expressive … you produce capital portraits of some of the characters, your performance in melodrame and farce are of the highest order … your talents are versatile – you rank A in our estimation – we should be sorry to part with you.[65]

Perlet was considered to be a first-rate actor: 'We noted that there were few performers on the English stage equal to him; he is quite as good an old man as Farren, he excels Harley as the intriguing valet, and he may be equal to Mathews in transformation from character to character.'[66] Above all, Perlet was considered natural and correct, adhering closely to the character and avoiding exaggeration to gain audience approval. His cross-dressing roles were equally appreciated: 'Perlet is quite a distinct personage in the old woman of "Le Legataire", to what he is in any of his male characters, and this part he makes altogether different from his young Englishwoman in "Les Anglaises pour rire".'[67] The writer generally found the women in the company to be less talented than the men, but Mlles Delia and St Ange were seen as superior artists.

---

63 John Russell Stephens, 'Rede, William Leman (1802–1847)', *ODNB*, accessed 18 November 2013. He was the brother of Leman Thomas [Tertius] Rede and born in Hamburg, Germany. He was very active in the 1833–41 period, writing for the Strand, the Olympic, the Adelphi and the English Opera House. He usually appeared as an actor in light comedy. After 1841 he turned to other forms of literature. He started a publication to rival *Punch*, called *Judy*, which only lasted for two numbers. His first play was *Sixteen String Jack*, presented at the Coburg in 1823.

64 *Everynight Book for 1826* (London, 1826), 108–20.

65 *Ibid.*

66 *Ibid.*

67 *Ibid.*

The *Everynight Book* critic profiled the theatre audience. In the public boxes:

> There is Miss Foote, pale, withered, and worn – a blighted lily … yonder is the well-known De Roos – we think he spells his name so; and in the box next to him sits the noble farce-writer, Glengall; farther off is my Lord Lowther; opposite lolls the Marquis of Hertford, and in a box on the right of the last mentioned gentleman we discover the brilliant eyes of one of the Queens of Fashion – the Countess St Antonio. The light-haired, lean, pale, rickety, cross-eyed gentleman in the large box on the left is Prince Esterhazy. Lord Belfast is another frequent visitor, Hughes Ball and his treasure, Mercandotti, are to be seen here almost every evening. Madame Brocard, the present premier danseuse at the Opera, is sitting in the last box from the stage of the lower tier humming 'Scots wha'hae;' and the Vice-Chancellor on the other side of the house looks as though he were mentally conning over a judgement …

Moving down to the pit:

> Here are fifty well-known faces about town – lords lounging for a few seconds with literati, and counsellors chatting with critics. Here is Charles Young … four-in-hand Savage, in a blanket great coat and a Belcher cravat, gazing at the performance, and laughing where he should, as though he really understood something about what was going on upon the stage; Monsieur Harmon, the Gymnast of St James's Street who is making our youthful nobility as nimble as mountebanks – the author of a clever production just from the press on the Gymnastic Exercises, and a Treatise on the Act of Fencing; Crowley the barrister – around him are several other of the legal profession … Mars, the redacteur of a very amusing French paper, published in London, entitled 'Le Furet' … the gentleman in white silk stockings and dark pantaloons with 'spectacles on nose,' and a book under his arm is Chatelain, who edits another French publication.[68]

The writer assured Cloup and Pelissié that he, along with many others, hoped that a company of French comedians could be permanently established in the metropolis in the near future.[69]

A short 1826–7 Beverly family season commenced in September and concluded in January 1827. John Kerr provided a new play entitled *The Monster & the Magician; The Fate of Frankenstein*, which was again based on Mary Shelley's original work.

By mid-December of 1826, *Les Soirées françaises* were presenting Scribe's *Une Visite à Bedlam*. In mid-January, *Le Tartuffe* was offered 'pour l'anniversaire de la naissance de Molière'.[70]

---

68   *Ibid.*
69   *Ibid.*
70   V&A: playbill.

On 30 May 1827, Mlle Georges, 'pensionnée du Roi de France et première actrice tragique du Théâtre Française'[71] (Plate 5), M. Eric Bernard-Leon, 'premier actor tragique du Théâtre de l'Odéon', Messrs Riquier and Leroux and Mlle Dupont, also from the Théâtre de l'Odéon,[72] made their appearances at the West London Theatre. The prices for admission were increased for this occasion: proscenium boxes £4 4s, boxes, circle and gallery £3 3s, pit 10s and parterre and gallery 5s. The repertoire included tragedy: Voltaire's five-act *Mérope* on 30 May; his *Sémiramis*, featuring Mlle Georges, on 1 June; and the following week, Pierre Corneille's *Rodogune*, in which Mlle Georges assumed the role of Cléopâtre. *Mérope* was repeated on 18 June, and on 20 June Jean Racine's *Iphigénie*, with Mlle Georges as Clytemnestre, was performed. Henry Crabb Robinson attended the performance:

> I had no pleasure. As before Mlle. George [sic] displeased me thoroughly. An entire want of truth and nature – her sudden changes of tone, mere artificial tricks, never inspired by the sentiment of the moment or that instinctive tact which goes at once to the heart …[73]

In the May–August edition of the *London Magazine*, a visitor to the theatre observed that the theatre had not been well supported after M. Perlet departed:

> and that is a wonder too … but Perlet was the fashion and Perlet certainly filled the house, and Perlet is unquestionably a very good actor; however he put no money in the pocket of the managers, because he took too much out for his own salary.[74]

Around mid-December, Beverly advertised a ten-week 1827–8 season. It was to be his last. W.R. Beverly arranged his wife's 28 January benefit without requiring her to appear on stage. Instead, Mr Wood's dogs, Bruin, in the role of a Lion, and Dragon, in *The Dog of Montargis*, were the featured performers for the evening. On 3 March 1828, Beverly senior took his farewell benefit and thanked the public for their faithful support. For the Beverly management success was often elusive and, when found, it was fleeting. W.R. Beverly's production of *Der Freischütz* (130 performances, 1824–6) was noteworthy, but an exception. Throughout his management at the West London, he relied on regularly changing bills featuring

71   Marguerite Joséphine George (1787–1867), biography at <http://www.theatre-odeon.eu/frCached>. She was born in Bayeux. She made her debut at the Comédie-Française in 1802. She soon became Napoleon's mistress. She was in St Petersburg in 1808 and returned to Paris in 1818. From 1822–40 she appeared at the Odéon. See also Gertrude Aretz, *Die Frauen um Napoleon* (Graz, 1932).

72   F.W.J. Hemming, *Theatre and State in France, 1760–1905* (Cambridge, 1994), 105–7. This theatre, considered second only to the Comédie-Française, was built in 1779 and opened in 1782 by Marie-Antoinette. The playhouse was managed by Louis-Baptiste Picard (1769–1828). It was here that *The Marriage of Figaro* was first performed in 1784. It was reconstructed in 1808, officially named the *Théâtre de l'Impératrice*, but it continued to be known as the *Odéon*. The theatre was destroyed by fire in 1818. The present structure was built in 1819.

73   Robinson, *Diary*, 118.

74   *London Magazine*, May–August, 1827.

melodrama, canine performers and action drama in an effort to remain solvent. The Beverly family were committed to life in the theatre, and W.R. Beverly's investment in the Regency/West London Theatre and the purchase of a long-term lease in London was a gamble that proved to be more risky than anticipated. When John Perry purchased the lease in 1828, the Beverly family was no doubt relieved. During their fifteen years (1814–28) as managers of the playhouse, the family typically spent part of the year, often several months, performing elsewhere in provincial theatres. By letting the playhouse to the French company and other managers, they were able to sustain their leasehold without default. Beverly sublet the theatre for thirteen months from December 1820 to January 1822 (to J.H. Amherst) and from September 1822 to March 1823 (to John Brunton). The French performers were at the theatre from 1821–8 for as many as fifty performances a year. In his tenure as manager of the West London, Beverly demonstrated courage, imagination and tenacity. It was at the West London Theatre that he proudly launched the artistic career of his son William R. Beverly.

In September 1828, Monsieur Chedel opened the West London Theatre. Messrs. Cloup and Pelissié had taken their *Soirées françaises* to the Lyceum for the 1828 season. Chedel was encouraged by his colleagues to engage a popular young French actor, Frédérick Lemaître (1800–76).[75] He had been performing in Calais when a lady arrived from London with a letter inviting him to play Georges de Germany in a series of performances of the French melodrama *Trente ans; ou, La Vie d'un joueur*, written by Victor Ducange (1783–1833) and Prosper Dinaux (1795–1859), at the West London Theatre. Lemaître was promised a large share of the profits. Chedel appealed to Lemaître's vanity and nationalistic pride by noting that several major English actors had played the part of Georges de Germany, but all of London was most eager to see the man who created the role. Lemaître accepted the invitation and appeared at the West London.[76] His performance in the play was described as powerful by one critic: 'one followed with certain anguish of soul this man, so elegant at the rising of the curtain, as he descended step by step, physically and morally, until he became a vulgar assassin'.[77] *The Times* critic, either not impressed by the appearance of Lemaître or without any idea who he was, never mentioning him by name, reported: 'the entertainments were respectably executed, though we recognised only two performers of Paris celebrity on the stage'.[78]

Chedel encountered legal difficulties almost immediately. He was either unaware of previous licensing arrangements or disparaging of authority when he elected to forego the required subscription season arrangements for the French performers. His boldness did not escape the watchful eyes of the patent holders and steps

75   Robert Baldick, *The Life and Times of Frédérick Lemaitre* (London, 1959), 58–9.
76   *Ibid.*
77   *Illustrated Sporting and Dramatic News*, 2 December 1876.
78   *The Times*, 5 September 1828.

were taken to close down his management. He was summoned to answer charges of operating a theatre without lawful authority on a complaint signed by Percy Farren, stage manager at the Haymarket Theatre, who swore he had gone to the West London and paid 2s 6d at the door for admission to the pit and saw a *comédie* in one act by Charles-Guillaume Étienne (1777–1845) entitled *Brueys et Palaprat*. A Mr Cater of Southampton Street gave similar evidence. In his defence, Chedel argued that similar performances had been given at the West London for eleven years under a magistrate's licence and that many distinguished citizens, including the Lord Chamberlain, had been subscribers. If money had been taken at the door of his theatre, Chedel claimed it was collected without his knowledge and certainly without his approval. He stressed the fact that his bills fully informed the public: 'No Money Taken at the Doors'. Farren and Carter were called again and testified that the man receiving money did not stand in the money taker's box, but instead met them at the door, demanded 2s 6d, told them no check was necessary, and said 'Go in'. Even with the aid of an interpreter, Chedel could not convince the court of his innocence. He was found guilty and required to pay a £50 fine.[79]

At the end of 1828, the Royal West London Theatre stood dark and empty.

---

79   *London Standard*, 22 September 1828.

Chapter Three

*The licensing laws, managers in
distress and the insatiable demand
for variety, 1829–1839*

John Perry of Charles Street, Fitzroy Square, had purchased the lease of the Tottenham Street property from W.R. Beverly early in 1828 and settled all taxes in arrears.[1] During the decade after Chedel's failure, Perry let the theatre to several different artists and managers. For him the lease was a business investment and there is no evidence that he was involved in theatrical production. Most managers did not remain at the theatre very long. Some enjoyed success, but only briefly.

The managers of the Tottenham Street playhouse were in competition with other minors and the patent theatres. Some were prospering while others were struggling to remain solvent. Charles Mathews and Frederick H. Yates were the managers and leading performers at the Adelphi. According to *The News* of 9 November 1828, they were enjoying full houses and strong revenues from a production of an opera entitled *The Mason of Buda*.[2] The Edward Fitzball melodrama *Red Rover; or, The Mutiny of the Dolphin* was also on the Adelphi bills in 1829.[3] The Surrey, under Robert W. Elliston's management,[4] presented T.P. Cooke in the first production of Douglas Jerrold's *Black-Eyed Susan; or, The Lover's Peril* with considerable success. Controversy over the production rights to Edward Fitzball's *Flying Dutchman* (the author apparently sold the script twice) prompted Elliston to commission a version

---

1   Holborn Public Library: Camden Local Studies and Archives Centre: St Pancras Rate Books: St Pancras Rate and Poor Tax, 1828.

2   A production with this title was licensed for the Adelphi on 21 October 1818. The author was J.R. Planché and the music was by G.H. Rodwell.

3   Alfrida Lee, 'Calendar for 1829–1830', *The Adelphi Theatre Calendar*, <http://www.umass.edu/Adelphi TheatreCalendar>, accessed 18 October 2012.

4   'Elliston, Robert W', in Highfill et al. (eds), *Biographical Dictionary*, vol. 5, 55ff.; and Christopher Murray, 'Elliston, Robert William (1774–1831)', *ODNB*, accessed 18 November 2013. See also Christopher Murray, *Robert William Elliston, Manager* (London, 1975). Elliston was an actor, singer, manager and playwright. His managements of the Surrey and Drury Lane, as well as provincial theatres in Manchester and Birmingham, and later the Olympic, were spirited, and as an actor he was highly respected by his contemporaries. He was regarded as a great talent with a perplexing personality.

by Douglas Jerrold. [5] In addition, John Braham and Mrs Waylett were popular in performances of *Guy Mannering* during the season.

The Olympic Pavilion was up for sale in 1829. The theatre would eventually be taken by Madame Vestris in 1830 and opened the following year. John Liston left the Haymarket in August of 1829 to perform at Drury Lane. [6] At the Theatre Royal, Covent Garden, Charles Kemble would be confronted with a magistrate's warrant issued for overdue rates and taxes. In an effort to avoid bankruptcy, he convinced his daughter, Fanny Kemble, to make her stage debut as Juliet. [7] Edmund Kean appeared at the Theatre Royal, Drury Lane in *Henry V* in 1830 and the American manager Stephen Price vacated the theatre in March after a stormy four-season tenure. [8]

From 1829 to 1839, several managers of the theatre in Tottenham Street tried to attract patrons from beyond the neighbourhood. Initially, John Chapman, Thomas Melrose and Alexander Lee, George Macfarren, Henry Mayhew and Gilbert A'Beckett, Louisa Nisbett and Henry Addison did establish a broader city-wide following, but after a few months they all succumbed to the uncertainties of managing a minor theatre. Success for Chapman, Melrose and Lee caused them to become embroiled in a battle over licensing law. The other managers struggled to respond to the unending demand for new plays and the expense of mounting them. Eventually, the managers were all forced to accept the reality that they could not risk alienating local theatregoers by producing plays that did not respond to prevailing neighbourhood tastes.

Throughout this period and continuing for the next several decades, the bills of fare at this theatre featured variety. Along with pantomime, farce, comedy and action-melodrama in all its forms, women-in-breeches roles were popular with Tottenham Street theatregoers. Mrs Waylett and Madame Vestris in 1830, Madame Céleste in 1831 and Mrs Nisbett in 1835 all enhanced their artistic reputations by portraying heroic male characters. Mrs Selby in 1833 played Othello for her benefit. The opportunity to appear in these roles gave women the freedom to explore new acting challenges and created for them a special, exotic actor–audience relationship. Cross-dressing men were also on the stage of the playhouse. In 1834 William Oxberry (1808–52)[9] was featured as a 'pauper Negress' and Mr Mitchell was Moll Chubb, commander of the female revolution in *Revolt of the Workhouse*. They were

---

5   Knight, *Major London 'Minor'*, 63.

6   Jim Davis, *John Liston, Comedian* (London, 1985), 77.

7   Robert Bernard Martin, 'Kemble, Frances Anne (1809–1893)', *ODNB*, accessed 18 November 2013.

8   Sheppard (gen. ed.), *Theatre Royal, Drury Lane and The Royal Opera House, Covent Garden*, 24.

9   Joseph Knight, 'Oxberry, William Henry (1808–1852)', rev. Klaus Stierstorfer, *ODNB*, accessed 18 November 2013. He appeared at a private theatre in 1825 and his first professional engagement was at the Olympic at a benefit for his stepfather, William Leman Rede. After performing in Chelmsford, Hythe, Manchester and Sheffield, he joined Hammond's company in York. In 1832 he acted at the Strand. He was four years at the English Opera House (Lyceum) before moving to the Princess's. In 1841 he succeeded Keeley at Covent Garden. He was a lively actor, a dancer in burlesque and a prolific author.

described in a review as 'superbly grotesque, and wantonly extravagant'.[10] Over the next several decades at this theatre, numerous actors and actresses continued this tradition, with women usually appearing as young, vital men and the males most often in comic roles.[11]

Early in 1829, Thomas John Dibdin (1771–1841) agreed to be the new manager of the West London Theatre. Dibdin was a writer of songs, verses and plays. He was a modestly accomplished actor and had experience as a theatre manager.[12] When he took the playhouse in Tottenham Street in 1829, Dibdin was in the latter years of his turbulent career. He would not recover his losses in the theatrical profession at the West London Theatre.

Thomas Dibdin's season opened on 12 January 1829. The press quoted John Perry as having said that he was following 'the only course by which they could hope to reap any benefit from the concern; that is, by having secured the services of Mr T. Dibdin, as manager. The gentleman's name attached to the bills of any theatre is sufficient guarantee that a few hours of real entertainment will reward its visitors.' A newspaper writer outlined the obstacles confronting Dibdin: 'The West London Theatre … is unfortunately situated at the extremity of the town; therefore, when it is considered that the majority of its auditors have to pass almost every other theatrical establishment, and that laziness is natural to us all, it cannot be denied that this theatre has to struggle against manifold disadvantages.'[13]

Dibdin chose four pieces for his opening bill: *T.T.S., or The Bar and the Stage*, a comic pasticcio; *Wedding Favours*, a pantomimic ballet; *Luck in the Lottery*, a new comic burletta of his own authorship; and *London Actor; or, Four Score Years Ago*, a musical piece. Prices were set at 4s, 2s and 1s with half-price tickets available at half-past eight; single or double free admission for the entire season was also available from the box office of the theatre. Responses in the first weeks were encouraging, in spite of bitter cold weather which required heating stoves to be placed in various parts of the house. A newspaper writer believed that 'the West London Theatre, when known, will equal the best of its competitors'.[14] The *Dramatic Magazine* 'wished him [Dibdin] every success'.[15]

Many of the plays presented at the West London were Dibdin's works, and during his five-month stay he revived other local favourites. By the end of January 1829, an earlier Sadler's Wells and Lyceum success was on the stage: *Suil Dhuv the Coiner;*

---

10   HC: clipping, November 1834.

11   Tracy C. Davis, *Actresses as Working Women* (London, 1991), 112–13.

12   John Russell Stephens, 'Dibdin, Thomas John (1771–1841)', *ODNB*, accessed 18 November 2013. See also Thomas Dibdin, *Reminiscences of Thomas Dibdin* (London, 1837). Two of his most noteworthy pieces, *The Dog of Montargis, or the Forest of Bondy* and *Harlequin Hoax; or a Pantomime Proposed*, were written and produced in 1814. He took the Royal Circus in 1816 and renamed it the Surrey. Following a brief interlude at the Haymarket, Dibdin found himself nearly £18,000 in debt as a result of losses at the Surrey and speculations in Ireland.

13   HC: clipping, January 1829.

14   *Morning Post*, 14 January 1829.

15   *Dramatic Magazine*, 2 March 1829.

13 Monsieur Gouffe, September 1829. Heal Collection, Camden
Local Studies and Archives Centre, London

or, The Eve of St John, based on a story in Gerald Griffin's *Munster Festivals* and featuring a 'Druidical Circle', a raging signal fire and a fierce combat. But it failed to draw. Dibdin's *Wolf of the Forest of Arden* (25), a fairy melodrama featuring settings described as 'a magnificent pavilion in nubibus' and 'my grandmother's enchanted cottage', proved more popular with audiences.

Dibdin recruited his friend and colleague from his Surrey days, Watkins Burroughs (1795–1869),[16] to be the leading man for his company. Unfortunately, the actor's reputation suffered from an observation by the *Mirror of the Stage* critic who thought Burroughs cursed with 'a cracking and whining voice'. Moreover, it was believed that for want of '*mind in his labours*', Burroughs often 'fell into the ridiculous in his performances'.[17] Dibdin enjoyed little success in March, and it was not until after the Easter holiday, when Mrs Young of the Olympic and W.H. Payne of Sadler's Wells were added to the company, that any production was repeated often. *Enchanted Will; or, Harlequin at the Lake of Killarney* (13) a pantomime, and the melodrama *Ninth Statue; or, The Irishman in London* (12) were on the April bills.

By May of 1829 Dibdin had left the theatre, and Burroughs assumed the role of manager. In an effort to attract audiences, the one shilling gallery tickets were reduced by half. Most of Burroughs's evenings as manager were devoted to guest performers and variety.

George Wild (1805–56) announced his plans to open the theatre for a summer season on 3 July 1829.[18] Wild's company was led by Miss Absolon, from the Surrey, Mrs Baker, from the Haymarket, and several players from the previous Dibdin troupe. Prices were reduced to 2s, 1s and 6d with no half-price admission, except to the boxes. The opening production of *The Old Chateau* in July of 1829 prompted a letter of warning, which Wild reprinted on his playbill, from the patent theatres about presenting legitimate drama.[19]

In August, Wild turned to sensational drama with Charles A. Somerset's *Zelina; or, The Heroine of the Cross*. Wild's comic antics and sensational drama offered a wide range of variety. Between August and October, Monsieur Gouffe (John Hornshaw, who had earned his reputation at the Surrey[20]) in *Jack Robinson and His Monkey* (18) was the primary attraction (Fig. 13). Wild engaged Gouffe beginning

---

16   Knight, *Major London 'Minor'*, 31–42. From 1822 to 1825, Burroughs managed the Surrey with other colleagues. One of his achievements was to engage Edward Fitzball to write for the theatre.

17   'The Minor-ies – No. 3', *Mirror of the Stage*, 1829.

18   'Memoir of Mr Wild', *Theatrical Times*, 6 March 1847. Blanchard, *Life and Reminiscences*, vol. 1, 44. Born George Brodie in 1805, he studied medicine as a young man, but his sole ambition was to become an actor. He made his debut on 25 October 1825 at the West London private theatre and then at the Olympic, which he managed from 1828–9. He performed with Edmund Kean at Richmond in 1832 and managed the Tottenham Street playhouse again in 1839. He managed the Olympic from 1841 to 1844.

19   *Theatrical Examiner*, 25 July 1829.

20   Knight, *Major London 'Minor'*, 146–7.

on 24 August for at least twenty-seven additional performances in plays written for his physical prowess and his ape costume: *Monkey of Arragon, Island Ape, John Adams, or the Monkey of Pitcairn Islands, Quadrupeds* and *Jocko, The Brazilian Ape*.

In September, Mr Coney and his talented dogs, Hector and Bruin, joined Gouffe on the bills. The canines appeared in *The Cherokee Chief; or, The Shipwreck'd Sailor & his Two Dogs, Knights of the Cross* and *The Forest of Bondy*. Nautical drama was also on the bills, with *The Pilot, Mutineers of the Bon Ton, Paul Jones* and *Spectre Pilot* being offered. Interspersed with the animals, floundering ships, Gouffe and sensational melodrama, were slack-wire performers, dancers and an occasional amateur actor.

John Chapman, Thomas Melrose and Alexander Lee, licensing laws and the patent theatres

John Kemble Chapman, Thomas Melrose and Alexander Lee took the theatre for the 1829–30 autumn season, which began on 23 November. They selected the name The Theatre, Tottenham Street for the playhouse. On bills circulated in the city, the managers confidently announced their plans to mount performances equal to those of the great houses. John Kemble Chapman (1806–52),[21] serving as the spokesman for the trio as well as acting manager for the company, had earned his theatrical reputation in provincial theatres. Thomas Melrose (1790–1834) was a singer and a promising musician.[22] The financially independent Alexander Lee (d. 1851) brought his skills as a composer and director of music to the management of the theatre. He also appeared in several productions.[23]

The lease was negotiated and the rental agreement signed (a weekly rate of £16, paid in advance), and the company was engaged. The prices were set at 4s, 2s and 1s with half-price beginning at half-past eight, curtain to rise at seven. Chapman, Melrose and Lee formed their company by hiring actors from the Theatres Royal Covent Garden and Drury Lane as well as from the English Opera House. The gentlemen included William Vining (1783–1861), from a large family of theatre artists,[24] and Percy Farren (1784–1843), the son of the well-known actor William Farren. Percy Farren, who was to serve as stage manager, suffered from an asthmatic condition and

---

21   An actor and theatre manager, Chapman was married to Ann Tree, sister of Mrs Charles Kean and Mrs Bradshaw. Erroll Sherson, *London's Lost Theatres of the Nineteenth Century* (London, 1925), 39–41. He rarely appeared as an actor in the company at the Theatre, Tottenham Street, but his wife Ann Tree did. After the 1829–30 season at the Theatre, Tottenham Street, he moved to the City Theatre, Cripplegate.

22   'Melrose, Thomas', in Oxberry, *Dramatic Biography*, 79–87. Upon his arrival in London from his native Felton, he studied music with Michael Kelly. In time this apprenticeship led to an engagement at John Brunton's theatre at Brighton. In the following years, he travelled to Edinburgh, Glasgow, Paisley, Aberdeen and Belfast before joining Chapman and Lee at the Theatre, Tottenham Street.

23   'Chapman, John K', in Sherson, *London's Lost Theatres*, 212; and Blanchard, *Reminiscences*, vol. 1, 87. After dissolving his partnership with Chapman and Melrose, Lee became the lessee at Drury Lane and an adversary of his former colleagues. He later married Mrs Harriet Waylett.

24   K.D. Reynolds, 'Vining, James (1795–1870)', *ODNB*, accessed 18 November 2013. William Vining is referred to in this entry.

performed only rarely as an actor. He was previously engaged as stage manager at the Haymarket where he also served as a friend and tutor of Helen Faucit as she prepared for a career on the Victorian stage.[25] Miss Ann Tree (Chapman's wife and the sister of Mrs Charles Kean) and Mrs Harriet Waylett were the two principal women in the company. Mrs Waylett (née Cooke, 1789–1851) was discovered by Charles and Maria-Theresa Kemble and brought to the Theatre Royal, Covent Garden in 1812 to play Desdemona. Prior to her appearance at the Theatre, Tottenham Street (Plate 6), Mrs Waylett had performed at several London playhouses.[26]

On Monday 23 November 1829 an enthusiastic audience attended *A Day of Folly, or, The Spanish Wedding* based on the Beaumarchais play *La Folle journée, ou, le mariage de Figaro*, with story elements borrowed from Mozart's opera *Le nozze di Figaro*. The music consisted of popular airs. The audience enjoyed the dramatic productions, the acting and singing (especially that of Ann Tree and Mrs Waylett). The orchestra was also thought to be excellent.[27] In the following week *Royal Travellers*, an operatic play based on the French opera by François-Adrien Boieldieu (1775–1834) entitled *Jean de Paris*, featured William Vining in the role of Phillipe de Valois and Mrs Waylett as the Princess of Navarre. On the same bill, Mrs Tayleure made her debut in the comic piece *Tit for Tat; or A Peep at the Mad-House* (21), adapted from the Eugène Scribe vaudeville *Une Visite à Bedlam*.

In the early days of the new management, the principal piece on the bills was often operatic. This represented an effort to attract audiences from beyond the neighbourhood. By the end of December *Spanish Barber, or the Fruitless Precaution*, adapted from Rossini's *Il barbiere di Siviglia*, 'was given in a style which, in regard to acting, singing, scenery, and costume, would have done credit to either of the winter houses'.[28] The first-price admissions declined after the first month, but the house was crowded at half-price.[29] The managers soon concluded that it would be difficult to survive on half-price receipts and that it would be necessary to increase the melodramatic and comic offerings on the bills.

On 14 January 1830, Percy Farren's new melodrama entitled *The Field of Forty Footsteps* (45) was first presented. It was based on a local legend about a love triangle involving two brothers and their violent deaths. The scene was set in Long Fields, an area behind the east side of Gower Street in the immediate vicinity of Bloomsbury Square. Percy Farren embellished the story by incorporating incidents

---

25 Carol Jones Carlyle, *Helen Faucit: Fire and Ice on the Victorian Stage* (London, 2000), 22–4.

26 Joseph Knight, 'Waylett, Harriet (1800–1851)', rev. J. Gilliland, *ODNB*, accessed 18 November 2013; and *Green Room Memoirs, Theatrical Library, c.*1820. She appeared in *The Blind Boy* at the age of sixteen in Bath and by 1819 she was in Coventry where she married a fellow actor, Mr Waylett. They performed at the Adelphi in 1820. Mrs Waylett appeared at Drury Lane in 1824 and the following year she was at the Haymarket. She acted and sang in Dublin and Cork in 1828. By 1834, she was the 'sole' manager of the Strand.

27 *London Standard*, 24 November 1829.

28 *Theatrical Observer*, 19 December 1829.

29 *Theatrical Observer*, 19 October 1829.

14 Frances Fitzwilliam as Fanny in *Maid or Wife*, 1834. Folger Shakespeare Library

from Walter Scott's *The Bride of Lammermoor* as well as from *Coming Out; and The Field of the Forty Footsteps*, published two years earlier.[30] The reviewer for the *Athenaeum* offered generous praise for the author and the leading actors, William Vining, Ann Tree and Mrs Waylett.[31] The play was exactly what the neighbourhood audiences desired.

Mrs Waylett next appeared in the title role of a burletta version of Thomas J. Dibdin's script *Don Giovanni* (29). Mrs Waylett's cross-dressing performance was an immediate success. Female cross-dressers became a popular addition to the playbills of this theatre as well as elsewhere in the city.[32] She appeared as Don Giovanni on the bills with *The Field of Forty Footsteps*, and the managers offered a special juvenile evening on 26 January, prior to the conclusion of the Christmas season. Admission was reduced to half-price for children under twelve years old. The entertainments, the managers promised, would conclude by eleven o'clock.[33] *My Wife's Husband* (25) premiered in February and *Midas* (17) opened on 18 March 1830 with Mrs Waylett appearing in the breeches role. According to the press, her Apollo was equal to that of any of her competitors at other theatres.[34] The theatre closed for nine days beginning 3 April for the Easter holiday. During the brief interval, Chapman, Melrose and Lee made several interior improvements.

Mrs Frances Fitzwilliam (1801–54) joined the company (Fig. 14).[35] On 12 April 1830 she made her first appearance at the theatre as Ellen Douglas in *Spectre Boat; or, The Weird Woman of Glenfellin* (15).[36] In late April Mrs Fitzwilliam and William Vining performed in *The Heart of Midlothian* (23). She had performed the Madge Wildfire role previously at the Surrey.[37] By May the critic for the *Morning Post* could not contain his enthusiasm for Mrs Fitzwilliam. He was 'delighted to find this justly favourite actress rather increases than otherwise in talent and energy and has

---

30 Jane Porter and Anna Maria Porter, *Coming Out; and the Field of Forty Footsteps*, 3 vols (London, 1828). See also John Timbs, *Curiosities of London*, new edn (London, 1868).

31 *Athenaeum*, 23 January 1830.

32 Davis, *Actresses as Working Women*, 114.

33 HC: playbill, 26 January 1830.

34 *Theatrical Observer*, 19 April 1830.

35 Joseph Knight, 'Fitzwilliam [née Copeland], Fanny [or Fanny] Elizabeth (1801–1854)', rev. J. Gilliland, *ODNB*, accessed 18 November 2013. She made her debut in Dover at the age of two. Upon hearing ten-year-old Frances Copeland sing, Charles Incledon suggested she abandon the stage to study voice seriously. She pursued a stage career and appeared four years later at the Haymarket under the management of George Coleman the younger. She was engaged at the Surrey by Thomas Dibdin, moved to the Olympic and later appeared at Drury Lane with Robert Elliston. During her career she performed at the Adelphi, Victoria and Sadler's Wells, which she co-managed with W.H. Williams in 1832.

36 The playbills attribute the play to the 'author of *Robert the Devil*' with special music by Alexander Lee. Two melodramas with the title *Robert the Devil* had been performed in London shortly before April 1830: Michael Rophino Lacy's *Robert the Devil, Duke of Normandy* (Covent Garden, 28 November 1829) and an anonymous melodrama *Robert the Devil; or, The Terror or Normandy* (Royal Pavilion, 16 March 1830). A version of the play, published in June 1830, lists Richard John Raymond as the author of *Robert the Devil; Duke of Normandy*. In that volume, *Spectre Boat* is listed as one of his works.

37 Knight, *Major London 'Minor'*, 25. Thomas Dibdin was so pleased with her reception in the role of Madge Wildfire at the Surrey in 1819 that he raised her salary by a pound a week.

lost none of that profusion of animal spirits which has always been the pleasing characteristic of her performances'.[38] Vining, too, had earned strong support from the *Morning Post*, whose writer thought him an actor 'whose abilities in the more lively characters of the drama are not surpassed by any actor on the stage'.[39] With these appealing entertainments, the managers enjoyed frequent full houses.[40] J.B. Buckstone (1802–79)[41] joined Mrs Fitzwilliam for her benefit on 10 May, and they performed his play *Dead Shot*. She continued at the theatre until mid-June. The managers kept the theatre open during the summer and hosted several leading London actors.

After seven months of management, Chapman, Melrose and Lee had attained a degree of success. They wisely altered their initial plans to perform primarily opera and musical entertainments and added more melodramatic pieces to their bills. With Mrs Fitzwilliam and Mrs Waylett in major roles, theatregoers flocked to the theatre. The full houses soon attracted the attention of the patent theatre holders.

The 1752 act of Parliament had redefined the authority of the patent theatres and enabled local magistrates to license theatres at their discretion. The patent theatres retained the authority to perform the 'legitimate' drama as they always had, and the new playhouses, or minor theatres, would present the burletta, a type of performance that would not make incursions into the patent theatres' prerogatives. The burletta was not defined in specific terms in the act of Parliament, which created considerable confusion. The burletta was a play with music, but uncertainty persisted as to how much music was required to make a distinction between the burletta and a 'legitimate' drama. By 1830, five songs in an act were viewed as sufficient to offset any spoken dialogue and thereby qualify the play as a burletta.[42]

As if the conflicts concerning production authority were not enough, the 1752 act also had the effect of intensifying competition for audiences among the managements of the major and minor houses. The law encouraged entrepreneurs to invest in playhouses, and several new theatres were built in London following the legislation. The newly licensed theatres were presenting pantomime, equestrian drama, aquatic drama, melodrama, ballad opera, burlettas and variety entertainments. The appeal of these offerings lured audiences away from the major houses: 'it was not merely that the inhabitants of London's new districts demanded their own theatres and entertainments. The playgoers of Drury Lane and Covent Garden demanded

---

38   *Morning Post*, 14 May 1830.

39   *Ibid.*, 23 March 1830.

40   *Ibid.*, 14 May 1830.

41   Donald Roy, 'Buckstone, John Baldwin (1802–1879)', *ODNB*, accessed 18 Novemer 2013. He began his career in the provinces and first appeared in London at the Surrey in 1823. He performed at the Coburg and after appearing at the Adelphi in 1827 he was back at the Surrey. He managed the Haymarket from 1853–77. As an actor 'he had great breadth and humour, and the mere sound of his voice, a mixture of chuckle and drawl, heard off stage was enough to set the audience laughing'. He was the author of around 200 plays, primarily melodrama and farces.

42   Rowell, *Victorian Theatre*, 10.

identical entertainments.'[43] Hence, by the late 1820s the differences between the offerings of the major and minor theatres were difficult to discern.

The holders of the patents became increasingly protective of their rights in this highly competitive environment and advocated strict enforcement of the burletta licensing restrictions. They identified offenders and filed prosecutions against the minor managers. While some viewed the prosecutions as petty and unwarranted, the law was the law, and until changes were made, the patentees were within their rights to protect themselves. To further complicate the situation, the minor managers routinely ignored the licensing restrictions, claiming the vagaries of the law prohibited any meaningful understanding, and produced whatever type of play they thought might attract audiences. By defying the law and offering 'legitimate' drama, however disguised, at their playhouses, the minor theatre managers provoked the anger of the majors. While popular support for elimination of the patents had grown steadily during the early part of the century, popular sentiment neither paid the fines nor changed the law. When a minor theatre management became too successful, it prompted closer scrutiny by the major theatres. Prosecution was inevitable.[44] Spies were sent to observe the activity at the minor playhouses with the expectation that they would testify in court proceedings about any perceived violations of the law.[45]

In June 1830 the managers at the Theatre, Tottenham Street received notification that information had been presented against them by the Drury Lane deputy box office book-keeper, John Parsons. Chapman, Melrose and their new partner George Perry (1793–1862)[46] – Alexander Lee having resigned, effective 1 June 1830, and moved to Drury Lane Theatre – were accused of presenting unauthorised entertainments. On the morning of 14 June 1830, the managers received the charges forwarded from the Bow Street Magistrates' Court. They shared the information with the public to elicit support for their cause:

> that you did, on the 10th day of March last, at the Parish of St Pancras, aforesaid, without authority by virtue of letters patent from our Lord the King or any of his predecessors, and without license from any Lord Chamberlain of the Household of our said Lord the King or any of his predecessors, unlawfully did cause to be acted, represented, and performed, for hire, gain, and reward, a certain entertainment of the stage – to wit, a certain musical entertainment called *The Gipsey's Prophecy*, contrary to the Statute ...[47]

43   *Ibid.*, 11.
44   Watson, *Sheridan to Robertson*, 20ff.
45   Jane Williamson, *Charles Kemble: Man of the Theatre* (Lincoln, NE, 1964), 196–200.
46   'Perry, George', in *Grove's Dictionary of Music and Musicians*, ed. J.A. Fuller Maitland, 2nd edn, 5 vols (London, 1904–10), vol. 3. He was born in Norwich. In 1822 he became the director of music at the Haymarket.
47   V&A: playbill, 22 June 1830.

There were nine violations cited in the charges and for each count a fine of £50 was to be levied. In addition the managers were required to appear before magistrates Thomas Halls and Richard Birnie on 24 June at twelve o'clock.

While a defence was being prepared, the managers continued to offer nightly entertainments. On their 22 June playbill, Chapman and Melrose responded to their accusers and advised them and the public that they would not feign contrition. Indeed, the managers were determined to challenge the laws that they considered to be outdated. Confidence ran high in Tottenham Street.

The newspapers warned the public that on the 24th 'a good deal of speechifying' would take place. With that prospect and the fact that leading theatre personalities were in attendance, the Bow Street Offices were crowded to capacity. William Dunn, treasurer of Drury Lane, W.P. Davidge, William Barrymore, T.F. Wilkinson, Frederick Vining, Henry Gattie and Joey Grimaldi were in attendance. Mr Adolphus, serving as legal counsel for the Committee and proprietors of Drury Lane and Covent Garden, including Messrs Willet, Kemble and Forbes, spoke in support of the information. He did not represent Alexander Lee, who was now lessee of Drury Lane. Alexander Lee chose to remain silent in the proceedings. He neither defended nor damned his former colleagues.[48]

C. Phillips, acting as counsel for Chapman, Melrose and Perry, arrived late and John Perry, the leaseholder, was not in attendance. The magistrates requested that John Perry appear at a later date. The case presented against Chapman attempted to prove that he was the acting manager at the time of the 10, 12 and 16 March performances of the plays cited in the information. The prosecutors alleged that Chapman's signature on an admission order clearly established that he was the acting manager on the specified dates. Witnesses were called to testify – Percy Farren, stage manager; George Perry, music director for the company; Mr Grey, copyist; and Mr Massingham, box book-keeper – but none could or would identify Chapman's handwriting with absolute certainty. In spite of the passionate appeals of Mr Adolphus, the magistrates agreed with Mr Phillips that the prosecutors had not succeeded in establishing that Chapman was the acting manager in violation of the licensing laws. After four hours of testimony and debate, the information against Chapman was dismissed, to general applause. Those present hailed the decision as a victory for Chapman and all minor theatres.[49]

Chapman circulated an open letter, published on a playbill, claiming victory over the duopoly and conveying the new motto of the Tottenham Street proprietors: 'Unflinching resistance to the oppressive Statute'. Chapman and Melrose decried the actions of Kemble and his associates whose selfish motives were not in the best interest of a legitimate and rational source of amusement. To close the minor

---

48   *Morning Post*, 25 June 1830.
49   *Ibid.*

theatres of London, they asserted, would be a blatant violation of the right to attend neighbourhood theatres and such an action would obviously be a foul conspiracy to deny the public what was rightfully theirs. Chapman and Melrose considered it flattering to have been singled out for prosecution. They vowed to contest the major theatres' traditional rights and solicited support from their faithful followers and friends.[50]

On 25 and 26 June, John Chapman and Mrs Chapman were joined by Miss Forde, George Bennett, James Vining and J.B. Buckstone to perform *African Gratitude* – a musical entertainment based, according to the playbills, on Henry Bishop's opera *The Slave* – and the popular nautical drama, *Black-Eyed Susan* (15). The *Dramatic Magazine* lauded the productions, noting that they had 'been got up in a style that would have done credit to our Winter Theatres'.[51] Both plays on the bill ensured that Chapman and Melrose would draw 'some very crowded houses'.[52]

The death of King George IV on 26 June delayed the court appearance of John Perry and he was put on the Bow Street calendar for 1 July. Once again Mr Adolphus appeared before magistrates Hall and Birnie to state the case of the patentees against John Perry. C. Phillips, attended by Mr Alley, spoke on behalf of John Perry. Adolphus was no more successful on this occasion than he had been previously. A correspondent in *The Times* suggested that Adolphus might have failed as the result of having earlier spoken at Bow Street in favour of the minor theatres. There was speculation that he purposely created a poor argument to ensure the dismissal of the charges. But such an explanation seems unlikely when it was reported that following the second dismissal and much squabbling between the counsels, Adolphus shouted in a rage that he had 900 more informations ready.[53] The defendants promptly issued playbills for the Theatre, Tottenham Street which bore the heading 'By Permission of the Lord Chamberlain'. The permission was granted temporarily at the time of the death of the sovereign and not as a result of a legal decision. This action may have fuelled the vengeful spirit of the patent holders.

John Chapman, Thomas Melrose and George Perry returned to the management of their playhouse confident that they enjoyed the support of both the public and the courts. Those who desired the abolition of existing restrictions were encouraged by the magistrates' decisions in June and early July. The *Athenaeum* stated a more conservative perspective: 'whatever may be our opinions as to the fitness of the law, we are bound to grant that the lessees of the patent theatres, from whom enormous rents could not be exacted but for the patent rights supposed to be granted to them, are fully justified, until some change shall take place, in resisting, to the utmost,

---

50   HC: playbill, 25 and 26 June 1830.
51   *Dramatic Magazine*, 1 July 1830.
52   *Ibid.*
53   *The Times*, 2 July 1830.

an encroachment, real or imaginary, on such rights'.[54] While the patent managers reviewed their legal strategies, performances at the Theatre, Tottenham Street were devoted to benefits to offset the legal expenses.

Popular pieces in July were the farce *Freaks and Follies*; *Blue Devils*, a musical entertainment; ΜΕΤΕΜΨΥΞΩΣΙΣ or *Metempsychosis* (11), probably authored by William Bayle Bernard (1807–75) with music by George Perry; and a version of *Faustus*, perhaps adapted from George Soane and Daniel Terry's romantic drama presented at Drury Lane in 1825. Alexander Lee was identified as the composer and musical director. George Bennett (1800–79)[55] from Covent Garden played major roles in the offerings. On 7 August a young actor, John Brougham (1810–80),[56] made his debut as Regular in a burletta entitled *Tom and Jerry; or, Life in London*, written by William Thomas Moncrieff (1794–1857),[57] and launched a career that brought him fame on both sides of the Atlantic. Brougham performed with the popular author-actor Tyrone Power (1795–1841)[58] in *The Irishman's Fortune or The Adventures of Paddy O'Rafferty*. On 24 August Power appeared in his new play *Etiquette Run Mad*, which showcased his stage Irishman to full advantage. Power succeeded in filling the theatre nearly every night until he left on 13 September.[59] In that same month, nautical drama was back on the stage with Douglas Jerrold's *Richard Parker; or, Mutiny at the Nore* (19) and *Black-Eyed Susan* (15).

In late October playbills conveyed the news that Madame Vestris (1797–1856)[60] had agreed to appear at the playhouse in November. She was well known for her singing and her beauty. She first performed on 15 November in *John of Paris* and two nights later appeared in *Don Giovanni*. The press concluded that her acting style and her plays were well supported by the 'small capacities of the house for

54   'Majors and Minors', *Athenaeum*, 27 November 1830.

55   Joseph Knight, 'Bennett, George John (1800–1879)', rev. Katharine Cockin, *ODNB*, accessed 18 November 2013; and Blanchard, *Life and Reminiscences*, vol. 2, 490. He appeared in London in 1822 and unsuccessfully performed *Richard III* at Covent Garden in 1823. The following year he played Conrad in the first production of *Der Freischütz* in England at the English Opera House. After the Tottenham Street engagement, he performed at Covent Garden for several years and then moved to Sadler's Wells to work with Samuel Phelps and Thomas Greenwood in 1844.

56   G.C. Boase, 'Brougham, John (1810–1880)', rev. John Wells, *ODNB*, accessed 18 November 2013. He was born in Ireland and educated to be a surgeon. He worked closely with Madame Vestris, and in 1840 he managed the Lyceum. He moved to the United States in 1842 and returned to London in 1860. In 1869 he opened Brougham's Theatre in New York City. He wrote nearly 100 plays.

57   John Russell Stephens, 'Moncrieff, William Gibbs Thomas (1794–1857)', *ODNB*, accessed 18 November 2013. Known on the bills as Thomas William Moncrieff, he wrote more than 170 theatrical pieces in his career and is remembered for his works written for Robert Elliston as manager of the Surrey, Olympic and Drury Lane.

58   Michael MacDonagh, 'Power, (William Grattan) Tyrone (1797–1841)', rev. Nilanjana Banerji, *ODNB*, accessed 18 November 2013. Power was born in Ireland and raised in Wales; his performances in a variety of pieces earned a reputation which later made him a favourite at the Haymarket with Benjamin Webster. On his return passage from an American tour in 1841, his ship sank, and the actor was lost at sea.

59   *London Standard*, 14 September 1830.

60   Jacky Bratton, 'Vestris [née Bartolozzi], Lucia Elizabeth (1797–1856)', *ODNB*, accessed 18 Nov 2013. She was born in London and trained as an actor and singer but best known as a theatre manager. She leased the Olympic Theatre in 1830 and established her reputation producing James Planché's farces and extravaganzas. She married Charles Mathews in 1838 and together they produced highly regarded productions and distinguished themselves as managers. See also Clifford John Williams, *Madame Vestris: A Theatrical Biography* (London, 1973).

pieces of this class'.[61] On the 24th she, a contralto, took the tenor role in *Fra Diavolo*, which would have had to be scored for her voice. Madame Vestris's performance was thought to be 'very lively and pleasant'. In her career, 'Madame Vestris … made a fortune by exhibiting her sexual attractiveness in breeches parts.'[62] Audiences, attracted by Power and Vestris, instilled optimism in the management but there was little opportunity to savour their successes. Without any warning, a playbill for the Theatre, Tottenham Street was circulated notifying the public that 11 December 1830 would be the last night of the company's season.

In November the patentees had filed new charges against Chapman, Melrose and Perry at the Court of King's Bench. Chapman and Melrose circulated playbills bearing a copy of the letter they had sent to the editor of the *Morning Herald*. The managers reaffirmed their challenge to the licensing laws. In addition they proudly announced that Madame Vestris had decided to join in the resistance against the patent coalition. Their adversary Charles Kemble was sharply criticised for his poor memory of the past: a group of generous individuals, including Chapman and Melrose, had helped rescue him from the forced sale of Covent Garden in 1829 when he failed to pay rates and taxes.[63] A writer for the 18 November 1830 issue of *The Age* asked the question of the day: 'Does this theatrical charlatan suppose that the public are blind to his quackeries, and persecution of his more able competitors, the Minor Theatres?'[64] In their open letter, Chapman and Melrose suggested that if his Covent Garden venture had failed, he would have gained first-hand knowledge of what conditions were like in the minor theatres, for he too would have been forced to earn his livelihood there. Appealing to public sentiment, Chapman and Melrose reminded their followers that several hundred people earned honest incomes from the minor theatres and these people would be unemployed if the minors were closed. The Tottenham Street managers found Kemble's ingratitude only slightly less objectionable than his attempts to intimidate them by hiring men to disrupt their entertainments.[65] That Kemble would stoop to such behaviour deeply disturbed them, and the managers warned him that the informers risked their safety by attending the theatre. Besides, why hold the minor theatres in contempt when the majors were in fact copying the latest successes of the minors for presentation on their own stages? Finally, Chapman and Melrose recalled that Adolphus, who served as Kemble's counsel, had publicly announced it was the intention of his client, Kemble, to close all the minor theatres. Chapman and Melrose reiterated

---

61   *The Times*, 19 October 1830.

62   Davis, *Actresses as Working Women*, 149–50.

63   HC: playbill, 18 November 1830. See also Henry Saxe Wyndham, *The Annals of Covent Garden Theatre*, 2 vols (London, 1906), vol. 2, 58–9.

64   Moody, *Illegitimate Theatre*, 43.

65   *Ibid.*, 42–3.

their determination to fight, 'steadily, openly, and honestly', against the 999 informations allegedly gathered against the minor theatres.[66]

Less than a month later, Chapman and Melrose posted notices that the Theatre, Tottenham Street would close.[67] They were forced to conclude their management when John Perry, the owner of the property, did not renew their lease. The original lease contained a clause that allowed for a renewal of one or five years at an annual rent of £832. If any other arrangements were desired, a new lease was to be prepared by Perry's solicitor. In advance of the expiration date, the managers notified John Perry that they wished to renew the lease for three years when the original one concluded on 27 November 1830. Perry did not respond for nearly six weeks, even though he had been on the premises several times. Finally, he notified the managers that the lease had been given to another person. When the managers proposed a renewal of three years, they had technically invalidated the original agreement with Perry, which stipulated that a renewal could be made for either one or five years. While there was no proof, Chapman and Melrose speculated that the patentees had intimidated John Perry with a threat of further litigation. Chapman and Melrose also accused Kemble of meddling. In the following days, a flurry of letters filled with allegations appeared in the press.

Perry had not been intimidated by Kemble. The change in management had been mandated by a judge. The patentees had appealed the earlier decision by the magistrates. Lord Tenterden of the King's Bench reviewed the findings of the magistrates and, in his reading of the law, he determined the defendants (Chapman and Melrose) to be guilty as charged; he ordered the Theatre, Tottenham Street closed. The managers were fined £350.[68] Their final night at the theatre was 11 December 1830. William Vining spoke briefly on behalf of Chapman, Melrose and Madame Vestris to express gratitude for all public support.

Chapman and Melrose were defeated in the courts, but they maintained their convictions concerning the licensing laws. They vowed that they would never recognise the legality of the patents. Perhaps Chapman and Melrose were consoled when the House of Commons convened a Select Committee on Dramatic Literature in 1832 to examine the theatrical monopoly. That committee, after hearing all arguments, concluded that 'the interests of drama will be considerably advanced by the natural consequences of a fair competition in its representation'.[69] Many theatre managers operated after 1832 as though the monopoly no longer existed. The official repeal would not occur until 1843.

---

66   HC: playbill, 18 November 1830.
67   *Ibid.*, 10 December 1830.
68   Moody, *Illegitimate Theatre*, 43.
69   *Report from the Select Committee on Dramatic Literature, 1832*, 2.

George Macfarren

The theatre remained dark for only a short time. George Macfarren (1788–1843), a gentleman, musician and dancing teacher, announced his intention to become the manager of the Theatre, Tottenham Street in January.[70] In honour of Queen Adelaide, Macfarren renamed it the Queen's Theatre, and he expressed hope that the new name would bring it respectability.

Macfarren hired James Winston, who had served as acting manager for Elliston at Drury Lane.[71] Prior to the official opening of the newly appointed playhouse, Macfarren invited select members of society and the press to view the renovations and to enjoy a gala ball held on the stage. The event was described in the press:

> The prevailing colour of the amphitheatre, or auditory, which has been greatly improved in form, is French white, relieved by rich ornamental scroll work and embossed decorations in burnished gold, some of which have been modelled from the designs of the tasteful age of Louis the Fourteenth. In accordance with propriety and the prevailing taste, those anomalies, the stage doors, have been removed, and a proscenium of very tasteful design has been constructed. The ceiling has been considerably raised and represents a dome, from the centre of which is suspended a new gas lustre, which serves also as a ventilator … The egress and regress to the theatre has been greatly improved, each part of the house now having its separate entrance.[72]

So extensive were the improvements at the theatre, the opening was delayed until 3 February. The first night was a success, in spite of inclement weather. One of the highlights of the newly decorated theatre was a new act drop curtain prepared by Clarkson Stanfield.[73]

Macfarren's acting company was a blend of experience and youth. The principal artists, under the guidance of stage manager J. Russell, were Mrs Julia Glover, Mrs Anne Humby (1800–63?),[74] Miss Pelham (her London debut) and Miss Dix

---

70   R.H. Legge, 'Macfarren, George (1788–1843)', rev. Rebecca Mills, *ODNB*, accessed 18 November 2013. After managing the Queen's Theatre in 1831, he became stage manager at the Surrey and then moved to the Strand. Cataracts caused him to go blind, but he became the principal force behind the formation of the Handel Society. Following the restoration of his sight in 1842, he served as editor and proprietor of *The Musical World*.

71   James Winston, *Drury Lane Journal: Selections from James Winston's Diaries, 1819–1827*, ed. Alfred L. Nelson and Gilbert B. Cross (London, 1974), xi–xiii. Winston was proprietor of the Richmond Theatre (Surrey) in 1799. Between 1796 and 1804 he was a strolling player. In 1805 he bought a one-eighth interest in the Haymarket Theatre. Winston was the acting manager of Drury Lane from 1819–27 under Elliston's management. In 1831 Winston was appointed secretary of the newly established Garrick Club.

72   London: British Library: 17th and 18th Century Burney Collection Database: theatre cuttings, nos 60–2, 1831.

73   Pieter van der Merwe, 'Stanfield, Clarkson (1793–1867)', *ODNB*, accessed 18 November 2013. He apprenticed as a painter in Edinburgh. He went to sea at the age of fifteen and was pressed into service in the Royal Navy in 1812. Soon after his discharge in 1814, he began his career as a scene painter, and by 1823 he was working at Drury Lane. He first exhibited his painting in 1820 and was a founder of the Society of British Artists.

74   Joseph Knight, 'Humby [née Ayre, other married name Hammon], Anne (1800–1863?)', rev. J. Gilliland, *ODNB*, accessed 18 November 2013. She was remembered by Charles Mathews for her 'intelligent by-play and the crisp smack of her delivery gave a fillip to the scene when the author himself had furnished nothing particularly witty or humorous'. Mrs Anne Humby was a well-respected actress and considered a leading London performer.

of the King's Theatre. The principal men in the company were Mr Green from Covent Garden; two young gentlemen from the Royal Academy of Music; George Bennett (who had appeared at the theatre in the previous season); and Arthur Edward Seguin (1809–52).[75] Macfarren's scenic artist William Leitch (1800–83) later became the drawing master to Queen Victoria and the royal family.[76] Doors opened at half-past six; performances began at seven. Prices were 4s, 2s and 1s, with half-price commencing at nine o'clock.

On 3 February *Galatea* (32), from John Gay's pastoral opera *Acis and Galatea*, a new operatic farce called *Three to One* (15) and Richard Ryan's *Everybody's Husband* (30) formed the opening-night bill. The receipts for the first night were £78 11s 6d, including £12 12s for private boxes, indicating that the playhouse was near capacity. The box office report notes that there were 434 in the audience when the evening commenced, including thirteen free admissions in the pit for the press and friends.[77] On the next night, 4 February, attendance totalled 423, and the receipts of £29 19s represented a more typical night at the Queen's over the ensuing weeks.[78]

Macfarren authored several of the plays produced under his management, and one of his most successful was a melodrama entitled *Danish Wife* (40). It shared the bill on 10 March with William B. Bernard's *Delusions* (18), a comic entertainment. *Danish Wife* was a convoluted work filled with familiar melodramatic elements: murder, suspense, mistaken identity and justice triumphant. Although critics noted that the plot was timeworn and that the production did not rise much above mediocrity, the *Danish Wife* proved attractive to the Queen's neighbourhood audience. Macfarren could offer opera, farce and musical entertainments, but local audiences entered the theatre at half-price for the melodrama.[79]

The playhouse improvements, new scenery and a large company of actors required a sizeable investment, which resulted in financial deficits from the onset of Macfarren's management. By March, Winston's account book offered a clear

---

75   R.H. Legge, 'Seguin, Arthur Edward Sheldon (1809–1852)', rev. Anne Pimlott Baker, *ODNB*, accessed 18 November 2013. Seguin was described as one of the finest bass voices ever heard. He performed at Drury Lane in 1833–4 and from 1835–7 he was at Covent Garden. After appearing successfully in G.V. Macfarren's *Devil's Opera* at the English Opera House in 1838, he went to America and appeared in New York at the Old National Theatre. He subsequently founded the Seguin Troupe which toured in the United States and Canada.

76   A. Macgeorge, *William Leighton Leitch, Landscape Painter. A Memoir* (London, 1844), 41ff. Leitch, primarily a watercolourist, was an acquaintance of David Roberts and Clarkson Stanfield and had learned scene painting while at the Theatre Royal, Glasgow in 1824. He devoted the better part of his career to teaching. He served the royal family for twenty-two years. See also Delia Millar, 'Leitch, William Leighton (1804–1883)', *ODNB*, accessed 18 November 2013.

77   V&A: account book signed by James Winston, January, February and March 1831. The revenue for 3 February at first price was as follows: boxes £6 12s, pit £24 6s and gallery £7 18s. The revenue collected at half-price was: boxes £3 4s, pit £5 5s and gallery £1 17s 6d. For the evening, private boxes totalled £12 12s and £15 8s was billed to the actors.

78   The revenues for 4 February at first price: boxes £3, pit £10 12s and gallery £3 11s. Half-price revenue was: boxes £4 2s, pit £5 17s and gallery £1 14s. One private box was taken for £1 1s.

79   V&A: account book signed by James Winston.

picture of the fragile state of the enterprise. A number of actors had agreed, in view of the 'extreme ill state of the receipts of the house last night', not to draw their expected salaries. The lengthy list of 'Actors Not Paid on Saturday' was an ominous sign for the manager. The cash in hand was £14 8s and the unpaid total was £106 5s.[80] The account-book summary for February and March shows receipts of £1,591 9s 6d, and expenditure totalling £1,691 11s ½ d.[81]

On 27 March 1831 Macfarren received a letter of resignation from James Winston. Winston wrote later about money owed him by Macfarren. He graciously says, 'You have mentioned remuneration, let that remain unthought-of by you, till the tide turns which I trust it will be soon, when you are getting plenty of money it will be time enough to think of me. As for the balance, I really would not ask for that were it not a time of the year when I have the least resources. When convenient, I will thank you for it.'[82] Winston continued keeping the accounts for the theatre and the balance sheet for 17 May 1831 shows expenditure of £3,213 11s 6d and total revenues of £3,120 15s. Clearly noted in the summary is the 'Balance due to Winston' of £92 16s 6d.[83] Macfarren, in the meantime, kept searching for a way to attract larger audiences.

In April Macfarren engaged a young French dancer and pantomime, Madame Céline Céleste (1810/11–82), who had appeared successfully on the Paris stage as a child, to make her dramatic debut at the Queen's. In 1827 she had travelled with dancers to New York. By 1830 she was dancing in London and the provinces. She had aspirations to become an actress but spoke no English.[84] Her highly successful cross-dressing career was launched at the Queen's on 4 April 1831. J.T. Haines's new military melodramatic spectacle *The French Spy* (58) presented Madame Céleste in a starring, albeit mute, role. She took the part of Mathilde de Grammont who, disguised as a military volunteer, follows her fiancé, Major Lafont, to the siege of Algiers. In her male disguise she woos the daughter of a sergeant, then disguises herself as an Arab boy (Plate 7) in order to enter the Algerian camp and rescue her beloved. As the Arab boy she performs an exotic dance and mime to learn the battle plans of the Algerians and, after Lafont is captured, she fights for his life on the battlements by torchlight. When she is discovered to be a woman, she is ordered to be dressed as a woman and added to the harem. She fights off the Arab leader with his own sword as the French break through the gates and blow up the

---

80   *Ibid.*

81   *Ibid.*

82   V&A: original letter, 27 March 1831.

83   V&A: correspondence.

84   Jane Moody, 'Céleste, Céline (1810/11–1882)', *ODNB*, accessed 18 November 2013. Her first English-language speaking role was 1838. In her later career, she managed the Adelphi and Lyceum theatres.

city.[85] In this role Céleste was 'crossing boundaries of sex and of ethnicity',[86] which made her an instant success with audiences and critics:

> Mademoiselle Céleste is rather tall than otherwise, but exquisitely made, and very graceful. Her countenance is intellectual if not handsome, and she has eyes sparkling with good nature. When she experiences any pleasurable feeling, her whole soul seems in her face, and she makes you as happy as herself; when she would express scorn, her countenance, so susceptible of passion, is dignified and determined; and during sadness, she equally impresses you with sentiment of pity and tenderness.[87]

The play allowed for 'a free-ranging fantasy that centres upon a woman doing astounding deeds of heroism and sexual play, distanced and also thrown into sharp relief by her silence, her eloquent movement and her extraordinary physical capacities'.[88] In addition, the production of *The French Spy* was well mounted: 'the scenery, the dresses, and the decorations, were really upon a scale of splendour far beyond what one might reasonably expect in so small a theatre'.[89] Madame Céleste received a weekly salary of £8, comparable to the leading actors in the company. Mr Seguin received £7 a week, Mrs Humby £8 and Mrs Glover £6. Mr Leitch, the scenic artist, received £2 10s.

At the conclusion of the seventy-five-night season, Macfarren continued to face serious financial problems. Nightly receipts for the winter season averaged only £32 9s 10d. A weekly deficit of £100 had accrued. There was little recourse for Macfarren. After 11 June 1831 he abandoned his management of the Queen's. In the days following, well-known artists like Thomas Potter Cooke (1786–1864)[90] appeared in the popular vehicle, *Black-Eyed Susan* (8). By mid-June Mrs Waylett was performing in a J.T. Haines play, *Russian Captive* (19). *Midas* (26) was also presented in June and July with Mrs Waylett in one of her favourite roles, Apollo. The summer season concluded on 14 July.

Several members of the Macfarren troupe reopened the theatre on 1 September. The September bills featured J.T. Haines's latest work, *Austerlitz; or The Soldier's Bride* (17), which focused on the vicissitudes of four young farmers from the village of Linselles, near Lille. The play contained all the requisite components for

---

85   J.S. Bratton, *The Making of the West End Stage: Marriage, Management and the Mapping of Gender in London, 1830–1870* (Cambridge, 2011), 137–41. See also Marjorie Garber, *Vested Interests: Cross-Dressing and Cultural Anxiety* (New York, 1997), 117.

86   Jane Moody, 'Illusions of Authorship' in Tracy C. Davis and Ellen Donkin (eds), *Women and Playwriting in Nineteenth-Century Britain* (Cambridge, 1999), 117.

87   *Morning Chronicle*, 5 April 1831.

88   Bratton, *Making of the West End Stage*, 140.

89   *The Times*, 6 April 1831.

90   Michael Slater, 'Cooke, Thomas Potter (1786–1864)', *ODNB*, accessed 18 November 2013. After the navy, he went on the stage in January 1804 at the Royalty, the winter home of Philip Astley and company. He worked at the Surrey under Elliston and moved to the Lyceum in 1820.

Tottenham Street audiences: soldiers, separated lovers, infidelity, a bomb explosion and a panorama of the battlefield. The world outside the theatre was also under siege. A cholera epidemic swept through London in October of 1831,[91] but the actors at the Queen's continued to perform. A Christmas pantomime called *World Turned Upside Down; or, Harlequin Reformer* (6) attracted the attention of the press. But the pantomime, devoted to the topic of reform,[92] was summarily dismissed as too unconventional and was soon withdrawn.

On 6 November 1832 George Wild returned to the Queen's (he had managed a brief 1829 summer season) with a new piece by Edward Fitzball called *The Wood Devil; or, The Vampire's Wife* (22). He obtained the new Fitzball script with the Queen's audience in mind and engaged Clara (Mrs Charles) Selby (1796/7–1873)[93] to play a 108-year-old woman. The reviewer for *The Times* reported that Fitzball's play was 'the most perfect piece of dramatic *diablerie* that we ever remember to have seen exhibited at a theatre of the dimensions of this. The lovers of horrors will do well to go and see it; it abounds with demons, vampires, pirates, witches, *et hoc genus omne* of German and Scotch romance.'[94] The writer noted that the house was well attended. Nearly all the boxes were taken and at half-price the pit and the back seats were filled.[95]

Wild hired Joey Grimaldi (1802–32), the son of the famous clown Joseph Grimaldi (1778–1837) for the season. Young Grimaldi had a reputation for erratic behaviour and occasional fits of madness. He received a weekly salary of £4 to play Black Caesar in *Fatal Thicket; or, a Slave's Revenge*, beginning Monday 26 November 1832. On 11 December, Joseph Grimaldi senior received news of his son's death at 24 Pitt Street. He died in a public house, apparently in a wildly insane state, dressed in costume and ranting lines from roles he had played in his career.[96]

Wild filled the 1832–3 season with *Cupid* (61), which was described on the playbills as 'a seriously-affecting, shriek-creating, and boisterous, glorious, uproarious, lovely, burlesque burletta'. To be competitive with other theatres, he lowered admission prices to boxes 3s, pit 1s and gallery 6d. *Cupid* continued to be played into December, and at Christmas the pantomime *Harlequin and the Elfin Arrow! or, The Basket Maker and his Brothers* (29), adapted from Sir Walter

---

91   Knight, *Major London 'Minor'*, 101.

92   The scenes for the pantomime identified on the playbills were: Reform of the Parliament House, Reformed Rakes, Reformed Bakers and Brewers, Medical Reform, Reformed Tailors, Legal Reform, Fashionable Reform, Reformed Rogues, Reform of the Clergy, Naval Reform, Dramatic Reform and Universal Reform. HC: playbill, 26 December 1831.

93   For Clara Selby [real name Sarah Susannah] see Joseph Knight, 'Selby, Charles [real name George Henry Wilson] (c.1802–1863)', rev. Klaus Stierstorfer, *ODNB*, accessed 18 November 2013. She was considered a competent actress specialising in middle-aged and elderly characters. The Selbys appeared under W.C. Macready at Drury Lane during the 1841–2 season.

94   *The Times*, 6 November 1832.

95   *Ibid.*

96   Charles Dickens, *Memories of Joseph Grimaldi* (New York, 1968), 286.

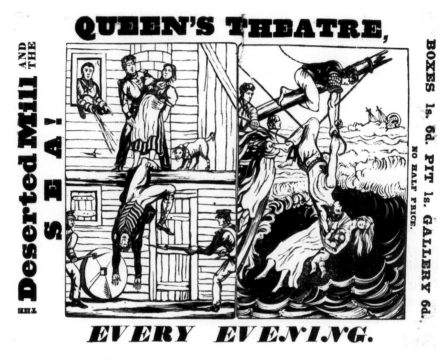

15 *The Deserted Mill* and *The Sea*, 1833. Heal Collection, Camden
Local Studies and Archives Centre, London

Scott's *Demonology and Witchcraft*, was added to the bill. In March the benefits commenced. Mrs Selby chose *Othello* for her night, and she took the title role. The event drew a large house and *The Times* reporter on 14 March 1833 concluded: 'notwithstanding the difficulties with which she had to contend in personifying a character so essentially masculine as that of the Moor, Mrs Selby was successful in the delineation of many of the beauties with which the part abounds, and depicted without apparent effort, and yet with great natural force and effect, the more tender passages of the author'.[97]

May 1833 playbills conveyed the news that a joint season of English and French performances, reminiscent of the Beverly years, would commence on 14 May. The English company would play Mondays and Fridays under the management of F.B. Pindar, and the French actors, headed by M. Theleur, would take the remaining nights. Wild abolished half-price tickets and lowered admissions. He advised his public on a 29 July 1833 bill that he was lowering prices to match those at the Surrey, Pavilion, Garrick and Sadler's Wells theatres. The new prices were fixed at: boxes 1s 6d, pit 1s and gallery 6d.

---

97   *The Times*, 14 March 1833.

After a summer of spectacle and farcical entertainments, Wild mounted two new successful productions that appeared on the same bill: Edward Fitzball's *The Deserted Mill; or, The Soldier's Widow* (62), opening on 16 September 1833, and Charles Somerset's *The Sea* (57), beginning a week later on 23 September (Fig. 15). Both productions were brimming with violence, revenge, madness, storms and pathos. A critic noted that *The Sea* deserved a better ship, and the script offended nautical propriety: 'Captains [were] familiarly discussing, disputing, squabbling and scuffling with their seamen; and discipline [was] so far forgotten that a common sailor orders out a boat as one might call for a hackney-coach.'[98] In early December Wild left the playhouse.

Gilbert A'Beckett and Henry Mayhew

The name of the theatre was changed to the Royal Fitzroy Theatre by Gilbert Abbot A'Beckett and Henry Mayhew when they opened their season on Thursday 26 December 1833. Both men were familiar with the theatrical world, but neither had any managerial experience. Henry Mayhew (1812–87) was the son of an attorney and had met A'Beckett at Westminster School where they were both students.[99] From the early days of his career, Gilbert Abbot A'Beckett (1811–56) was involved in the publication of several periodicals. He studied at Gray's Inn in 1828 prior to starting the comic weekly *Figaro in London* in 1831.[100]

The popular actor-writer William Henry Oxberry was to be the leading performer in the company. Oxberry was described as a very little man, a lively actor and dancer in burlesque with a quaint manner; he is said rarely to have known his part on first nights. A contemporary said of him: 'There were few theatres at which he was not seen.'[101] The other gentlemen in the company were Benjamin Manders of the Strand, John Parry (1809–81)[102] and Mr Mitchell of the Theatre Royal, Covent Garden. The women were Miss Mason (a niece of Mrs Siddons and J.P. Kemble) from the Victoria, Mrs Brindall of Drury Lane and Miss Crisp of the Strand. Admissions were boxes 3s, pit 2s and gallery 1s. Half-price began at 8:30 initially, but was later changed to 8:45.

---

98 HC: clipping, 29 September 1833.

99 Deborah Vlock, 'Mayhew, Henry (1812–1887)', *ODNB*, accessed 18 November 2013. After running away from school and going to sea, he was articled to his father, but soon turned his energies to literary pursuits and joined A'Beckett as co-publisher of *Figaro in London*. Mayhew was one of the co-founders of *Punch* and served for a time as editor. In addition to his comic writing, he authored *London Labour and London Poor* and *The Boyhood of Martin Luther.*

100 Paul Schlicke, 'À Beckett, Gilbert Abbott (1811–1856)', *ODNB*, accessed 18 November 2013. Of the more than fifty plays he wrote, most were topical burlesques filled with satire. He was also a regular contributor to *Punch*. In his later years he served as a magistrate at the Greenwich and Woolwich police court and at Southwark.

101 Joseph Knight, 'Oxberry, William Henry (1808–1852)', rev. Klaus Stierstorfer, *ODNB*, accessed 18 November 2013.

102 'Parry, John', in Boase, *Modern English Biography*. He began his acting career in 1827 in Leeds followed by Sheffield, Sheffield and Pontefract. He first appeared in London at the Victoria Theatre in 1833 where he later became stage manager. He was an actor and the stage manager at the Queen's from 1839–47.

On 26 December 1833 *The Templar; or, the Effects of Passion*, a domestic drama, *Who's Right? Or, Who's Wrong?*, a new farce, and a pantomime called *Harlequin Merman! or, The Mysteries of the Deep* were presented. The audience was rowdy, and the noise and screams of laughter emanating from the 'gallery gods' made it difficult for the reviewers to hear, much less evaluate, the first two pieces on the bill. Once the pantomime began, the audience grew quieter. The laughter and noise continued on the first night until one o'clock in the morning, and the plays were all announced for the next evening. Both audience and critics warmly applauded all the performers. It appeared the new management was launched successfully.[103] The *Athenaeum* provided a different response to the evening:

> *The Templar* and two following pieces, appear to us to have all been written by the same person – and we should further say, that that person has seldom, if ever, written for the stage before. The language generally is respectable, in some cases decidedly smart and good, but it is essentially undramatic, and the construction of the pieces is very faulty.[104]

The new plays may have been disappointing, but the *Athenaeum* writer expressed appreciation for the ambience of the playhouse:

> The price of admission is fairly and distinctly stated to be intended to cover every expense. Thus you enter, are shown to a seat, without having to pay a shilling for what you have already bought. A bill of the performance you have paid to see, is furnished you gratis – and if you happen to have a cloak or an umbrella – convenient outside but anything else within – the servants of the house take charge thereof – *without* charge and restore it to you of course on demand. The management deserves much credit for these wholesome regulations.[105]

A'Beckett's new farce, *King Inco* (20), opened on 9 January 1834. Neither the critics nor audiences found it particularly appealing, but it did not prevent the managers from putting it on the bills several times during the season. Writing in *Figaro* on 14 January 1834, A'Beckett mused about the challenges of writing for the popular stage:

Commenced on Friday,

Finished on Saturday,

Copied by Monday,

Parts distributed on Tuesday,

---

103   *The Times*, 27 December 1833.
104   *Athenaeum*, 11 January 1834.
105   *Ibid.*

Rehearsed on Wednesday,
Acted on Thursday,
and, for what we know,
Dead and d – – d by Friday.[106]

Wandering Minstrel (75), Mayhew's one-act farce debuting on 16 January, proved more popular. Mistaken identity was the foundation of the plot. Allegedly, Mayhew had based his play on the life of Charles Cochrane, the natural son of Basil Cochrane, a nabob residing in Portland Place, who assumed a disguise as a Spanish minstrel and wandered about Great Britain and Ireland in 1828–9, speaking no English and professing to raise money for Spanish émigrés.[107] Mayhew's play was filled with puns and buffoonery, broad, comic, working-class trickery and pretentious upper-class characters.[108]

A'Beckett's *Son of the Sun* (37) was first presented on 13 February 1834. The play borrowed heavily from a Madame Vestris production at the Olympic Theatre. Entire passages were copied to depict the 'classical, satirical, musical, mythological and whimsical' view of the Phaeton.

On the evening of 24 February, *The Revolt of the Workhouse* (50) was performed before a full house. It was a burlesque ballet-opera based on an earlier Covent Garden ballet entitled *The Revolt of the Harem*. The original had received poor reviews. Henry Crabb Robinson had found it 'a tedious long ballet but rendered endurable by some very beautiful scenery – especially a moonlight mountain scene near Granada and parts of Alhambra. The evolutions of the female army were also very pleasing – but the dancing was only second rate.'[109] The Royal Fitzroy production featured cross-dressed Oxberry as Sally Slack, a 'pauper Negress', and Mr Mitchell as Moll Chubb, commander of the female revolutionaries. A'Beckett's burlesque lampooned both the inanity of the subject matter and the incompetence of the dancing in the Covent Garden original. The harem revolt and a controversial bathing scene were transformed into a paupers' revolt and the scrubbing of linen – an activity that quickly deteriorated into a pitched battle with soapsuds. Critics and audiences were amused by the satire, but concern was expressed that it was a breach of good taste and decorum. A'Beckett was accused of placing vulgarity on the stage of the Royal Fitzroy. He defended his efforts:

I will admit that there is *prima facie* something low in the notion of a revolt of paupers; but after all, is the workhouse more likely to give rise to indelicate ideas than the seraglio? There may be inelegance in the pirouettes of Mr Oxberry, as a pauper negress in long white

---

106   *Figaro in London*, 14 January 1834.
107   James Winter, *London's Teeming Streets, 1830–1914* (London, 1993), 121.
108   Winter, *London's Teeming Streets*, 122. Charles Cochrane admitted in later life to having written the play.
109   Robinson, *Diary*, 140–1.

drawers and merino gown, but are they more likely to corrupt the mind than the antics of a French danseuse as a concubine in no drawers at all and short gauge petticoats?[110]

The letter was signed 'One of the Proprietors of the Fitzroy Theatre'.

On 31 March a new season began. Mayhew appears to have assumed a less active role in the daily activity at the theatre. A'Beckett next produced a 'fairy ballet opera' called *The Frolics of the Fairies; or, Puck in a Pucker* (24) which began on 7 April. The story was inspired by the quarrel between Oberon and Titania in *A Midsummer Night's Dream*. Audiences responded well to the offerings at the Fitzroy, but the ongoing demand for new plays and changes on the bills strained resources.

At the end of April, A'Beckett and Mayhew were summoned to the Marylebone Magistrates Office to answer a demand for wages filed by Messrs Arthur, Kent, Owens, Terry, Gastons, Gunn and Burrows. These gentlemen, carpenters and scene-shifters at the Fitzroy, sought payment for labour performed. When they received only three of the twenty shillings due each of them, they went on strike in the middle of a performance. The managers did not appear, hoping to settle the matter privately. The court proceeding signalled the end of their management. By June, the managers had left the theatre, and Gilbert A'Beckett was in the Insolvent Debtors' Court the following month.[111] He testified that his income averaged £15 a night, but his expenses were £22.[112] He would later claim that part of the problem at the Royal Fitzroy Theatre could be traced to their colleague James Ollier who, as acting manager, withheld money from his colleagues and 'in a fit of extreme consequence, in fact in the very last stage of a severe attack of dignity, called himself sole manager of the Fitzroy'.[113]

Edward Edwards advertised on 1 July 1834 his intention to change the company, the playbills and the prices for the theatre. Oxberry was to continue for a time. Prices were reduced to 2s, 1s and 6d and the bills changed to 'the blood and murder system' that best met the 'altered taste of the cheap and nasty audience'.[114] Edwards opened his season on 6 October with *Nero! The Murderer of His Mother* (13). According to his playbill, it was a spectacular melodrama with ferocious scenes of combat, the conflagration of the imperial city, fountains of real wine and the spectre of Nero's murdered mother making strategic appearances.

Louisa Nisbett

The brothers Bond, one of whom was a moneylender, offered Louisa Cranstoun Nisbett (1812–58) a salary of £20 a week to become the manageress of the renamed

---

110   HC: clipping, 28 February 1834.
111   *The Times*, 31 July 1834.
112   *Examiner*, 3 August 1834.
113   Arthur William A'Beckett, *The A'Becketts of 'Punch'* (New York, 1903), 51.
114   *Figaro in London*, 12 July 1834.

Queen's Theatre for a season commencing in January of 1835.[115] Described as a tall woman of considerable beauty, Mrs Nisbett's strengths as an actress were found in comedy; she also played young men quite well. Those who heard her laugh described it as one of the most rippling, joyous and musical ever heard.[116] When the young manageress assumed the direction of the Queen's, she was twenty-three years of age.

Louisa Nisbett's first night at the Queen's was 19 January 1835. The house

> has been completely painted, decorated, ornamented, &c., in short the interior is so perfectly changed from what it was … the curtains of the private boxes are of white and crimson and are particularly elegant … the house was crowded in every part with the most respectable auditors, and the lobbies were filled with visitants anxious to catch a glimpse of what was going on on the stage.[117]

Prices were restored to the higher, more traditional 4s, 2s and 1s. Children under twelve were admitted for half-price. Half-price for other patrons was at nine o'clock. The company supporting Mrs Nisbett consisted of Messrs Morris Barnett (from the Macfarren management of the Queen's), Edward William Elton (1794–1843)[118] who also served as stage manager, Benjamin Wrench (1778–1843),[119] William H. Tilbury and John Parry, who had performed at the theatre in 1833. The women in the company were Jane Mourdant and Miss Mourdant (Mrs Nisbett's younger sisters) and Mlles Chapman, Williams and Brindal. The first evening consisted of four pieces: *The Farmer's Son* (2), *The Maid of Castile* (2), *Station House* (28) and *Is He Jealous?* (3). The first two pieces were poorly received and hissing accompanied the final curtain for *The Maid of Castile*, an awkward debut for Jane Mourdant. *Station House*, by Charles Dance,[120] appealed to the audience and calmed the crowded house. Despite some dissent, the pieces were called for the following evening.

---

115 Joseph Knight, 'Nisbett [née Macnamara, later Lady Boothby], Louisa Cranstoun (1812–1858)', rev. J. Gilliland, *ODNB*, accessed 18 November 2013. Louisa Nisbett performed Juliet, Miss Hardcastle and Jane Shore before she was ten years old. She took the role of Angela in Monk Lewis's *The Castle Spectre* at the English Opera House in 1822. She played in the provinces, performing at Bristol, Cardiff, Stratford-upon-Avon, Northampton, Southampton and Portsmouth. Following the Queen's, she became manageress of the Olympic. In 1837 she was at the Haymarket with Benjamin Webster. She appeared at Covent Garden with Madame Vestris in 1839 in the first production of *London Assurance*.

116 Blanchard, *Life and Reminiscences*, vol. 1, 190–1.

117 *The Times*, 20 January 1835.

118 Joseph Knight, 'Elton, Edward William (1794–1843)', rev. Katharine Cockin, *ODNB*, accessed 18 November 2013. His real surname was Elt. He made his stage debut at the Olympic in 1823. He was at the Surrey, the Haymarket and Covent Garden from 1832–6 and in the Macready Company at Drury Lane in 1839.

119 Joseph Knight, 'Wrench, Benjamin (1776x8–1843)', rev. Nilanjana Banerji, *ODNB*, accessed 18 November 2013. He declined a commission in the army and turned to the stage, making his first appearance at Stamford. He received an offer from Drury Lane in 1806 and remained with the company until 1815. He later appeared at the Adelphi in 1820. By 1826 he was at Covent Garden.

120 John Russell Stephens, 'Dance, Charles (1794–1863)', *ODNB*, accessed 18 November 2013. Charles Dance worked for thirty years in the office of the Insolvent Debtors' Court. He collaborated with J.R. Planché among others. His greatest successes were light pieces and extravaganzas for Madame Vestris.

Among four new plays presented in February were *Family Peculiarities! or, Sisters Three* (24), Charles Selby's comedy *The Married Rake* (37),[121] Douglas Jerrold's *Schoolfellows* and Charles Dance's *In Status Quo; or Romance and Romancers*. In *The Married Rake* Mrs Nisbett assumed the dual roles of Mrs Trictrac and Cornet Fitzherbert Fitzhenry. She was alluring in female attire and a dashing figure in trousers as the Cornet (Plate 8). The contrast and sexual ambiguity created by such a performance drew audiences to the Queen's.[122] Disguised as a young cavalry officer, Mrs Nisbett is discovered at the feet of Mrs Frederick Flighty by Mr Flighty. His jealousy is compounded by the fact that he has been philandering. His errant ways are exposed, he learns he has not been cuckolded by his wife and pledges to reform his ways. *The Times* was enthusiastic: 'We are content to be merry under petticoat government at the Queen's Theatre. Five or six pieces of a night, full of song, fun and sentiment, are sufficient to satisfy anybody. There is something for persons of all tastes and dispositions, except the grave.'[123] On 17 February Douglas Jerrold's comedy *Schoolfellows* (27) began a successful run. William Creswick (1813–88) made his first London appearance in the role of Horace Meredith.[124]

Mrs Nisbett's productions were popular and frequently the house was filled. The evenings consisted of farce and light comedy but the narrowness of the repertoire soon became evident. Critics and theatregoers bemoaned the lack of variety. The manageress's only recourse was to change the bills regularly. T.H. Bayley's *Volunteers* (30) premiered on 24 March with Mrs Nisbett as Captain Helen Bang putting her corps of young ladies through military manoeuvres in splendid costumes. Expecting an invasion by the French, the Captain takes the place of her brother, whose fear of guns makes him a poor leader of the volunteers. Benefits began in late March, featuring J.B. Buckstone and Mrs Glover, and the season concluded 11 April.

Changes to the Queen's acting company had occurred when the season resumed on 20 April 1835. Creswick and Wrench had left the company and Mary Ann

---

121 Joseph Knight, 'Selby, Charles (*c.*1802–1863)', rev. Klaus Stierstorfer, *ODNB*, accessed 18 November 2013. His real name was George Henry Wilson. In 1832 he was a member of the Strand Theatre company. He wrote more than ninety plays, many adapted from the French. He was a productive author, a 'useful' actor and supplied himself and others, including Louisa Nisbett, Harriet Waylett and Frederick Yates, with very popular plays.

122 Jim Davis, 'Presence, Personality and Physicality: Actors and Their Repertories, 1776–1895', in Joseph Donohue (ed.), *The Cambridge History of British Theatre*, 3 vols (Cambridge, 2004), vol. 2, 272–91.

123 *The Times*, 16 February 1835.

124 Joseph Knight, 'Creswick, William (1813–1888)', rev. Katharine Cockin, *ODNB*, accessed 18 November 2013. He joined Samuel Phelps at Sadler's Wells in 1846. He appeared with William Macready and Helen Faucit. With Richard Shepherd, he managed the Surrey from 1848 to 1862.

Orger (1788–1849),[125] Miss Murray and Mrs Laura Martha Honey (1816?–43)[126] were added. The premiere of Charles Dance's burletta *The Tame Tigers; or, No Harm Done* (23) on 6 April featured the Mourdant sisters as two fashionable ladies who compete for the attentions of gentlemen admirers. The ladies' maids, Mrs Nisbett as Rose Jennings and Miss Chapman as Phyllis Jennings, also portray young men, Captain O'Blazes and Ensign Walter Scott Byron. The piece incorporated a familiar mixture of audience-pleasing ingredients, including mistaken identity and manipulative maids. The comic confrontations were enhanced by the cross-dressing characters which greatly amused the playgoers.

In September of 1835, Mrs Nisbett presented two of her most highly regarded productions: *The Spirit of the Rhine* (24), a musical drama written by a member of her company, Morris Barnett, and *Zarah* (42), created for her by George Soane.[127] *The Spirit of the Rhine* was a melodramatic piece starring Mrs Laura Honey and featured two new songs: 'My Beautiful Rhine' and 'The Dream'. *Zarah* (Fig. 16) was an immediate success. As Zarah the gipsy heroine, Mrs Nisbett loves and is loved by a young gentleman whom she rescues from a villainous, knife-wielding member of her own band. She conceals her lover in a cavern, arranges his escape and then is shot by one of her fellow bandits. Her dying words, 'I knew it would be thus!', were spoken, according to reviewers, with a 'most thrilling expression'. Mrs Nisbett captivated audiences and critics with her compelling performance and her exotic costume. She was attired in bright colours and glittering ornaments. Her performance as Zarah was 'nightly advancing in public estimation' and she demonstrated a 'versatility of talent' for which she had not been previously credited.[128] *Zarah* was an important departure from light comedy for Mrs Nisbett.

A playbill was posted on 10 November 1835 with startling news: Mrs Nisbett announced the end of her management. She thanked her followers and advised them that her final performance would be on 13 November. Three days later, she was appearing at the Adelphi Theatre where she remained until 23 December. On Boxing Day, Mrs Nisbett returned to the Queen's and told those in attendance that the Bond brothers had, without warning, cancelled their contract with her. She announced that she and M. Laurent's troupe of French actors would share the Queen's stage. On 29 January 1836 Mrs Nisbett and M. Vizentini, the French

---

125 Joseph Knight, 'Orger, Mary Ann (1788–1849)', rev. J. Gilliland, *ODNB*, accessed 18 November 2013. After performing in the country and Scotland, she made her first appearance at Drury Lane as Lydia Languish in 1808. She also performed at the Lyceum. In 1813 she returned to Drury Lane. By 1845 she was at the Olympic with Madame Vestris and at Covent Garden.

126 Joseph Knight, 'Honey [née Young], Laura Martha (1816?–1843)', rev. J. Gilliland, *ODNB*, accessed 18 November 2013. She made her first stage appearance under the name of Laura Bell. By 1826 she was at the Olympic with her mother. In 1832 she was at the Strand with Mrs Waylett. After appearing at several London theatres, she undertook the management of the City of London theatre.

127 Emma Plaskitt, 'Soane, George (1789–1860)', *ODNB*, accessed 18 November 2013. He was the younger son of Sir John Soane and graduated from Pembroke College, Cambridge in 1811. He authored plays and novels, and translated works from French, German and Italian.

128 *Morning Post*, 15 September 1835.

16 Louisa Nisbett as Zarah in *Zarah*, 1835. Widener Library, Harvard University, 11432.48

director, offered three pieces: *Borrowed Feathers*, *Le Mariage de raison* and *Les Gants jaunes*, which earlier had been performed at the Adelphi under the title *Yellow Kids*. The response to the new arrangement was positive. The plays were amusing and considered in the best of taste. The French actors performed with exceptional felicity 'which in French actors seems almost instinctive, and gives to dramatic representations the appearance of real life and society'.[129] By the end of February, Mrs Nisbett had concluded her days as manager of the Queen's. In the end it became impossible for her to meet the demand for constant variety.

During the next few months, several individuals performed benefits or played short seasons. Evenings at the Queen's had deteriorated, according to the reporter who attended Master Henry O'Connell's benefit performance of *Douglas* on 16 June 1836. The audience found him dull and rose to exit immediately following the tragedy. An agitated man, identifying himself as the manager, confronted the audience and loudly demanded money for the rent of the theatre. After a protracted debate, the band, followed by O'Connell, retired, leaving the audience bewildered. A few members of the band reappeared, but they wisely did not remove their hats. Those in attendance, angered by the contempt of the management, pelted the musicians with orange peels, gooseberries and halfpennies. A general barrage of abusive language followed, and a few brief scuffles broke out. Order was finally restored to the nearly empty house. As the actors attempted to complete the bill, the man claiming to be the manager continued his tirade at the top of his lungs.[130]

Also in June 1836, two familiar artists appeared at the Queen's for a short season: Messrs Cloup and Laporte. The French actors, having performed at the theatre many times during the 1821–8 period, presented *Les Gants jaunes*, *Les Memoirs d'un Colonel*, *Les Suites d'un mariage de raison* and *Les Malheurs d'un joli garçon*.

On 2 August 1836, Henry Robert Addison (1805–76) assumed the management of the Queen's. He gave the evening of 5 August to M. Cloup for his benefit, as an expression of his gratitude for those who had supported the French performers and also to advertise his upcoming season. Addison was a playwright and army officer. His early plays were written for Mrs Waylett and several were performed at the Adelphi.[131]

His first night consisted of the farce *Striking Beauty* (20), the burletta *West Country Wooing* (34) and the operettas *The King's Word* (3) and *Midas* (3). Reactions on the first night were not encouraging, and it appeared ominous for Addison. Harriet Waylett played *West Country Wooing*, but her appeal barely offset the perceived weaknesses of the acting company. *The Times* predicted disaster for

---

129   *The Times*, 30 January 1836.

130   *Ibid.*, 17 June 1836.

131   John Russell Stephens, 'Addison, Henry Robert (1805–1876)', *ODNB*, accessed 18 November 2013. He was well known in literary circles as a journalist. He subsequently became a lieutenant-colonel, but his reputation as a writer of sixty farces and plays exceeded his military exploits.

the management: 'the theatre was attended last night but indifferently, and without amendment it cannot be otherwise. There are too many good public amusements in London for people to waste their time in witnessing the performance of a company of whom only one is excellent, while most of the others are not above mediocrity, and the rest are at an immeasurable distance below it.'[132]

In the next month, a new romantic piece by William Collier entitled *Kate Kearney; or, The Fairy of the Lakes* (15) was judged as the best production of the Addison management. Still, one critic suggested that if the actors took the pains to perfect themselves in their parts, they might enjoy longer runs of the plays. Mrs Waylett played Kate Kearney throughout October, but by the end of month she shared the bill with H. Smith and his dog, Hector, in the reliable *Forest of Bondy* (5). Soon after, Mrs Waylett and Captain Addison left the Queen's.

From March to October of 1837 the Queen's had no official manager. Much of the activity during this period consisted of benefits. The reputation of the Queen's was at a low ebb:

> Were we required to give a new name to this establishment; we should term it 'a new theatrical house of correction, to which the public is obliged to pay for admittance.' In no other theatre is intellect put to such *hard labour*, in tracing the meaning of the trash which is nightly foisted on the audience as dramatic entertainment, and which, compared with the productions at other houses, is like prison-fare after sumptuous food. Never did dog kennel suffer from worse management … the prompter is more frequently heard than the performers! However, it once more closes to-night; and, we should imagine it will be long ere it re-opens. It is, in truth, an Augean stable, requiring a second Hercules to cleanse it.[133]

In the autumn of 1837, Miss Desborough arrived in London from the Richmond Theatre to become the manageress of the Queen's. The *Morning Chronicle* offered Miss Desborough encouragement for success in her London venture.[134] She was also forewarned by others in the press: 'The Queen's Theatre is again in the hands of a lady – a Miss Desborough – whose friends, if they have any sincere wishes for her present or future welfare, will make an empyrosis of this ruinous property, and avenge the hundreds it has destroyed.'[135] By December, when Miss Desborough was unable to pay her rent, she found John Perry a most impatient landlord:

---

132 *The Times*, 4 August 1836.
133 HC: clipping, 1837.
134 *Morning Chronicle*, 7 October 1837. See Frederick Bingham, *A Celebrated Old Playhouse: The History of Richmond Theatre, from 1765 to 1884* (London, 1886), 31. Miss Desborough had opened the 1837 season at the Richmond Theatre. She announced that the Richmond's stage would hereafter be 'brilliantly lighted with gas'.
135 HC: clipping, 14 October 1837.

On Thursday Mr Deering Montague, one of the principal comedians at the Queen's Theatre, entered the office, accompanied by about twenty other actors and actresses, for the purpose of obtaining advice from the sitting magistrate, Mr Shutt, under the following circumstances: The applicant stated that for some time past he and the other persons who were present had been performing at the above theatre, which was under the management of Miss Desborough, and the landlord had put an execution in the house that morning, while the company were rehearsing a new comic piece. The broker and his man were not satisfied with seizing the machinery, scenery, and other properties attached to the house, but, in spite of the most urgent and vehement remonstrances, they laid their sacrilegious hands upon the dresses, wigs, pantaloons, boots, and other articles belonging to the actors and actresses assembled, and which did not belong to the theatre, but were of course private property.[136]

Perry was provoked to action as the result of unpaid rent. Miss Desborough and Perry had reached a stalemate: the manageress would not vacate the theatre and the landlord appeared powerless to evict her.[137] While the two factions struggled, the playhouse interior was methodically stripped of everything of value. Perry had defaulted on mortgage payments. Thus, the holder of the mortgage ordered a deed of covenant with powers of sale prepared.[138]

George Robins of Covent Garden printed the sale particulars and circulated information concerning the playhouse to be sold at the Auction Mart on 27 February 1838. The property located at number 3 Tottenham Street, adjoining the playhouse to the east, was also advertised for sale. Robins's materials were filled with puffery. He described the 'snug little theatre' as having a seating capacity of more than 1,500 persons: two circles of boxes for about 1,000, eleven private boxes and a spacious pit for 500 more patrons. The seating capacity of the playhouse never exceed 500–600.[139] He added that an 'enterprising and skilful proprietor' might render the building attractive and profitable.[140] A parody of Robins's advertisement was circulated by one fully aware of the history of the playhouse:

This dog hole having ruined about two hundred lessees, and returned at least four members annually to each of the Metropolitan prisons, has at last wound up the proprietor himself, who is compelled, by the mortgagees, to sell the Property! George Robins, who would throw the poetry of puffery over a freehold watch box, and invest with attraction the copyhold of a cooler's stall, uses his utmost ingenuity, to tempt the

136 *Examiner*, 24 December 1837.
137 *The Town*, 27 January, 1838.
138 *Morning Post*, 23 February 1838.
139 Richard Lorenzen, 'The Old Prince of Wales's Theatre: A View of the Physical Structure', *Theatre Notebook*, 25 (1971), 132–45. All the data strongly argue for a seating capacity around 560. See also Chapter Six of this book for an analysis of the theatre plans.
140 V&A: copy of sale bill and particulars.

'*enterprising capitalist*,' to fling away his money upon this regular millstone round the neck of the muses …We think the truest description that Robins could have given, would have been the following:

'IMPORTANT TO LUNATICS'
MR. GEORGE ROBINS has the honour to announce that
the Proprietors having resolved to get out of
the thing upon any terms, have instructed
him to look out for a victim for THE QUEEN'S THEATRE.
As a medium (for getting rid of surplus
cash) it may be pronounced the
MOST DESIRABLE CONCERN IN THE MARKET![141]

The prophecy of doom did not discourage Benjamin Lisle from submitting a successful bid of £2,650 for the theatre.[142] He was to be the proprietor for nearly three decades.

In April of 1839 the newspapers issued a warning to the public about the impending return of George Wild to Tottenham Street. Wild announced that he was the lessee of the theatre for a third time and that he would commence his season with a benefit for himself. Wild's bravado aroused an already suspicious press:

Wild, who has previously disgusted the locality, is again permitted to do so. We do not forget his former tricks and shall keep a sharp look out, he is one of those fellows who only care for themselves, and is utterly regardless of any persons he may draw into the vortex … If a theatre will not answer under a man of talent, it will never do so under George Wild, who when he had the Olympic turned it into a complete nursery of crime and indecorum.[143]

Despite adverse publicity, Wild enjoyed the support of the Duke of Brunswick, the Earl of Waldegrave and others during his first few weeks. In early May he offered *Perpetual Motion* (11), a ballet, and revived Edward Fitzball's *The Deserted Mill; or, The Soldier's Widow* (10) to capitalise on the 1833 success of the play. Shortly thereafter, French actors, under the direction of M. Cloup, began performances.

In late May, Wild offered the *The Cook Sylph; or, The Footboy's Dream* (42) and *Venus and Her Hobby; or, The Painter and his Four Daughters* (14). To strengthen his bills, he engaged Master Hutchings, the Lilliputian Wonder, to play the comic

---

141   V&A: copy of paradoy sale bill.
142   *The Times*, 1 March 1838.
143   HC: clipping, April 1839.

interlude *Little Tiger* (5) and to sing 'I'm Quite a Ladies' Man'. J.P. Hart's drama *Freemason! or, The Secret of the Lodge* (18), with the author in the cast, was being played in early June as part of a series of benefit nights featuring Mrs Nisbett, Mr Fitzjames and Mrs Honey. On the occasion of Fitzjames's benefit on 1 June 1839,[144] the company included Mrs Nisbett playing Lady Teazle to Samuel Phelps's Joseph Surface in *The School for Scandal*. The better part of July was devoted to George Dibdin Pitt's *Phantom Ship; or, Son of the Doom'd* (31). The nautical drama featured a scene in which the pilot of the ship was thrown screaming overboard and another that included the sensational rescue of the hero's son from the bottom of the sea. Wild kept admission prices at 2s, 1s and 6d. It was his most successful season at the theatre. On his 5 August 1839 bill, he confidently advised the public that he would return after a brief closure for redecorating.[145]

But it was Charles James James who opened the Queen's Theatre as the manager in September. A change of management at the Queen's was never surprising.

---

144   HC: playbill, 1 June 1839.
145   HC: playbill, 5 August 1839.

Chapter Four

The Charles J. James management:
melodrama, pantomime, nautical
drama, the dogs and American
novelties, 1839–1865

In September of 1839, Charles James James (1804–88) became the manager of the Queen's Theatre, and he continued in that capacity for the next twenty-six years. C.J. James was a scenic artist who designed, painted and arranged the scenery for his productions at the Queen's.[1] His father, who specialised in glass painting, educated and trained him as an artist. By the time he reached his mid-twenties, C.J. James 'had already established in both England and America repute, not only for artistic ability, but for strict probity'.[2] Visual artists sometimes sought gainful employment in theatre circles, and James upon his return to London worked as a scene painter for Madame Vestris at the Olympic from 1834 to 1836. He was engaged for a time at the Victoria, and then took the lease of the Queen's in 1839, at the age of thirty-five.[3]

The Queen's Theatre was a small playhouse, and the resources available from box office receipts dictated what the manager could invest in production. The parallel limitation was the small stage area which meant that elaborate scenic display would not be possible. The action drama and pantomime which were central parts of his repertoire could not be presented with the more elaborate settings of his competitors, but James could, on a lesser scale, mount productions taking full advantage of his artistic skills and mechanical imagination. Edward Wedlake Brayley's *Historical and Descriptive Accounts of the Theatres of London* provides a description of the playhouse from 1826:

---

1   'James, Charles James', in Boase, *Modern English Biography*. See also Blanchard, *Life and Reminiscences*, vol. 2, 623. James apprenticed under his father for several years, and together they created transparent views of John Martin's works. In 1830 their view of *Joshua Commanding the Sun to Stand Still* was shown in London. An early sketch of the work is in the Ashmolean Museum. That piece, along with several others, was taken to the United States and exhibited between 1831 and 1834. When Marie Wilton and Henry J. Byron took the playhouse in 1865, they invited James to be their acting and business manager, which he did for eleven seasons. In August of 1876, he retired after thirty-seven seasons at the playhouse.

2   Blanchard, 'History of the Prince of Wales's Theatre'.

3   'James, Charles James' in Boase, *Modern English Biography*.

The interior is small, but neatly fitted up. It has two tiers of boxes; the lowermost consisting of nine divisions, of which the three central ones are public, and very large; the others are private boxes. The upper tier has only one private box on each side. The gallery is sufficiently capacious for 200 persons: the pit, which is 39 feet in depth, and 22 feet wide, will also contain about the same number. Elevated on each side, above the pit, are four private boxes, fitted up in an elegant style. The proscenium is 21 feet wide; and from the front of the stage to the back wall the extent is 36 feet. Over each of the stage doors, which are white and gold, is an extensive box.[4]

In 1841 the proscenium opening of the Queen's stage was measured at 18 feet.[5] It was a small picture frame, with little enough stage space for the actors, much less cascading streams of water or burning buildings. Yet James persevered and created first-rate scenic display, albeit in miniature. James was highly regarded by critics and audiences for his achievements as a scenic artist, especially in his annual pantomime. Throughout his management, he freely revived past successes, which enabled him to draw upon his extensive inventory of scenery without incurring great expense.

By 1839 the population in the immediate vicinity of the Queen's Theatre had increased to nearly 25,000. The Greenwood map of 1827 (Fig. 17), contrasted with the Rocque map (Fig. 1), illustrates how the empty fields had been developed and new streets created. The area adjacent to the playhouse on Tottenham Street consisted of a mixture of shops and private dwellings. Among the inhabitants of the area were shoemakers, carpenters, tailors, bricklayers, printers, plumbers, glaziers, shopkeepers, cabinet makers, upholsterers and labourers. Many of the women worked as domestic servants, cooks, charwomen, milliners, seamstresses, washerwomen, manglers and laundry keepers. Around the present-day site of the University of London and in nearby Bloomsbury, a more educated community of artists, engineers, surgeons, musicians and the like resided. They, too, were potential theatregoers.[6] The Queen's audiences during the James management were largely uninterested in poetic tragedy, sophisticated comedy or subtle sentiment. They attended the theatre for 'thrilling action, stirring emotion, spectacle, jolly farce and an ideal image of themselves and their own lives'.[7]

From the onset of his management, C.J. James planned his bills to respond to the local preferences for pantomime, sensational drama, nautical drama, melodrama

---

4   Edward Wedlake Brayley, *Historical and Descriptive Accounts of the Theatres of London* (London, 1826), 83–4. Architectural plans prepared by the Metropolitan Board of Works at the request of the Theatres and Music Hall Sub-Committee in 1882 corroborate this information.

5   *Theatrical Journal*, 17 July 1841. The measurements provided at this date are: width of the stage 35 feet and depth 32 feet. Only the Strand's stage depth was less than the Queen's.

6   Jim Davis and Victor Emeljanow, *Reflecting the Audience: London Theatregoing, 1840–1880* (Iowa City, 2001), 137–64. Providing important demographic, historical and social profiles of London theatregoers, this invaluable study includes a section on the audience and the area around the Queen's Theatre.

7   Michael Booth, *Prefaces to English Nineteenth-Century Theatre* (Manchester, 1980), 25.

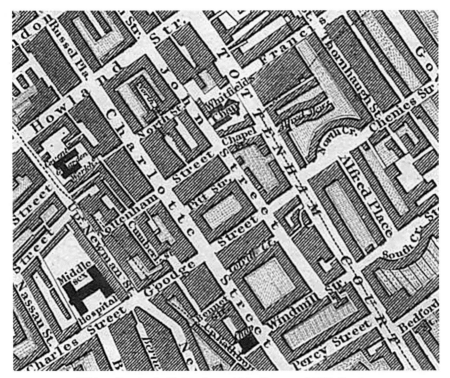

17 Map of London by Christopher and John Greenwood, 1827. Courtesy
of Mark Annand. Site hosted by Bath Spa University

of all types and traditional farce and spectacle, including canine performers. He
frequently depicted the neighbourhood in his productions. In September of 1842,
his scenes for *Lawless of London* featured views of nearby London locations, and
for the 1840–1 Christmas pantomime, *Georgy Porgy; or, Harlequin and Aunty
Paunty*, the chase scene included the interior of the Queen's Theatre and local
shops and streets.

The Queen's Theatre and its competition
Theatre managers continued to be confronted with financial difficulties throughout
the 1840s and 1850s. Under the best of circumstances theatre management was
a challenging profession. James competed with the Adelphi, the Surrey, the
Haymarket (where Benjamin Webster became manager in 1837), the Royal Victoria
and Sadler's Wells. The Islington location of the last-named theatre was an eight-
penny fare from Regent Street,[8] and Sadler's Wells served a largely local audience

---

8   Shirley S. Allen, *Samuel Phelps and Sadler's Wells Theatre* (Middletown, CT, 1971), 79.

until Samuel Phelps, Mary Amelia Warner and T.L. Greenwood became the managers in 1844. Astley's Amphitheatre provided equestrian entertainments from early in the century, and the Olympic, under frequent changes of management after J.R. Planché left in 1839, offered entertainments similar to those presented at the Queen's by James. In 1842, John Mitchell took over St James's Theatre, producing mostly French plays with the leading stars of the French stage. William Charles Macready was manager of Covent Garden (1837–9) and Drury Lane (1841–3). The Princess's Theatre in nearby Oxford Street offered promenade concerts and opera until Charles Kean became manager in 1850.[9] In the East End, the Standard opened in 1835, the City of London in 1837, the Britannia in 1841 and the Grecian in 1843.[10] Theatregoers had many options.

Many of James's predecessors at the Queen's Theatre had experienced financial ruin, and the new manager was keenly aware of the need to attract as many patrons as possible by offering quality entertainments at a reasonable price of admission. As a result, he lowered and raised ticket prices nine times while managing the Queen's. Initially he set prices at 2s for boxes, 1s for the pit and 6d for the gallery with half-price only for the boxes. In 1841 he adopted half-price for boxes and pit. By 1848, his prices were at the lowest levels: boxes and stalls were 1s, the pit was 6d, and the gallery 3d. The Lord Chamberlain's records indicate that if the house was full, the revenue for the Queen's would be £50 a night.[11] To develop a successful season required very careful planning. Theatre management was after all a business. The financial foundation of the Queen's season became the Christmas pantomime, as it was at many theatres. The pantomime revenue was a significant part of the annual income and a long run of the pantomime served to offset losses incurred from mounting less popular pieces.[12] James's pantomime productions were performed between thirty and sixty nights each season, a reasonable run considering the size of the neighbourhood and the competition from other theatres in the city.[13]

Nautical drama was also popular at the Queen's and over five seasons, beginning 1842–3, James offered more than 300 performances of at least 30 different plays on his bills. The most popular productions, *Ship of Fire* (47) and *Hour of Retribution* (24), were presented in the 1845–6 season, but the popularity of nautical drama soon faded after this date. Melodrama filled the void left by the demise of nautical drama. Audiences began to look beyond nautical drama for entertainment and engagement:

---

9   Booth, *Theatre in the Victorian Age*, 27–57.

10   Michael Booth, *English Melodrama* (London, 1965), 53–4.

11   Davis and Emeljanow, *Reflecting the Audience*, 157.

12   Booth, *Theatre in the Victorian Age*, 36–7.

13   Booth, *Prefaces to English Nineteenth-Century Theatre*, 149–58. See also Jim Davis (ed.), *Victorian Pantomime* (Basingstoke, 2010), and Russell Jackson (ed.), *Victorian Theatre* (London, 1989), for more detail about the popular form and its production.

They were the new uneducated and largely illiterate urban masses who lived in bleak and depressing circumstances; what they wanted from the stage was thrilling action, stirring emotion, spectacle, jolly farce, and an ideal image of themselves and their own lives. All of this they obtained from melodrama, which simultaneously satisfied their desires for escapist entertainment, for a better world where such as they received the happiness and rewards proper to the virtuous poor, and for a quasi-realistic presentation of the every-day occurrences of their own domestic existence. For the first time in English dramatic history, they themselves were the heroes of a drama written especially for them in a language and with a simplicity they could understand, a drama concerned with their own lives and dreams.[14]

Mounting productions that would attract audiences for at least twenty nights in a season was a goal of every theatre manager, but it was difficult to achieve with a relatively small, mostly neighbourhood audience. The Christmas pantomime inevitably held the stage of the Queen's for a long run, but for the remainder of the season James was required to change the bills frequently. From 1839 to 1854 James presented more than 450 performances of thirty-five melodramas and comic pieces written by Thomas Mildenhall. The manager's son, C.S. James, provided at least thirty dramas and pantomimes that were presented in more than 500 performances from 1845–53. From 1856 to 1864, William E. Suter wrote around fifteen plays a season for James. Many of the plays by these authors were revived more than once. C.J. James also obtained plays from many other dramatists and commissioned adaptations or versions of successful plays produced at other theatres. Among the most frequently produced authors at the Queen's were John Johnstone, Thompson Townsend, Thomas Wilks, Edward Fitzball, C.Z. Barnett and George Soane.

Blackface minstrel shows and plays were also presented at the Queen's. These performances, having originated in the United States, 'became, in Britain, one of the most popular forms of entertainment for the rest of the century'.[15] Dramatisations of *Uncle Tom's Cabin* and *Dred* could be seen at the Queen's and on stages throughout London. Theatre managers viewed the American negro, whether in minstrel shows or dramatic productions, as another inexpensive source of melodrama and variety that would appeal to working-class audiences.

The newspaper critics and theatrical writers of the day documented the artistic achievements of Madame Vestris at the Olympic (1831–8), William Macready at Covent Garden (1837–9) and Drury Lane (1841–3), Samuel Phelps at Sadler's Wells (1844–62), Charles Kean at the Princess's (1850–9)[16] and Benjamin Webster at the Haymarket (1837–53) and the Adelphi (1844–74). In the early years of

---

14 Booth, *Prefaces to English Nineteenth-Century Theatre*, 25.

15 Sarah Meer, *Uncle Tom Mania: Slavery, Minstrelsy, and Transatlantic Culture in the 1850s* (Athens, GA, 2005), 150.

16 Michael Booth, *English Plays of the Nineteenth Century*, 5 vols (Oxford, 1969), vol. 1, 3.

James's management, the critics visited the Queen's too, but their interests in his productions waned over time. By the early 1850s reviewers rarely visited and their observations all but disappeared from the press. When they did visit the playhouse, the critics inevitably praised James's scenery. His artistry as a scene painter earned him a reputation in theatrical circles even though his repertoire was limited to the specific tastes of his neighbourhood patrons. Ultimately, the critics left him and his audience to their own amusements.

The Queen's acting company was characterised by its loyalty to C.J. James. Their other opportunities may have been limited but they had earned the respect and appreciation of both the Queen's audiences and the manager. Several actors performed for multiple seasons: Mrs John Parry for sixteen, Tom Manders and Mr Fortune for fourteen, Mr Randall thirteen, John Parry ten, Marian Rogers and Charles Sennett for nine each and Miss Wrighten for eight.

The James management: 1839–1850

C.J. James's first season, 1839–40, began in September. He hired John Parry, son of Thomas Sefton Parry, to play leading roles as well as to serve as acting and stage manager. Parry had appeared at this playhouse in 1833 under the A'Beckett-Mayhew management and was a member of Mrs Nisbett's company in 1835. He served as acting and stage manager at the Queen's for the next ten years (Fig. 18). He played both villains and serious roles and, later in his career, he became a member of the company at the Britannia, where he appeared from 1856 to at least 1875.[17]

In late October James engaged Lee Morton (pseudonym of Dion Boucicault, 1820–90) to perform for six nights following his successes at the New Strand and the St James's.[18] The Christmas pantomime, written by Richard Nelson Lee, was *Peter Piper; or, Harlequin and the Magic Peck of Peppers* (24). Lee (1806–72) authored nearly two hundred pantomimes during his career and served as manager of several London theatres.[19] C.J. James enhanced the production's appeal by preparing a diorama at the conclusion that depicted Mont Blanc, the Glacier des Boissons, the Valley of Chamouni (or Chamonix) by moonlight, a view of distant,

---

17   *The Britannia Diaries, 1863–1875: Selections from the Diaries of Frederick C. Wilton*, ed. Jim Davis (London, 1992), 64. In the Britannia Diaries, Wilton notes that Parry had appeared extensively in the provinces and in London at the Victoria, the Standard and the City of London prior to the Queen's. In 1874, John and Mrs Parry were sued by their landlord and Wilton's notes indicate that they were earning £2.50 a week, he as an actor and she taking tickets.

18   Peter Thomson, 'Boucicault, Dion (1820–1890)', *ODNB*, accessed 18 November 2013. His name was originally Dionysius Lardiner Boursiquot. He was born in Dublin, son of a French refugee and Irish mother. He appeared as an actor under the name Lee Moreton or Morton in the English provinces. Having left London University in 1840, he wrote *London Assurance* in 1841. It was his first great success at Covent Garden with Madame Vestris. Benjamin Webster encouraged him to adapt French plays and sent him to Paris in 1844. He travelled to New York in 1853 and returned to London in 1860. He took the lease of Drury Lane in 1862.

19   Alan Ruston, 'Lee, (Richard) Nelson (1806–1872)', *ODNB*, accessed 18 November 2013. He was a writer, actor and juggler and involved with travelling fairs in and around London. He was also a utility player for Robert Elliston at the Surrey in 1827. In 1849 he took the City of London Theatre and managed it until 1868.

18 John Parry in *The Secret Witness*, 3 July 1847, *Theatrical Times*. Harvard
Theatre Collection, Houghton Library, Harvard University, TS 30.22F

perilous passes and a mysterious monastery. The *Theatrical Journal* noted: 'it is impossible to refrain from laughing heartily at the fun of the opening scene, nor of feeling gratification and delight at the beautiful diorama – Mont Blanc and the Moselle and the Vale of Chamouni appear in glowing reality before the admiring spectator. Mont Blanc with its cloud capt summit by moonlight is very beautiful.'[20]

The press offered the new manager praise: 'If Mr James does not make a fortune, we shall be very surprised, every novelty being good, and success is certain.'[21] Constructive criticism was also forthcoming: 'we could however just hint to the spirited lessee, the necessity of a little renovation and cleansing of the interior of the theatre, which from neglect and the poverty of former managers has become in a dilapidated state.'[22] Reservations regarding the quality of the acting company were expressed: 'with the exception of Parry and his wife, Miss Rogers, and the danseuse Miss Gooderman, more inadequate representations of passions and qualifications of action, cannot easily be found.'[23]

Variety was an important part of the first season. Arnold Buck, the 'Wizard of the South', was engaged to imitate the popular Mr Anderson, who was known as the 'Wizard of the North'. The high point of the performance was his gun illusion. A volunteer loaded the pistol in full view of the audience, retired to the rear of the auditorium, aimed the weapon and fired at M. Buck. The Wizard of the South then stepped forward, removing the bullet from his mouth for the audience to behold. One night, after the discharge of the pistol, M. Buck haltingly exclaimed, 'Ladies and Gentlemen, here is the ball, but something else has been put in the gun – I am wounded.' He staggered to the rear of the stage and the curtain dropped immediately. A doctor was summoned, as well as the police, and upon examining the victim and the sizeable number of holes in the back scene, it was determined that the pistol had been loaded with small shot or steel filings. The wounds were superficial, however, and within two weeks M. Buck returned to the stage with his 'Magical Illusions' and famous 'Gun Trick'.[24]

Monsieur Cloup, who had appeared at this playhouse in the 1820s in *Les Soirées françaises*, had left the St James's Theatre and arranged with C.J. James to perform two nights each week in the months of April and May. As the *Morning*

---

20   *Theatrical Journal*, 28 December 1839.

21   *Ibid.*, 4 January 1840.

22   *Ibid.*, 12 January 1840.

23   *Ibid.*, 14 March 1840.

24   *Ibid.*, 4 April 1840. A letter to *The Times* on 3 April 1840 offered an explanation of the trick: 'Sir, the Conjuring trick performed by Mr Buck is generally performed by German wizards in the following manner: A small hollow globe of extremely thin glass is filled with quicksilver, which gives it the weight and appearance of a leaden bullet. Being put in the barrel of the gun, the glass is bruised by ramming it forcibly down. Upon discharging the gun, the quicksilver will flow out, and no injury be done to the person fired at. Should, however, the glass globe have been of a considerable thickness, and the gun be discharged at so short a distance that the broken pieces of glass may attain the conjurer, such result might ensue as has been the case with regard to Mr Buck's accident. Your obedient servant, W.K.K.'

Post observed, 'A good French company in a good London theatre is a *desideratum*, and nothing would give us greater pleasure than to be an accessory toward its establishment. Some improvement in M. Cloup's *corps dramatique* is, however, wanted before it can reasonably expect to obtain extended support.'[25]

On 9 May 1840 a writer for the *Theatrical Journal* offered an early assessment of James's management:

> The visitors are night after night inflicted with pieces which baffle the acutest ingenuity to find out merit or meaning: the policy which continues this system, is really much to be regretted; for with extreme liberality and effectiveness in the scenic department, there should be something of talent in the dramas and the acting to correspond. The introduction of female warriors into every production, no matter how constructed, is carried on ad nauseam; and cannot, though the eye be for the time pleased, counterbalance the absence of average merit.[26]

The 1840–1 season is not well documented. Tom Manders (1797–1859),[27] H. Reeves and Miss Wrighten were added to the acting company. While it is possible that James was experiencing full houses, especially for his pantomime productions, it is more likely that he wished to convey that impression. He announced a new policy to be implemented at the Queen's. Effective immediately, the box office keeper was instructed to advise people purchasing tickets when the house was full and only poor standing space was left in the pit. It was seen as a good policy and it earned him commendation in the *Theatrical Journal*.[28]

A Thomas Mildenhall play, *Santhanas in Love; or, The Peri of Beauty* (18), did well in March. Miss Wrighten narrowly avoided disaster in the role of the Peri of Beauty (in Persian mythology a mythical superhuman being, originally represented as evil but subsequently as a good or graceful genie or fairy). One evening she 'was performing the part of the fairy, in which character she has to be suspended in air at a height of at least 25 to 30 feet: the bandage by which she was supported gave way, and she was precipitated on the stage with great force upon her head; fortunately her fall was in some degree broken, in consequence of a fillet, which was attached to one of her legs, but which also gave way'.[29] Her fall left her in a badly bruised state, but she returned to the stage in April and continued as a member of

---

25 *Morning Post*, 20 April 1840.

26 *Theatrical Journal*, 9 May 1840.

27 Blanchard, *Life and Reminiscences*, vol. 2, 227. Manders worked as a clerk in the Bank of England from 1814–21 until his office was abolished. He turned to acting in the provinces with his wife Louisa Powell. He made his London debut at the City Theatre, Milton Street. He appeared at the Strand and Olympic theatres, but he spent 'upwards' of sixteen years at the Queen's where he was a great favourite. He later became proprietor of the Sun Tavern, Long Acre, a popular establishment with the theatrical profession.

28 *Theatrical Journal*, 2 January 1841.

29 *Ibid.*, 3 February 1841.

the company for the next seven seasons.[30]

In May, James chose an action-filled drama, *Claude du Val; or the Ladies' Highwayman* (20), featuring Miss Rogers in the breeches role. She appeared in five revivals of the play during the nine years she was a member of the company.

During the summer recess, James initiated repairs to the playhouse. On his bills prior to the opening of the 1841–2 season, he reported that 'new staircases have been erected from the Upper to the Lower Boxes, the Private Boxes decorated and furnished. The Pit and Gallery seats have been raised affording each auditor a perfect and uninterrupted view of the stage which has been materially improved on a novel scale.' As a part of his improvements, James installed a water tank under the Queen's stage. Throughout the city 'real water' on stage was considered essential for nautical as well as sensational drama. Critics were not always enthusiastic about the novelty: 'we are deluged with water: not content with natural sources, artificial means are resorted to, to inundate us with liquid streams. Water on the stage destroys the fire of the performer.'[31] Sadler's Wells, the Strand, the Adelphi and the Pavilion had earlier been fitted for the use of water on their stages, and the Queen's, with the production in October of Mildenhall's *Giselle; or, The Phantom Dancers of the Danube* (12), appeared to be 'working double tides by introducing water-spirits and fiery-spirits destroying the attributes of the other.'[32]

Giselle was an adaptation of a ballet produced at the Paris Opera earlier in the year. The performers in the piece were thought competent, but it was James's scenery that once again received special notice: 'we have often had the pleasure of noticing this man's paintings … nothing can be so charming and so truly natural as the opening scene of the Vine Dresser's hut on the banks of the Danube. It reminds me of one of Claude's never to be sufficiently admired landscapes.'[33] Additional interest in the aquatic scene was created by 'oxy-hydrogen' light[34] reflected through the streaming water to create a prismatic effect of colour.

Prior to the 1841 Christmas pantomime, T.P. Taylor's version of *Susan Hopley* (20), based on George Dibdin Pitt's play, was performed. In February 1842 Edward Stirling (1807–94)[35] provided a new play for James entitled *The Queen of Cyprus; or, the Bride of Venice* (30). The manager's scenic contribution was a representation of the moat surrounding the city of Nicosia with part of the city engulfed in flames in the background. The last charge of the Cypriots was an exhilarating moment in the evening's entertainment, and the audience cheered enthusiastically.[36]

---

30 V&A: clipping, 25 March 1841.
31 *Theatrical Journal*, 3 November 1841.
32 *Ibid.*
33 *Ibid.*, 16 November 1841.
34 Most likely a light produced by the incandescence of some substance, quite probably lime, in an oxy-hydrogen flame.
35 Stirling was known for his adaptations of Charles Dickens's novels for the stage.
36 *Theatrical Journal*, 12 February 1842.

A writer for the *Theatrical Journal* summarised James's achievements in his first three years: 'It has been our gratifying lot to award unlimited praise to the management of this little theatre for its skill, tact, and liberality in the production of novelties, which are generally well chosen and put together upon the stage with every appliance of well-painted scenery, fanciful costumes, and other appliances.'[37]

C.J. James started the 1842–3 season in September. By 12 September he had found audiences for *Lawless of London; or, The Sharper's Progress* (25) and in early October *The Shadow; or, The Poisoned Flower* (23), adapted by Mildenhall from the opera *L'Ombre*, was popular. The ethereal appearance of the Shadow (Miss Wrighten) and a cascade of real water were acknowledged by the press: 'the last scene, with its countless fountains of real water, has not its equal in London, and it reminds us of the good old days of Sadler's Wells.'[38] *Jack Sheppard* (22) was presented on 24 October. It was to become a Queen's favourite and was revived in each of the next four seasons.

Nelson Lee's pantomime for December and January was *Polly Put the Kettle On; or, Harlequin, Robin Hood and the Magic Cat* (44). It was well received and the long run was guaranteed. The boisterous audience nearly overwhelmed the antics on stage:

> Monday evening a crowded and merry audience were congregated to witness the vagaries of the pantomimic heroes at this little theatre. For some time the majority of those who were present seemed to entertain a decided conviction as to the superiority in sweetness of their own voices to those of actors or singers. Ultimately, however, when 'the gods' had adjusted their rivalries and settled in their respective positions, the tumult abated, and the Page of Naples … became partly intelligible to the mass of the auditory …[39]

At the conclusion of the evening, C.J. James's diorama was displayed. It contained the principal scenes and incidents connected with 'Her Gracious Majesty's Visit to Scotland', including the departure from Woolwich, Royal Arsenal, Passing the Nore Light, The Camper Down, 120 Guns, Tynemouth Cliff and Castle, Fern Islands, Longstone and the Scene of Grace Darling's eventful exploits, Berwick Light House and Harbour, Royal Squadron, Bass Rock and Pier at Granton, General View of the City of Edinburgh, and Arrival of Her Most Gracious Majesty and Prince Albert. The scenic artist and the mechanics dominated the evening and reflected the general changes occurring in pantomime.[40] *Polly Put the Kettle On* served as

---

37   *Ibid.*, 29 January 1842.

38   *Ibid.*, 23 October 1842.

39   *Ibid.*, 26 December 1842.

40   Booth, *Prefaces to English Nineteenth-Century Theatre*, 196–7. A writer in *The Times* for 28 December 1840 had earlier expressed concern about the reduction of Clown's role in pantomime and the emergence of 'mechanical ingenuity and dioramic painting' as the focal point of the evening.

inspiration for toy theatre plates prepared by John K. Green. A costume sheet (Fig. 19) bearing the title conveys the character of the production and its costumes.

On 20 February a new Mildenhall military spectacular, *Lady Sale! or, the Affghan* [*sic*] *War* (38), was presented. The playbills advised the public that the drama was based on recent events in India and it embraced the major points of a campaign that had aroused worldwide interest.

For July of 1843, C.J. James produced a new action drama written by T.P. Taylor called *Herne the Hunter; or the Wizard Oak* (40), based on Harrison Ainsworth's romance *Windsor Castle*. The convoluted plot defied logic, but the scenes in the forest and caves, the historical figures and the intense action made the play popular with audiences.

In 1843 the Theatre Regulation Act was passed. It rescinded all previous acts relevant to the control of the stage. Licensing and regulation of theatrical activity was consolidated in the office of the Lord Chamberlain, and that office held the sole authority for the licensing of plays and theatres for all of Great Britain. In effect, local jurisdiction, which had created different types of licences, most notably the burletta licence, was now abolished in favour of a more unified policy. The minor theatres could produce any type of drama approved by Her Majesty's Examiner of Plays without restrictions, but the playbills remained largely unchanged. Managers continued to offer the types of entertainment they had in the past.[41]

In December of the 1843–4 season all attention was focused on Nelson Lee's pantomime *Pat a Cake, Pat a Cake Baker's Man, or Harlequin and the Magic Cake* (40). The popularity of pantomime at the Queen's was firmly established.

Margaret Mellon's *The Jewess* (24) opened in early April with Marian Rogers in the title role. It was one of the many adaptations of René-Charles Guilbert de Pixérécourt's *La Juive*. The story focused on two thwarted lovers, the Jewess and Prince Leopold, a Christian, and their eventual union. The *Theatrical Journal* offered further encouragement to James:

the proprietor of the Queen's stage, is one of the safest whips on the road, and a journey down Tottenham Court Road, will repay the seeker after amusement. The Queen's stage has never yet been upset under his gentleman's guidance. He is civil, obliging, and very enterprising, offering to the visitors who may occupy the box seats, comfort and respectability, and to those on the roof, a ceaseless variety of amusement during the journey, which generally begins about seven, and ends towards midnight. The fares are exceedingly low, there being so much competition of late with other stages of heavier weight, and rail-roads who wait for no one.[42]

---

41 Booth, *English Melodrama*, 13–38; Watson, *Sheridan to Robertson*, 21–57. See also Moody, *Illegitimate Theatre*.
42 *Theatrical Journal*, 14 April 1844.

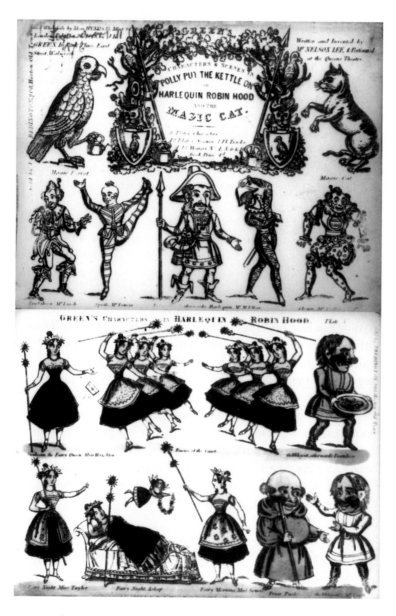

19 *Polly Put the Kettle On, or, Harlequin, Robin Hood and the Magic Cat*, pub.
by John K. Green, 1843. Scenery by C.J. James. Author's collection

In early June, a disaster was averted by a quick response. Between eleven and twelve o'clock in the morning, a fire broke out in the theatre. A rehearsal was about to begin when an explosion occurred and a thick cloud of smoke immediately filled the building. A match had accidentally ignited a quantity of fireworks and dresses. The Queen's staff made their way to the origin of the blast and extinguished the fire. *The Times* reported that the theatre and its contents were not insured.[43]

The 1844–5 season commenced on 9 September, and James described at length on his playbills the alterations undertaken during the three-week interval. The newly developed space was created

> for the assembling of the audience (for the purposes of Promenade and refreshments) and erected at great expense, which the encouragement of the past seasons and the prospect of the future alone have authorized. This novel attraction represents the Caverns of Enceladus in its general construction; yet, from effects of light upon the shells and spars, the falling, and the sounds of the real water; the statues, among them Eve at the Fountain, it may be termed the Grotto of Beauty. Through the different vista of the Caverns, are seen the following tableaux – Ehrenbreitstein, Coblentz, and Lausanne; Edystone, Allun Bay, and Netly Abbey [*sic*], by Moonlight. It is believed that the above novel addition to the convenience and pleasure of the audience, by Mr James, will be appreciated by the patrons of this theatre.[44]

The 'Caverns of Enceladus' was open free of charge to the patrons of the pit and boxes. The 'gallery gods' were excluded. The Queen's Theatre was thriving. According to a September visitor:

> This theatre has been doing good business since their opening. On the night we were there, the pit and gallery were crammed, and the boxes not by any means bad … Our friend Manders, and Miss Wrighten, are as humorous as ever and continue to keep the house in one roar every time they open their mouths … Mr James has also provided a beautiful lounge for his box and pit audience … It is one of the most perfect specimens of the painter's art that was ever exhibited to the public …[45]

James next engaged the American tragedian J. Hudson Kirby, the son of John Kirby who was clown at the Surrey for thirty years. Kirby had appeared at the Surrey in late June and moved to the Victoria in September where he became embroiled in a conflict with the management.[46] He was at the Queen's in early October and performed *Hamlet* (5), *A New Way to Pay Old Debts* (3), *Richard III* (6), *Othello*

---

43   *The Times*, 5 June 1844.
44   HC: playbill, 9 September 1844.
45   *Lloyd's Weekly Newspaper*, 22 September 1844.
46   Knight, *Major London 'Minor'*, 208–12.

(2) and *Macbeth*. The bills also featured the American Southern Minstrels who presented 'Ethiopian Entertainments' for eighteen nights beginning 7 October 1844.[47] Mildenhall's *Alma; or, Daughter of Fire* (22), from the opera *La Fille de feu*, was the major production from late November through to 26 December. *Harlequin Wat Tyler, or The Lord Mayor of London* (38), authored by Charles Sloman, was the Christmas pantomime.

On 6 January of the New Year, 1845, James mounted a play adapted from Charles Dickens, *The Chimes; or a Goblin's Story* (24). It was not the first dramatic version of the story to appear on the London stage. Other productions had been licensed earlier at the Lyceum, Albert Saloon, Adelphi and Apollo.[48] Another successful burlesque opened in May – Charles Sloman's *Cherry and Fair Star* (23). In June, James offered his audiences Thompson Townsend's nautical drama *The Lost Ship; or, The Man of War's-man, and the Privateer* (17), and the American strongman Mr Canfield, who lifted a 400-pound cannon to his shoulders and held it securely while his assistant fired it.

The 1845–6 season began on 1 September with a very popular bill, the nautical drama *Ship on Fire; or, Romance of the Deep* (47) by C.Z. Barnett and *Major Domo* (26), a comedietta by Margaret Mellon. The nautical drama contained the usual components: death-defying action, intrigue, fear and confusion. The innovative staging included two levels for scenes to be performed simultaneously. The audience viewed concurrent actions in different parts of the ship. This spectacle, with fires, a storm, real cascading water and vigorous combat, held the stage for seven weeks.

In late September of 1845, C.J. James presented a new burlesque entitled *A Night with Blue Beard; or Something Curious* (25), written by his son Charles Stanfield James. C.S. James, named for the artist Clarkson Stanfield, earned his reputation as a scenic artist and an author under the tutelage of his father. C.S. James wrote at least thirty plays for the Queen's.[49]

In January James offered a newly acquired version of *The Cricket on the Hearth; or, a Fairy Tale of Home* (28). Adaptations of the Charles Dickens work appeared at

---

47   *Ibid.*, 143–5. The first blackface shows in London date from around the 1830s. In 1836, Thomas D. Rice (a white American actor who performed in blackface) appeared in London at the Surrey. His Jim Crow character was popular and prompted many imitators.

48   Allardyce Nicoll, *A History of the English Drama, 1660–1900*, 6 vols (Cambridge, 1965), vol. 6, 78.

49   'James, Charles Stanfield', in Boase, *Modern English Biography*. C.S. James left the Queen's in the early 1850s and became a scenic artist at Drury Lane, Sadler's Wells (1857 under Phelps) and Sefton Parry's Holborn Theatre in 1866. At the Prince of Wales's, he designed and painted the scenery for *Society, Little Don Giovanni, £100,000, Ours* and *Caste* for the Wilton-Byron-Bancroft managements after 1865. Some of his most successful plays were *Hand of Fire; or the Demon Hunter of the Hartz* (1849), *Old London Bridge, The Dogs of the Grange* (1850) and *Corn Field; or, Clouds and Sunshine, Sun and Sorrow* (1850). He also wrote seven pantomimes for the Queen's, including *Cinderella and the Fairy Glass Slipper! or, Harlequin and the Silver Lily* (1851), *Beauty and the Beast: or, Harlequin Prince Agor, the Queen of the Roses, and King of the Thorns* (1852) and *The King of the Carbuncles; or, Harlequin Prince Peerless and the Enchanted Beauty of the Diamond Castle* (1853), all featuring scenery prepared by his father and him. In 1868, in his early forties, C.S. James met an untimely death at Setubal near Lisbon.

metropolitan theatres throughout the month.[50] In this month James also produced *Old Mint of Southwark; or, Admiral Sam & the Orphan Sailor Boy* (24), written by his son C.S. James.

In February of 1846 Henry Thomas Betty (1819–97), the son of William Henry West Betty (1791–1874), was welcomed to the Queen's for a series of performances: *Macbeth* (8), *Hamlet* (6), *Richard III* (4), *Pizarro* (1) and *The Royal Oak* (1).[51] He shared the bills with *The Cricket on the Hearth* and the popular nautical drama *Gale Breezley* (11). The audiences were uncertain about the plays: 'They applauded Mr Betty, it is true, in those portions of the tragedy with which they were in a measure familiar; but beyond this, bestowed all their attention upon Polonius.'[52]

Audiences at the Queen's continued to hold nautical dramas in very high regard. Eight were offered between June of 1845 and April of 1846. James added another to his offerings, jointly authored by C.Z. Barnett and G.J. Walker, entitled *The Hour of Retribution; or, A Mariner's Prophecy* (24) for April.

W.J.A. Abington

W.J.A. Abington (1807–48), a provincial actor and barrister, recently from the Theatre Royal, Southampton and on his way to the Richmond Theatre, took the Queen's for a summer season to begin in July of 1846.[53] His season of Shakespeare directly competed with Samuel Phelps's season at Sadler's Wells. Abington opened on 11 July; Phelps started his two weeks later.[54] Abington's acting company consisted primarily of performers from Richmond and a few London personalities: Charles Selby and Clara Selby; Thomas Hailes Lacy (1809–73), the future publisher of Lacy's Acting Editions of Plays;[55] and the celebrated lecturer Clara Seyton, known for her precise and engaging readings of Shakespeare.

Prior to his opening, Abington invited the press to view his improvements to the theatre decor: 'The whole of the interior has been restored to what it was originally

---

50   Nicoll, *History of the English Drama*, vol. 4, 96. The Lyceum version was the first, having been licensed on 17 December, but several other theatres, including the Princess's Theatre, Albert Saloon, Adelphi, Marylebone, City of London, Haymarket and Apollo Saloon, soon followed.

51   Giles Playfair, *The Prodigy: A Study of the Strange Life of Master Betty* (London, 1967), 177–8. Henry Thomas Betty first appeared in 1835 at Gravesend. He acted in the provinces from 1838–43. He first performed in London as Hamlet at Covent Garden in 1844. He retired from the stage in 1854. See Paul Ranger, 'Betty, William Henry West (1791–1874)', *ODNB*, accessed 18 November 2013.

52   *Illustrated London News*, 21 February 1846.

53   *Gentleman's Magazine*, 32 (1849), 660–1. William James Achilles Abington, Esq., MA, barrister-at-law, was a graduate of Trinity College, Cambridge and was called to the bar in 1834. He managed the Norwich circuit and for several seasons was the manager of the theatre in Southampton. He was also the lessee of the Richmond Theatre where he died in 1848.

54   Allen, *Samuel Phelps*, 102.

55   John Russell Stephens, 'Lacy, Thomas Hailes (1809–1873)', *ODNB*, accessed 18 November 2013. He was an actor and publisher. His first London appearance is thought to have been in 1828 at the Olympic. He managed the Windsor Theatre, and in 1841 became manager of the Theatre Royal, Sheffield. He joined Samuel Phelps at Sadler's Wells in 1844. He went into the bookselling business in 1849. By 1857 he was at 89 Strand and soon began publishing Lacy's Acting Editions of Plays.

MR ABINGTON, AS HAMLET.

ACT. V.

LONDON, THOS MC LEAN, 26, HAYMARKET.

PRINTED BY STANNARD & CO 7 POLAND ST

20 W.J.A. Abington as Hamlet, undated. Print made by E. Noyce and published by Thomas McLean. © Trustees of the British Museum.

when the French plays were performed here.'[56] Admission prices for the refurbished playhouse were increased to the standard 4s, 2s and 1s. Abington's first night, 11 July 1846, began with *As You Like It* (6), followed by Miss Hartley and G.H. Gilbert in the new polka 'La Gradiska' and musical selections from the band, directed by Mr Ridgway. The evening concluded with Charles Selby's *Ask No Questions* (7). In the Shakespeare piece, Thomas Hales Lacy appeared as Jacques; Mr Craven portrayed Orlando; Clara Seyton made her dramatic debut as Rosalind; and Mrs Selby played Audrey. The critics responded favourably, if not enthusiastically, and encouraged the public to visit the Queen's on the second night when Mrs R. Gordon was to make her London debut.[57] Interest was generated also by the manager's appearance as Shylock in *The Merchant of Venice* (4). Critical reservations disappeared, and the manager was lauded for his work: 'Mr Abington deserves the support of the public for the praiseworthy manner in which he is carrying on the management of the theatre. He made his first appearance in London last week as Shylock, and gave a careful and intellectual delineation of the character. It is gratifying to see a gentleman of education and position taking upon himself the management of a theatre with such laudable intentions.'[58] Abington was called for at the conclusion of his Shylock, and he announced the company would perform *Venice Preserved*, *School for Scandal*, *You Must Be Married*, *My Husband's Secret* and *Honey-Moon*. The *Theatrical Times* praised Abington's acting and his choice of plays, though the critic was disappointed by Miss Seyton's inability to project her voice with the clarity and lyricism required of a stage actor: 'This young lady has great talent, but what can induce her, or the management, to suppose she has the slightest vocal ability? It is one thing to be able to read Shakespeare with 'discretion', and quite another to attempt a display of musical power, without the slightest knowledge of the rudiments of the art.'[59] Not only did she lack technical skills, the critic noted, she also had the temerity to acknowledge her claque in the pit by repeating a song on more than one occasion. Nevertheless, the critics and public encouraged Abington to offer a second, short summer season.[60]

Abington next offered productions of *Bertram* (6), *Othello* (4), *Hamlet* (8), *Katherine and Petruchio* (3) and *Romeo and Juliet* (1) with supporting pieces repeated from the earlier part of the summer: *Spectre Bridegroom* (7), *Speed the Plough* (7), *Rendezvous* (4) and *Sketches in India* (2). Abington's performance in *Hamlet* (8) was considered meritorious but lacking the '*ars celare artem*' of an outstanding actor (Fig. 20). However, the reviewer for the *Illustrated London News*

56   *The Times*, 10 July 1846.
57   *Theatrical Times*, 17 April 1847. Her maiden name was Harriet Gurney Read. She was born in Norwich in 1817. She made her dramatic debut there in 1837. She moved to the Olympic where she remained for the next decade.
58   *Illustrated London News*, 25 July 1846.
59   *Theatrical Times*, July 1846.
60   *Ibid.*

found Abington's work superior. Also, the critic appreciated the scenic excellence of the production, especially 'the appearance of the Ghost [which] was managed by a very ingenious effect; the platform of the castle, and the portrait in the closet, being painted on a very transparent medium, which when light was thrown on the figure, blended the scene and the spirit so curiously, that the latter had the appearance of being seen through'. In his version of the play, Abington restored scenes that were often omitted, and as a result, the production lasted for four hours. Yet *Hamlet* was regarded as Abington's crowning achievement.[61]

A writer for the *Theatrical Journal* expressed concern about the state of drama on the London stage: 'the general impression on us is that we are more in want of good plays than good players; our minor drama is certainly in a most deplorable state; and we shall not do well, until our playwrights shall work better, to copy or adopt the sparkling vaudevilles of our French neighbours'.[62] The author concluded that plays at the Queen's, as at most theatres in the city, were formulaic:

> a villainous noble, and some subordinate villains – a persecuted female – a defender of innocence, always a match for at least three opponents – interspersed with the variety of a comical butler, and a prying chambermaid – occasionally red and blue fire – and in the end vice abashed and virtue triumphant, – not however without sore loss occasionally in the course of the piece by deaths and other casualties.[63]

On a bill advertising the 1846–7 season, James announced reduced ticket prices for the theatre: front boxes became 2s, boxes and stalls 1s, pit 6d and gallery 3d. The new admission prices were approximately half of those charged in 1839. James was following other minor theatre managers in an effort to attract more patrons. The *Illustrated London News* offered an assessment of the situation:

> The different theatres which are now open with threepenny galleries – and other prices in proportion – mention the competition on all sides, in the singing taverns, &c., as their motive for reducing the admission money. We cannot conceive that this plan will benefit them. Few, however poor, who turn out to make a holiday night of it, care whether they give sixpence or three pence, and look chiefly to the entertainment offered, which cannot possibly be a good one at this miserable pittance, if even the barest expenses of the different stock departments of the humblest establishments are taken into consideration.[64]

---

61   *Illustrated London News*, 29 August 1846.
62   *Theatrical Journal*, 6 October 1846.
63   *Ibid*.
64   *Illustrated London News*, 28 November 1846. In December the managers of the Britannia, Standard, City of London, Albert, Bower, Victoria and Queen's were among those called to the Lord Chamberlain's office to account for their reduction in prices. The Lord Chamberlain licensed the theatres with the understanding that there was an agreed upon price to be charged for admission and that the theatres were exercising a prerogative that was not theirs. Wilton, *Britannia Diaries*, 222, note. 2, citing the LCP, LC7/6, PRO.

In the New Year several plays were presented for more than twenty nights: a drama by Thompson Townsend, *Temptation; or, The Fatal Brand* (30); a nautical drama by Thomas Higgie, *Laid Up in Port; or, Sharks Along Shore* (24); and a new Mildenhall play entitled *Ship of Glass* (29).

On 21 April 1847 ten entertainers called the 'New York Ethiopian Methodists' began performing for twelve nights, and the 'Alabama Serenaders' followed them on 5 May. Thompson Townsend's *Death Signal; or, The Night Watch* (22) opened in mid-May; and a week later, Thomas Higgie's new work entitled *Devil's Mount* (23) was presented and continued on the bill into June. On 31 May, a production of *Somebody in the House with Dinah, or, The Invitation to the Nigger Ball* (14) featured 'a whole bevy of black females' who performed the piece with members of the Queen's acting company. The play offered a harsh picture of angry, ungrateful freed slaves.[65] From the end of June, W.J. Lucas's new drama, *Rag Picker of Paris; and the Dress Maker of St Antoine* (32), played until the season concluded.

During the 1847–8 season, interest in America continued at the Queen's Theatre: 'Increasingly, America had come to exercise a certain fascination over the English mind, as it expanded its commerce and trade, and territory. It offered such contrasts – the new against the old, the republic against the monarchy, a people's militia against the soldiers of the Crown.'[66] At London playhouses 'blackface was perceived as a cross-class, even a family entertainment. Troupes like the Serenaders attracted the fashionable upper echelons, and blackface seems to have been patronised by the respectable types, including clergymen, who avoided other forms of theatre.'[67]

At the Queen's Theatre a 'Wild West' show featuring cowboys and Native Americans in conflict followed the Negro minstrels and variety entertainments on the stage. Margaret Mellon's *Bride of the Prairie* (21), set in the 'wild west of America', premiered on 13 September 1847 and featured Kataba the Indian Chief, authentic Indian dances, a near scalping, a treacherous Frenchman and scenes depicting the 'jungle' near the Indian encampment. James created a new curtain and act drop for the start of the season, and he raised the pit prices to 8d from 6d and the gallery to 4d from 3d.[68]

London audiences also responded well to the strong emotional appeal of temperance drama, which prompted James to acquire George Dibdin Pitt's new play entitled *The Bottle; or, The Drunkard's Fate* (43). It opened on 12 October 1847. It was a grim story about a man whose drinking led him to abandon his family, kill his wife in a drunken rage and die a depraved maniac in an asylum. Versions of the play were being offered at several London theatres, and the *Theatrical Times* considered the Queen's production to be among the best. Miss Rogers (whose

---

65   Hazel Waters, *Racism on the Victorian Stage* (Cambridge, 2007), 120–2.

66   *Ibid.*, 90.

67   Meer, *Uncle Tom Mania*, 151.

68   HC: playbill, 13 September 1847.

21 John Hudspeth in *The Irish Rebellion*, 12 August 1848, *Theatrical Times*. Harvard Theatre Collection, Houghton Library, Harvard University, TS 30.22F

acting elicited several hearty rounds of applause) and Mr Parry were called before the curtain at the conclusion of the play. The *Theatrical Times* reviewer found John Hudspeth's (Fig. 21) performance as Comus the gardener-grenadier in the farce entitled *The Post of Peril* a welcome relief from the tension of *The Bottle*: 'he kept the very crowded house in a continual roar of laughter'.[69]

C.S. James was the author of the holiday pantomime, *Fair Rosamond; or, Harlequin and the Magic Rose* (36). *Fifteen Years of a Soldier's Life; or, Scenes at Home and Abroad* (22) began in late April with Miss Marian Rogers as Jessie Ashdown (Fig. 22). *Sister and I* (15), a farce by Mildenhall featuring Miss Wrighten as Rose (Fig. 23), was also on the bills. The two women were particular favourites at the Queen's. Miss Wrighten appeared at the Queen's for nine seasons; Miss Rogers performed for eight.

Documentation for the 1848–9 season is sparse. C.J. James again lowered admission prices to match what his audiences were willing to pay: boxes and stalls 1s, pit 6d and gallery 3d. Not until April of 1849 and the production of C.S. James's *Haymakers; or Vice and Virtue* (22) did the company perform any work frequently that year. In May C.S. James's *Seven Dials; or, The Beggars of London* (25) was the popular production. The Queen's remained open throughout the summer months. On 2 July, C.S. James's new historical drama, *Old London Bridge* (50), commenced and became one of the longest-running productions in the James management period. Audiences were captivated by the fire on the bridge and the brave apprentice's death-defying rescue of the heroine by traversing a beam precariously spanning the distance between the burning shops on the bridge.

On 27 August C.S. James's *The Hand of Fire; or, The Demon Hunter of the Hartz* (27) opened the 1849–50 season. Magic and wizards were frequently part of a night at the Queen's. *The Hand of Fire* bore more than a passing resemblance to *Herne the Hunter*, a success from the 1843–4 season. The play was filled with special effects and action: a secret panel behind a tapestry, a tree bridge over a gaping chasm, and bolts of fire shooting from the demon Wolfgang's awesome 'hand of fire'. James offered Dibdin Pitt's new play *The Sea Lion; or, The Frozen Ships and the Hermit of the Icebound Bay* (25) in November.

The Christmas pantomime by C.S. James, *Sleeping Beauty in the Wood; or, Harlequin and the Golden Horn* (51), opened on 26 December and played well into the New Year. On his playbills, C.J. James noted that he had painted twenty new scenes for the production. Benjamin Pollock (1856–1937)[70] reissued plates

---

69   *Theatrical Times*, 19 August 1848. John Hudspeth was a native of Manchester where he made his stage debut and performed for three years. He first acted in the north and later appeared at the Pavilion in London in 1839. He arrived at the Queen's in 1846. He appeared at the theatre for three seasons.

70   George Speaight, *The History of the English Toy Theatre*, rev. edn (London, 1969), 148–9. Benjamin Pollock married John Reddington's daughter and acquired Reddington's toy theatre plays and shop. He reprinted the inherited plays for sixty years.

22 Marian Rogers in *Fifteen Years of a Soldier's Life*, 6 May 1848, *Theatrical Times*.
Harvard Theatre Collection, Houghton Library, Harvard University, TS 30.22F

2 'Blowing up the Pic-Nics; or, Harlequin Quixote Attacking the Puppets; Vide Tottenham Street Pantomine' by James Gillray, 2 April 1802. © National Portrait Gallery, London

Mr BRAHAM in the character of ORLANDO.
to Mr THOs DIBDIN (the Author of the CABINET &c) this PRINT
is inscrib'd by his FRIEND   Robt DIGHTON.
Drawn, Etch'd & Pubd byDighton, Char Crofs. March. 22. 1802.

3 John Braham as Orlando, 1802. © Victoria and Albert Museum, London

LE COMÉDIEN D'ÉTAMPES
(GYMNASE 1821)
LES QUATRE RÔLES JOUÉS PAR PERLET

4 Adrien Perlet: 'Le Comédien d'Étampes, Gymnase, 1821: quartre rôles de Perlet'.
Bibliothèque nationale de France

5 Mlle Georges (Marguerite-Joséphine Weimer). Collection of Théâtre national de l'Odéon, Paris

6 Mrs Waylett, by Thomas Hodgetts, after F. Meyer, 1830. © National Portrait Gallery, London

7 Madame Céleste as the Arab Boy in *French Spy*, 1834. Courtesy of the New York Public Library

8 Louisa Nisbett as Cornet Fitzherbet Fitzhenry in *The Married Rake*, 1835.
© National Portrait Gallery, London

23 Miss Wrighten in *Sister and I*, 22 July 1848, *Theatrical Times*. Harvard
Theatre Collection, Houghton Library, Harvard University, TS 30.22F

24 *Sleeping Beauty in the Wood; or, Harlequin and the Golden Horn*, 1849.
Reissued by Benjamin Pollack. Scenery by C.J. James. Author's collection

that had originally been produced by J. Green[71] (Fig. 24) and based on the Queen's production. The actors from the Queen's company are identified on the plates. According to James, the 'Magic Tower and Palace of Enchanted Light and Pillared Hall of Diamonds' was especially compelling because it was one of the 'most beautiful and novel effects ever produced on any stage, the entire setting being composed of Jets of Gas'.[72]

Plays doing well this season were C.S. James's *The Bronze Statue; or, The Virgin's Kiss* (29) and Mildenhall's *The Shark of the Atlantic; or, The Fight for the Beacon* (23), revived from 1843–4 and 1845–6. In April C.S. James's demonstrated his versatility by writing a canine drama entitled *Dogs of the Grange; or, The Old Inn Yard* (24), starring Henry Smith and his dogs Hofer and Bruin. A new C.S. James work, *The Corn Field; or, Clouds and Sunshine, Sun and Sorrow* (27), was the principal play from 20 June.

In late August and early September, James refurbished the playhouse interior. His playbill for 23 September 1850 detailed the improvements: 'Boxes, public & private have been refitted [with] a new ceiling [and] the centre has been raised, the front of the gallery re-modelled & ornamented with gilt frames containing figures of tragedy, comedy, poetry, music & dancing'.[73] Staff artists also produced the decorations for the house, including 'busts of Cerito, Taglioni, Charlotta Grisi, Lucille Grahn, and Duvernay'. The circle contained medallions of Shakespeare, Milton, Otway, and Massinger. A new curtain 'unequalled in grandeur of effect' containing a portrait of Her Most Gracious Majesty was painted by C.J. James.

The 1850–1 season began well in September. James increased admission prices for the season: boxes and stalls were 1s 6d, the pit was 8d and gallery 4d. Half-price was boxes 1s, pit 6d and no half-price for the gallery. The season featured *The Valley of Diamonds; or, The City of the Stars* (40) by an unknown author, and in November *The Pirate Queen; or, The Cataract of the Giant's Rock* (26), by Mildenhall, was on the bills. In December, C.S. James's pantomime *Cinderella and the Fairy Glass Slipper! or, Harlequin and the Silver Lily* (45) delighted the Christmas audiences.

In early February *Belphagor, the Conjurer; or, Woman's Constancy* (24) and *Three Naughty Boys of 1851* (24), a piece by John B. Johnstone, were the featured plays. *Azael the Arab; or, The Profligate of Memphis* (25) by C.S. James opened on 31 March.

The James management: 1851–1855
The C.J. James management changed after James's son, C.S. James, left the Queen's to pursue his career as a scenic artist. In his first eleven years at the Queen's Theatre,

---

71 *Ibid.*
72 HC: playbill, 26 December 1849.
73 HC: playbill.

C.J. James had produced a number of new plays by Thomas Mildenhall and C.S. James. Beginning in 1851, the year his son departed, James began to rely heavily on revivals to fill his bills. This practice allowed him to draw upon his extensive repository of plays and scenery accumulated over the years and kept production expenses at a minimum. At the same time, he also chose to limit his newspaper advertising. This decision effectively isolated the Queen's and reduced its visibility. As a result, reviewers visited the theatre less frequently than in the past and the reputation of the theatre suffered:

> when we see two theatres, such as the Victoria and the Queen's (Tottenham Court Road), devote themselves to the drama of crime and intrigue, we cannot but lament that the talent and capacity they possess should be so sadly misapplied. When we see anything really exhibiting a desire for better things we shall be only too glad to notice and applaud them.[74]

C.S. James's Christmas pantomime *Beauty and the Beast; or, Harlequin Prince Agor, the Queen of the Roses, and the King of the Thorns* (46) was the most successful production of the 1851–2 season. The remainder of the year consisted primarily of revivals.

The J.B. Johnstone adaptation of Harriet Beecher Stowe's novel *Uncle Tom's Cabin* (12) was a noteworthy production in the 1852–3 season. The novel was published in England in May of 1852. Theatre managers rushed to mount a dramatic version of the highly popular book. The Standard Theatre production was licensed for 13 September and preceded the Victoria Theatre and Queen's versions by one week. The play appealed to 'working class audiences all over London. South of the river there were two productions at the Victoria; in the East End *Uncle Tom* was playing at the Pavilion, the Standard, and the City of London; and in the West Stowe's hero appeared at the Royal Surrey and at the Royal Marylebone.'[75] The Christmas pantomime was *The King of the Carbuncles; or, Harlequin Prince Peerless and the Enchanted Beauty of the Diamond Castle* (40).

The Queen's Christmas pantomime for the 1853–4 season was *Harlequin King Richard III; or, the Magic Arrow and the Battle of Bosworth Field* (38). An impressive diorama of Constantinople and the Dardanelles, painted by Mr James, concluded the performance. By late February of 1854 the drama *Gin and Water* (18) was at the Queen's, while competing versions were being performed at the Victoria, Pavilion and Standard. In early March *Wilkins and His Dinah* (27), an anonymous farcical piece, was on the bill. J.B. Johnstone's drama *Woman and Her Master* (28) was offered in May and June.

---

74   *Tallis's Dramatic Magazine*, November 1850.
75   Meer, *Uncle Tom Mania*, 144.

The 1854–5 season began on 2 October. C. Fenton's drama *Edward, The Black Prince; or, The Battle of Cressy* (26) was presented on 30 October. The Christmas pantomime *Hop O'My Thumb; or, The Giant Ogre and His Seven League Boots* (49) was the most frequently performed production in the season. Anonymously authored, it was the first pantomime in eight years not penned by the manager's son. In January and early February *Black Rainbow; or, The Weird Woman of Novgorod* (25) was the most popular offering. *The Emperor's Gift* (27), a musical drama, was mounted in the middle of the month and on 23 April a revival from 1835–6 of Morris Barnett's *Spirit of the Rhine* (23) was on the bills. *A Night with Blue Beard; or Something Curious* (24), a revival of the C.S. James 1845 extravaganza, was offered in late May. *Jack Sheppard* (34), too, was revived in August. It proved to be so popular that it was presented at the Queen's for twenty-four more performances the following season.

In October of the 1855–6 season the farce *The Ratcatcher's Daughter* (31) was often performed. *St George and the Dragon; or, Harlequin & the Demon King and the Fay Queen of the Golden Lake* (52) was the Christmas pantomime. *Jack Sheppard* (24) was re-presented in February. It was the seventh revival of the play at the Queen's under C.J. James's management. Mr Sidney appeared as Jack Sheppard, breaking the tradition of having the title role performed by a woman at the Queen's. Thompson Townsend's *Spectre Robber* (25) was also on the bills in March.

The James management: 1856–1865

In the last ten years of James's management of the Queen's, he resumed the production of new plays as an integral part of each season. William Suter (1811–82) replaced C.S. James as the 'resident dramatist', and from 1856 to 1865 he provided James with about fifteen plays a season.[76] Suter's forte was melodrama and pantomime. His pantomimes were highlights of the season and usually performed for more than fifty or sixty nights. Beyond the pantomimes, few productions exceeded twenty performances, which required James to change the bills frequently. Charles Sennett was appointed acting and stage manager at the commencement of the 1856–7 season.

On 25 October Suter's adaptation of Harriet Beecher Stowe's novel *Dred; or, The Dismal Swamp* (24) opened at the Queen's.[77] A production at the Surrey had opened five days earlier. The play climaxes with the death of Dred and his ascension into the bosom of the angels. The scenery for the Queen's production was designed

---

76 Notice of death in *Reynolds's Newspaper*, 4 June 1882. Suter was an actor at the Lyceum and Sadler's Wells before pursuing a career as a dramatist. He worked for several theatres, including the Grecian and the Surrey.

77 Waters, *Racism on the Victorian Stage*, 179–82. *Dred* was published in August 1856. Waters notes that it was 'a response to "legal" and extra-legal attempts to extend slavery to Kansas and, by implication, to the rest of America'. The novel sold 150,000 copies in America and 165,000 in Britain. Like *Uncle Tom's Cabin* it was soon adapted for the stage. By October/November 1856, *Dred* was being performed in London at the Queen's, the Victoria, the Surrey, the Britannia and the Standard.

25 *Dred*: 'Ascent of Dred into the Bosom of Angels', pub. by J.K. Green, 1856. Author's collection

and created by C.J. James.[78] In December J.K. Green issued toy theatre illustrations inspired by the Queen's production. The apotheosis scene was depicted on one of Green's plates (Fig. 25).

The December pantomime was *Sinbad the Sailor; or Harlequin King One Eye* (49), under the direction of Charles Sennett. A Queen's Theatre favourite, *Herne the Hunter* (34), was the popular production in April. In July of 1857 John Douglass (1814–74) and the Great National Standard Company came to Tottenham Street.[79] His summer season was eclectic: *The Merchant of Venice* (1), *Hamlet* (1) and *Othello* (1) as well as *The Miller and His Men* (2), *Camp Follower; or the Mystery of Twenty Years* (4) and *Death Ship; or, the Wild Woman of the Wreck* (2).

---

78   C.J. James and C.S. James were praised for their scenic excellence by Fitzball. See Edward Fitzball, *Thirty-five Years of a Dramatic Author's Life*, 2 vols (London, 1859), vol. 2, 262.

79   'Douglass, John', in W. Davenport Adams, *A Dictionary of the Drama* (London, 1904). An actor and manager, he began his career as a super, aged eleven, in a Covent Garden pantomime. He was known for his nautical characters. He managed theatres between 1833 and 1845, including Gravesend and Chelsea. He began his connection with the Standard in 1845 and the New Standard in 1867 where he remained manager until 1874. He was also manager of the Pavilion and Marylebone theatres during that time.

The 1857–8 season commenced on 29 August with a production of a 'romantic drama' entitled *The Poison Flower; or, The Shadow Bride and the Demon Nun* (27), that continued to play throughout September and October. James Fernandez (1835–1911) made his London debut in this production.[80]

On 21 December 1857 William Suter's *King Teapot the Great; or, Harlequin the Spirit Queen* (52) began its lengthy run. Mrs John Parry took the role of Alcoholia, the 'Spirit Queen and Queen full of Spirit, highly adulterated with envy and malignancy, the proprietor of a Bad Spirit Vault'. New scenery was prepared by C.J. James. Charles Sennett produced and directed the pantomime. In March and April 1858 two new Suter plays were mounted, *Highland Jessie Brown; or Lucknow Rescued* (22), set in India at the time of the 1857 rebellion,[81] and *Giant's Tomb; or, Eleanor the Accursed; or, The Sins and Sorrows of Twenty Years* (33).

During this season W.B. Donne, the Examiner of Plays at the Lord Chamberlain's office, visited the playhouse for a routine inspection. He found the Queen's to be in disrepair. James received notification that improvements must be made. His last serious renovation had been in 1850. Donne noted that the theatre was 'scandalously dirty and very defectively ventilated. I find that it goes in the immediate neighbourhood by the name of the dust-hole.'[82] James undertook the necessary renovations and by 1860, when the Examiner of Plays revisited and reviewed the conditions, the Queen's had attained commendable standards of cleanliness.[83] A drawing of the Queen's Theatre interior (Fig. 26) in the Harvard Theatre Collection provides a general view of the auditorium, including the act drop, the old proscenium doors, the narrow forestage, the footlights and the decoration of the playhouse.[84] The similarities between this and the Schnebbelie drawing (Fig. 7) are considerable, the exception being Schnebbelie's depiction of decorative details.

The 1858–9 season began on 4 September. In November Lady Clara Cavendish's new work, *Woman of the World* (23), was on the Queen's stage. During the second half of the nineteenth century the villainess became an increasingly important character in melodrama.[85] In this play, the villainess Joanna is involved in a plot to sell her attractive cousin to a libertine duke and assist in the poisoning of the cousin's uncle. She is in league with Monti, an evil Italian hypnotist. Her plans are

---

80   'Fernandez, James', in Charles E. Pascoe, *Our Actors and Actresses: The Dramatic List*, rev. and enlarged edn (London, 1880), 142–3. Fernandez was born in St Petersburg, Russia on 28 May 1835. He made his debut at the Queen's Theatre, Hull in 1853. His first London appearance was at the Queen's under C.J. James in 1857. He performed at many provincial and London theatres, including the Adelphi, Princess's and Drury Lane, and was at the Lyceum with Irving in 1878.

81   The rebellion occurred from 30 May to November 1857.

82   Davis and Emeljanow, *Reflecting the Audience*, 142.

83   Tracy Davis, *The Economics of the British Stage, 1800–1914* (Cambridge, 2000), 105.

84   Cambridge, MA: Houghton Library, Harvard University: Harvard Theatre Collection: A. Boycott, Drawings of Interiors of London Theatres, MSThr 434.

85   Booth, *English Melodrama*, 156.

26 A. Boycott, Drawings of Interiors of London Theatres: The Queen's. Harvard
Theatre Collection, Houghton Library, Harvard University, MS Thr 434

thwarted, and she realises that she must flee to London to live as a 'woman of the
world'. In a moment of conscience, she denounces Monti, is stricken with remorse,
bursts a blood vessel and falls dead.[86] While the play was popular, Suter's new
Christmas pantomime, *Forty Thieves; or Harlequin Ali Baba* (52), proved the most
successful production of the season, as usual.

Suter's Christmas pantomime for the 1859–60 season, *Harlequin Blue Beard, and
the Great Bashaw* (52), began on 26 December 1859. The remainder of the season
was devoted to revivals of *The Corn Field*, *The Ship of Glass*, *The Giant's Tomb* and
The Jewess.

In autumn of 1860–1 the Queen's bills consisted of familiar offerings: *One
Handed Monk*, *Dred* and *John of Paris*. The farce *Travelling in Bed* (21) was
presented in October. William Suter's 1860–1 pantomime was *The Children in
the Wood; or The Cruel Uncle and the Fairies of the Golden Vines* (52). Other
noteworthy productions were Suter's *The Three Brothers of Mystery* (28) in
February, *The Irresistibles* (26) in March and *The Syren of Paris* (21) in April. June
was devoted to *Brigands in the Bud* (21).

The 1861–2 season opened in September with revivals until December when
William Suter's *Harlequin Aladdin and the Wonderful Lamp* (61) opened the
Christmas season. This piece became the longest-running pantomime under
James's management. The scenery was the work of the indefatigable manager and
scenic artist C.J. James. The success of the production was marred by an unpleasant
disturbance outside the theatre – a reminder that the neighbourhood was still
somewhat untamed:

---

86   *Ibid.*, 156–7.

Long before the time of opening the entrances to this Theatre were besieged by an immense crowd, the principal portion of which seemed to comprise 'roughs' of the lowest grade and boys of young age, and the scene of uproar that took place was disgraceful, and at one time assumed a somewhat threatening aspect. All respectable persons who wished to enter the theatre could not for a time get near the doors, and to add to this, fights were of most frequent occurrence, the whole forming a scene of confusion and uproar seldom equalled.[87]

The 1862–3 season commenced on 13 September. Marian Jackson and Jenny Slade were added to the company. In December, William Suter's pantomime *Harlequin Kenilworth; or, The Golden Days of Good Queen Bess* (60) became the second-longest-running pantomime under James's management.

Lady Audley's Secret (31) premiered on the Queen's stage on 21 February 1863. The play was adapted by Suter from the Mary Elizabeth Braddon[88] novel. The character Lady Audley was a further development of the villainess character, which became a popular feature in West End melodrama for many years.[89] Suter's *Aurora Floyd; or, The Deed in the Wood* (33), another adaptation of a popular Mary Elizabeth Braddon novel, had a long run beginning on 4 April.[90] Suter next adapted French playwright Eugène Scribe's *The Glass of Water; or, Causes and Effects* (15), which opened on 2 May.

The 1863–4 season featured Suter's *The Highwayman's Holiday* (26), a musical comedietta in September, and his *The Spirit of Mercy* (17) was offered from 26 October. *Harlequin Ivanhoe; or the Fair Maid of York* (52) was Suter's pantomime for 1863. In March of 1864 Suter's *Perseus; or, A Rocky Road to Travel* (24) proved popular. The bills changed frequently during the next three months.

The 1864–5 season was to be C.J. James's last season as manager of the Queen's Theatre. In October *The Detective; or, The Ticket-of-Leave Man* (10) was performed. In December of 1864, William Suter's and C.J. James's final Christmas entertainment at the Queen's, *Old Dame Trot and Her Comical Cat; or Harlequin Little Boy Blue Who Lost His Sheep* (59), was staged, and it continued well into the following year.

In March, at the closing of the pantomime, James concluded his long tenure

---

87   *The Era*, 29 December 1861.

88   Katherine Mullin, 'Braddon, Mary Elizabeth (1835–1915)', *ODNB*, accessed 18 November 2013.

89   Booth, *English Melodrama*, 156–76.

90   John Russell Stephens, *The Profession of the Playwright: British Theatre 1800–1900* (Cambridge, 1991). William Tinsley, the publisher of *Lady Audley's Secret* in 1862, brought legal action against T.H. Lacy, the publisher of Lacy's Acting Editions of Plays, for copyright infringement. Tinsley claimed that Lacy, by publishing William Suter's dramatisations of Mary Elizabeth Braddon's novels *Aurora Floyd* and *Lady Audley's Secret*, had violated Tinsley's copyright. In court Suter did not claim that his plays were abridgements of the novels. He testified that his plays had indeed been published. The court decided that the plays had been produced and not published, and as a result, there was little the court would feel compelled to do. But when Suter's plays were printed, he was subject to the letter of the law. Tinsley won a perpetual injunction against Lacy.

as manager of the playhouse. *The Corsican Brothers* was mounted for his benefit performance. The darkened stage, a ghostly apparition and the chilling sound of an eerie melody were familiar elements at the Queen's under James's management. However, James was not receiving his ticket of leave from the profession. He had accepted an offer from Marie Wilton and Henry J. Byron to continue as the sole lessee and business manager of the theatre. The theatre was scheduled to reopen, after a brief closure, on 15 April 1865.

E.L. Blanchard described C.J. James's management as one of 'sagacity, perseverance and honourable conduct'.[91] While he may not have attained the artistic heights of some of his contemporaries, James did manage to survive for a number of years as manager of a minor theatre, facing intense competition from the growing number of minor houses, with his character and reputation intact. That was a singular achievement and it earned him respect within the profession. An illustration of James's humanity was recalled by E.L. Blanchard shortly after a chance encounter between the two men which occurred on 12 April 1880. Blanchard noted in his diary: 'Visit from my old friend, Charles James, the old manager of the Queen's Theatre, seventy-seven years of age, looking wonderfully well; he presses on me a cheque for £5 for unremunerated services of long ago, and restores to me a copy of my old farce, *The Angel of Islington*, dated 1838.'[92]

In addition to his personal attributes, he possessed both a keen understanding of his audience and their tastes as well as sufficient business acumen to keep his enterprise solvent. He appreciated the fact that his largely neighbourhood audience wanted to be transported to the ends of the earth, to the frozen north, to the deck of a listing ship in a raging storm or to the murky world of ghosts and spirits. They wanted to visit, however briefly, a time and place where they might be rescued from the dangers and injustices of life by an honourable person, perhaps even a faithful dog. James's audiences embraced the romantic ideal that justice can and should prevail, and they were comforted and reassured when good triumphed over evil. They also relished the madcap frivolity of the Christmas pantomime, the annual uproarious escape into that fantastic world where rules and logic were suspended for a time. More than 1,000 performances of pantomime were offered by James during his management of the Queen's. His well-executed scenery was considered a significant factor in the success of these productions and a high point of the season.

What audiences could and would pay to attend the Queen's required James to plan carefully. He met the challenge of maintaining a steady revenue stream by keeping the theatre accessible to his audiences. Selling more tickets, even at a lower price, was better than nothing. In his first season, 1839–40, James set prices at boxes 2s, pit 1s and gallery 6d. By 1848–9 prices were reduced to boxes 1s, pit 6d

---

91   *Era Almanack*, October 1888.
92   Blanchard, *Life and Reminiscences*, vol. 2, 500.

and gallery 3d. In the following year he increased the pit to 8d and the gallery to 4d. For his final season, 1864–5, prices at the Queen's were: boxes 1s, pit 6d and gallery 4d. James, with a keen sense of the fortunes of his neighbourhood, kept the Queen's an affordable destination for its patrons.

James's audiences were comfortable with the predictable plots and outcomes of the plays, the easily recognised and understood characters and the even more familiar scenery, costumes and properties. The loyalty of the largely neighbourhood audiences sustained James's management for his twenty-six years of tenure. His achievements as a scenic artist, particularly in pantomime, earned him the respect of his colleagues, his audiences and the critics. Loyalty extended to the Queen's acting company as well. Many actors in the company performed at the theatre for multiple seasons. Undoubtedly they were well-known celebrities in the Tottenham Street area, and they endeared themselves to their audiences. James contributed the physical trappings of popular entertainment: the startling trap doors, the novelty of the water tank, the raging fires, the tumultuous seas, the peals of thunder and the din of combat. Thus, the Queen's audiences were entertained and returned for more.[93]

That James was a well-respected businessman and an experienced manager was not lost on Marie Wilton and Henry J. Byron as they negotiated the lease for the playhouse. Having accepted their invitation to continue at the theatre as business manager, James performed the duties of that office until his retirement in 1879. His integrity, honesty and years in the profession made him an ideal colleague for the inexperienced new managers.

An article in the *Era Almanack* reviewed James's managerial career at the Queen's in 1861, and it was a thoughtful summary of his achievements:

> This very compact and remarkably well-ordered little Theatre is pursuing 'the even tenor of its way' in its quiet and unostentatious manner – just the sort of manner which, if we mistake not, denotes it being what is understood in commercial phraseology as 'well-to-do in the world.' Mr C.J. James … is a man as shrewd as he is enterprising, and knows exactly how to manage to keep up the celebrity of his establishment, to earn credit for his Management, and to increase the exchequer. Although voluminous Tragedies and five act Comedies are not within the scope of the Theatre before us, yet Dramas and Melodramas, Farces, Operettas, Comediettas, and the like flow in constant profusion, and well succeed in drawing very respectable houses.[94]

H. Barton Baker in his *History of the London Stage*, written nearly forty years later, unkindly observed that the Queen's Theatre, under James's management, shared

---

93   Booth, *English Melodrama*, 13–39.

94   *Era Almanack*, 17 November 1861.

with the Bower Saloon 'a reputation of being the lowest theatre in London'.[95] Baker's judgement was not supported by either the 1861 *Era Almanack*'s assessment of C.J. James or Marie Wilton's memory of her visit to the Queen's in 1865 prior to becoming the manageress of the playhouse. She observed the theatre to be 'a well-conducted, clean little house'.[96] Indeed, the Lord Chamberlain's Examiner of Theatres praised the efforts of James in an 1861 report and in 1867 commented that the improvements undertaken over the previous eight or nine years rendered it 'one of the handsomest and most commodious of the smaller Theatres in London'.[97]

95   H. Barton Baker, *History of the London Stage: And its Famous Players (1576–1903)*, 2nd edn (London, 1904), 317.

96   Squire Bancroft and Marie Bancroft, *Mr. and Mrs. Bancroft: On and Off the Stage*, 2 vols (London, 1888), vol. 2, 178–9.

97   Davis, *Economics of the British Stage*, 288–9.

Chapter Five

The Prince of Wales's Theatre and the Bancroft legacy: artistry and antimacassars, 1865–1880

Marie Wilton and Henry J. Byron

The new management of the playhouse in Tottenham Street was a partnership formed by a successful twenty-five-year-old burlesque actress, Marie Wilton (1839–1921), and a thirty-year-old playwright, Henry J. Byron (1835–84). They planned to begin their management in mid-April 1865. Marie Wilton[1] was determined to advance her acting career and had applied to leading managers seeking an engagement to play comedy parts. She did not want to continue performing as a burlesque boy. With the support and a loan of £1,000 from her brother-in-law Francis Drake, she set out to become the manager of her own theatre.[2] She concluded that managing her own theatre would enable her to achieve her professional goals. She had begun performing early in life and William Macready, Charles Kemble and Charles Dillon were impressed with her skills as a child actress. Dillon brought her to London in 1856 to perform Henri in Charles Webb's *Belphegor* at the Lyceum. Upon her arrival, she received news that the young lady cast as Perdita in William Brough's production of *The Winter's Tale*, which shared the bill with *Belphegor*, had been taken ill. Marie Wilton was asked to prepare the additional role of Perdita. She had only a few days of rehearsal and barely enough time for her mother to create a costume. The *Morning Post* gave her a warm notice for her two performances:

> Miss M. Wilton is a young (apparently *very* young) lady quite new to us, but her natural and pathetic acting as Henri, the son of Belphegor, showed her to possess powers of no ordinary character, which fully entitled her to the recalls she obtained at the end of the second act. She appeared also as Perdita, the Royal Milkmaid, and made still further inroads in the

---

1   George Taylor, 'Bancroft [née Wilton], Marie Effie, Lady Bancroft (1839–1921)', *ODNB*, accessed 19 November 2013. She was born in Doncaster and appeared on the stage as a child.
2   Squire Bancroft and Marie Bancroft, *The Bancrofts: Recollections of Sixty Years* (London, 1909), 55–9.

27 Marie Effie Wilton as Pippo in *The Maid and the Magpie*,
1858. © Victoria and Albert Museum, London

favour of the audience; indeed, anything more dangerous to throw in the way of a juvenile prince it were difficult to imagine. She is a charming *debutante*, who hails from Bristol. She sings prettily, acts archly, dances gracefully, and is withal of a most bewitching presence.[3]

In the next few years she distinguished herself at the Haymarket under the direction of J.B. Buckstone, at the Adelphi with Benjamin Webster and at the Strand, where she quickly became very popular in burlesque under the direction of Mrs Ada Swanborough (1845–93). In her reminiscences she recalled with some nostalgia her 1858 appearance in Henry J. Byron's *The Maid and the Magpie* (Fig. 27). The piece was written especially for her by the young, virtually unknown writer. The critics were impressed with her command of the stage. She captivated audiences, including Charles Dickens, who wrote to John Foster:

> I really wish you would go between this and next Thursday to see 'The Maid and the Magpie' burlesque. There is the strangest thing in it that ever I have seen on the stage – the boy Pippo, by Miss Wilton. While it is astonishingly impudent, must be or wouldn't be done at all, it is so stupendously like a boy and unlike a woman that it is perfectly free from offence. I have never seen such a thing. She does an imitation of the dancing of the Christy Minstrels wonderfully clever which, in the audacity of its thorough-going, is surprising. A thing you cannot imagine a woman doing at all; and yet the manner, the appearance, the levity, impulse and spirit of it are so exactly like a boy, that you cannot think of anything like her sex in connection with it. It begins at eight and is over by a quarter past nine. I have never seen such a curious thing and the girl's talent is unchallengeable. I call her the cleverest girl I have ever seen on the stage in my time, and the most singularly original.[4]

Marie Wilton implored H.J. Byron to write a play for her that allowed her to appear in women's clothing, but before this was accomplished she became the manager of her own theatre. She invited Byron to become her partner and serve as resident author.[5] Theatre management was a male-dominated world, and for a young unmarried woman and an actress there were potential questions about propriety and legal responsibilities.[6] Marie Wilton agreed that Byron would invest no capital and that she would indemnify him against any losses incurred.

Marie Wilton realised she would have to appear in burlesque and new comedies before she could redirect her career. Byron was expected to provide new plays to facilitate her development as an actress. Wilton and Byron agreed to draw weekly

---

3   *Morning Post*, 17 September 1856.

4   Sherson, *London's Lost Theatres*, 220–1.

5   Blanchard, *Life and Reminiscences*, vol. 2, 560–1; and Peter Thomson, 'Byron, Henry James (1835–1884)', *ODNB*, accessed 19 November 2013. In his career Byron wrote 150 burlesques and extravaganzas and served as the editor of *Fun* and the *Comic News*.

6   Davis, *Actresses as Working Women*, 3. See also Davis, *Economics of the British Stage*, 282–4.

salaries of £10 each and share the responsibility of the £20 a week rental for the playhouse.[7] Wilton and Byron visited the Queen's Theatre together with Byron's wife to see one of the last performances offered by C.J. James. They wanted to inspect the premises and observe the patronage. Marie Wilton recalled the evening:

> It was a well-conducted, clean little house, but oh, the audience! My heart sank! Some of the occupants of the stalls (the price of admission was, I think, a shilling) were engaged between the acts in devouring oranges (their faces being buried in them), and drinking ginger beer. Babes were being rocked to sleep, or smacked to be quiet, which proceeding, in many cases, had an opposite effect! A woman looked up to our box, and seeing us staring aghast, with, I suppose, an expression of horror upon my face, first of all 'took a sight' at us, and then shouted, 'now then, you three stuck-up ones, come out o' that, or I'll send this 'ere orange at your 'eds.[8]

Both Wilton and Byron questioned the wisdom of their new venture. They recognised that it was a colourful neighbourhood with rather specific theatrical interests.[9] For them to transform the playhouse into a destination for the fashionable from the West End, they would have to redecorate the interior and carefully manage every detail of their productions to attain their goals.[10] They engaged C.J. James at £20 a week to pay for rent of the playhouse and for his services as business manager. His knowledge of the business of the theatre, the playhouse and the neighbourhood gave them confidence. They petitioned His Royal Highness, the Prince of Wales, who later became a loyal patron of the theatre, with a request to change the name of the playhouse. His approval was given in mid-February. The playhouse in Tottenham Street would reopen as the Prince of Wales's Theatre.

The playhouse closed on 18 March 1865 while workmen cleaned and painted the interior and installed new seats. The necessary improvements nearly exhausted Wilton's financial resources, and she was left with only £150 in reserve on opening night. A reporter for the *Illustrated London News* described the appearance of the refurbished theatre:

> The interior of the house has been entirely reconstructed and richly decorated, under the direction of Mr E.W. Bradwell, of Great Portland Street. The front of the boxes presents

---

7   Bancroft and Bancroft, *Recollections*, 57.

8   Bancroft and Bancroft, *On and Off the Stage*, vol. 2, 178–9.

9   Davis and Emeljanow, *Reflecting the Audience*, 149. By 1861, the majority of inhabitants in the St Pancras parish were employed in industrial and domestic trades, according to Davis and Emeljanow. See also Joyce Mekeel, 'Social Influences on Changing Audience Behavior in the London Theatre, 1830–1880', PhD thesis (Boston University, 1983), 132. She notes, 'one finds on Tottenham Street itself in 1865, five bootmakers, two beer retailers, one pub … three grocers, two timber merchants, a baker, an undertaker, a plumber and an artist. Fifteen years later in 1880, the pattern remains much the same; there is one more pub, a coffee house, three tobacconists, and a few more grocers.'

10   Bancroft and Bancroft, *On and Off the Stage*, vol. 1, 176–9.

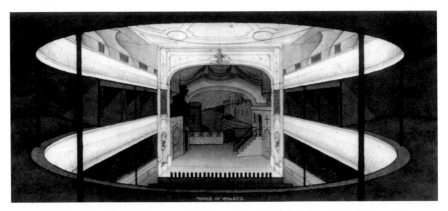

28 A. Boycott, Drawings of Interiors of London Theatres: Prince of Wales's Theatre.
Harvard Theatre Collection, Houghton Library, Harvard University, MS Thr 434

an ogee, with white and gold trellis picked out with blue; and the ceiling is divided into six panels, with gold stars and a blue centre. The arch of the proscenium is framed with white enamelled scroll, the panels in blue, and the Prince of Wales's feathers in white and relief forming the centre. A niche with an ornamental stand of flowers graces each side of the proscenium – an arrangement, we understand, due to the taste of Miss Wilton. There are four commodious rows of stalls, consisting of fifty-four in number, all spring-stuffed and cushioned, and covered with blue leather and white enamelled studs. The box seats, entirely new, are similarly stuffed and covered; and the whole circle, brilliantly illuminated, is lined with rosebud chintz.[11]

A drawing (Fig. 28) in the Harvard Theatre Collection provides a view of the interior. It depicts the fourth scene, 'A Well Known Spanish Square', from the 26 December 1865 production of *Little Don Giovanni*. The white antimacassars in the stalls were a crowning touch of Victorian civility. They were placed there at the suggestion of Miss Wilton to make that section of the theatre more appealing and 'homey' for the patrons. As the carriages crowded the streets around the theatre, the Tottenham Street neighbourhood gathered to view the proceedings:

The reopening of the edifice so familiar to the neighbourhood, under such altered circumstances, naturally caused a large crowd of Tottenham-court-road natives to assemble at the doors of the theatre on Saturday evening. The poorer among them being accustomed to view the establishment as one intended for plebeian patronage looked with timid wonder at the fashionably-dressed persons who now entered the brilliantly-lighted portals. To their eyes the change was as marvellous as anything recorded in the pages of fairy fiction.[12]

---

11   *Illustrated London News*, 22 April 1865.
12   *The Times*, 17 April 1865.

PRINCE OF WALES'S THEATRE.

RE-NAMED BY SPECIAL PERMISSION.

Licensed by the Lord Chamberlain. [Tottenham Street, Tottenham Court Road.] Sole Lessee, Mr. C. J. JAMES.

This Theatre, Re-Constructed and Elegantly Decorated, by Mr. E. W. BRADWELL, of Great Portland Street,

OPENS FOR THE SEASON, ON SATURDAY, APRIL 15th,
UNDER THE MANAGEMENT OF

MISS MARIE WILTON

ON SATURDAY, APRIL 15th, EASTER MONDAY, APRIL 17th, 1865, AND DURING EASTER WEEK

The Performances will commence at half-past 7, with a New and Original Comedietta, in One Act, by J. P. WOOLER, Esq. Author of "Founded on Facts," &c. entitled

A WINNING HAZARD

Colonel Croker		Mr E. DYAS	
Jack Crawley		Mr SIDNEY BANCROFT	From the Prince of Wales's Theatre, Liverpool, his First Appearance in London.
Bodley Croker		Mr F. DEWAR	From the Royal St. James's Theatre.
Aurora		Miss LILIAN HASTINGS	From the Theatre Royal, Bath and Bristol, her First Appearance in London.
Coralie		Miss BELLA GOODALL	From the Theatre Royal, Liverpool, her First Appearance.

To be followed by a New and Original Operatic Burlesque Extravaganza, entitled

LA! SONNAMBULA!
OR THE SUPPER, THE SLEEPER, AND THE MERRY SWISS BOY.

Being a passage in the life of a famous Woman in White : a passage leading to a tip top story, told in this instance by MR. J. BYRON, ESQ., author of "Aladdin," "Orpheus and Eurydice," "Mazourka," "Ill Treated Il Trovatore," "Miss Eily O'Connor," "Maid and the Magpie," Etc., Etc. The New Scenery by Mr. CHARLES S. JAMES and Assistants. The Overtures and Incidental Music, Composed and Arranged by Mr. J C VAN MAARKE. The Costumes, by Mrs. NIEUWS, Mr. S MAY and Assistants. The Appointments, by Mr. JONES. Burlesque By CLARKE. The Extravaganza produced under the direction of the Author.

The Count Rodolpho	Misanthropical, Metaphysical, Metaphorical, Dyspeptic, Bilious, and Disagreeable	Mr F. DEWAR
Village Notary	Marriage Contracts, Paternal Blessings, Title Deeds, Rightful Heirs, and other Stage Requirements, on the shortest notice	Mr M. W. MONTGOMERY, from T. R. Surrey
Alessio	The Merry Swiss Boy	Village Barber and Chatterbox, combining two extreme solitary ranks, being at once Private Inquirer and General Gossip	Miss MARIE WILTON
Elvino	The Nice Young Man of the Village	Miss FANNY JOSEPHS
A Virtuous Peasant	by the kind permission of the Legitimate Drama	Mr HARRY COX, from T R. Brighton, his 1st appearance in London
An Ingenuous Rustic	Mr BROWN	A Simple minded Villager	Mr JONES	A Gallerious Clodhopper	Mr ROBINSON
Amina	the Village Beauty—in her own opinion	Mr J. CLARKE, from the St. James's, Adelphi and Strand Theatres
Teresa	Aunt to Amina—or the Opera-cha—Amina's Mother, but at the present Drama one aren't	Miss LILIAN HASTINGS
Elvira }		Miss BLANCHE WILTON
Lisetta }	a pretty little piece of Alp-ite hide	Miss AUGUSTA WILTON
Liza	Mistress of the Village Inn, but one sad herself, who having been thrown over by Elvino, naturally feels considerably upset	Miss BELLA GOODALL

Peasants and Populace regardless of expense.

SCENE 1.—THE VILLAGE OF TRA-LA-LAL-LA IN THE PICTURESQUE MOUNTAINS OF LURLIETY.

THE HAUNTED CHAMBER,

SCENE 2—EXTERIOR OF THE 'GOLDEN FLEECE' INN.

SCENE 3. NUMBER SIX.

THE PHANTOM.
THE VILLAGE KLEPTOMANIAC.

SCENE 4—EXTERIOR OF THE 'GOLDEN FLEECE' INN.

SCENE 5. — THE OLD WATER "MILL," OR "HOSTILE MEETING OF THE WATERS."

DREAMLAND!
WHICH, IT IS HOPED, CONCLUDES THE PIECE TO THE SATISFACTION OF EVERYBODY.

IN THE COURSE OF THE EVENING,

GOD SAVE THE QUEEN, & GOD BLESS THE PRINCE OF WALES

To conclude with A. G. TROUGHTON, Esqr.'s famous Farce of

VANDYKE BROWN

Vandyke Brown	(his Original Character)	Mr J. CLARKE
Mr Robinson	Mr E. DYAS	Mr Footman	Mr E. W. MONTGOMERY
Mrs Robinson	Miss COLLIER	Mrs Brown	Miss B. WILTON
Rebecca	(her Original Character)		Miss LAVINE

THE NEW ACT DROP, BY MR. CHARLES. S. JAMES.

Previous to the commencement of the Performance, will be exhibited

Prices of Admission—Stalls . 6s. Dress Circle . 3s. Pit . 1s. 6d. Amphitheatre Stalls . 1s. 6d. Gallery . Sixpence.

29 Playbill for Prince of Wales's Theatre, 15 April 1865. Heal Collection,
Camden Local Studies and Archives Centre, London

From the first night, it was evident that fashionable society had little difficulty finding the way to the Prince of Wales's Theatre. The writer for the *Illustrated London News* described the admission prices as being at 'aristocratic' levels.[13] Stalls were 6s, dress circle 3s, pit 1s 6d, amphitheatre stalls 1s 6d, gallery 6d, boxes £2 2s, £1 11s 6d and £1 1s. Half-price was not offered.[14] Babes in arms were not admitted. As the audience found their seats in the theatre, the Wilton-Byron acting company anxiously awaited the start of the evening. The managers had assembled a relatively young, but experienced, group of performers:

Gentlemen: Frederick Dewar, H.W. Montgomery,[15] Harry Cox, Mr Brown, Mr Jones, Mr Robinson, John Clarke,[16] Sydney Bancroft, Mr Tindale, E. Eyas, Mr Hilland, Mr Bennett.

Ladies: Fanny Josephs,[17] Lilian Hastings, Bella Goodall,[18] Blanche Wilton (Marie Wilton's sister), Miss Lavine, Miss Collier, Mrs Saville, Miss L. George, and Marie Wilton.

The opening night of the abbreviated 1865 season was 15 April. It was filled with excitement and anticipation. The bill (Fig. 29) consisted of three pieces.[19] J.P. Wooler's *A Winning Hazard* (45) was the first piece performed. It was a farce about an old gentleman's efforts to marry off his two wards. Making their London debuts were Bella Goodall, Lillian Hastings and Sydney Bancroft. Immediately following the curtain-raiser, Miss Wilton appeared in Byron's piece written for the first night,

---

13   *Illustrated London News*, 22 April 1865.

14   The new managers ended the tradition of half-price tickets at this theatre and continued to increase ticket prices over the next several years. In 1867 the dress circle was increased from 3s to 4s. In 1869 the stalls were increased from 6s to 7s, the dress circle from 4s to 5s, the pit from 1s 6d to 2s, the amphitheatre stalls remained 1s 6d and boxes were increased from £2 2s to £3 3s, £1 11s 6d to £2 2s and the £1 1s remained the same. In 1874 the stalls were increased from 7s to 10s, the dress circle from 5s to 6s, the pit from 2s to 2s 6d and the boxes were unchanged.

15   Joseph Knight, 'Montgomery, Walter (1827–1871)', rev. Nilanjana Banerji, *ODNB*, accessed 19 November 2013. Blanchard, *Life and Reminiscences*, vol. 2, 401–2. Montgomery (real name Richard Tomlinson) was American and made his name in England performing at Bath and Bristol. In London he appeared at the Princess's, the Haymarket and Drury Lane.

16   Blanchard, *Life and Reminiscences*, vol. 2, 484. John Clarke (1830–79) first appeared at the Strand in January 1852. He toured the provinces and returned to the Strand as principal comedian in 1855. His first hit was Ikey the Jew in Leicester Buckingham's burlesque of *Belphegor* in 1856. From 1858 he appeared in extravaganzas produced by Ada Swanborough and written by H.J. Byron and Francis Talfourd.

17   'Josephs, Fanny', in Pascoe, *Actors and Actresses*, 215–16. Frances Adeline (Fanny) Josephs (1842–90) made her debut on the London stage at Sadler's Wells in 1860. She worked at the Strand in 1861. In 1879 she became the lessee of the Olympic Theatre.

18   'Goodall, Isabella', in Pascoe, *Actors and Actresses*, 61. Isabella Goodall was born in Liverpool on 10 August 1851. She performed in Liverpool and made her debut on the London stage on 15 April 1866 in *A Winning Hazard*.

19   Bancroft and Bancroft, *On and Off the Stage*, provides cast lists for most productions and revivals at the theatre.

La Sonnambula! Or, the Supper, the Sleeper and the Merry Swiss Boy (91). *The Times* reported: 'Never was seen a smarter "little Swiss boy," and never was the feeling of a large audience towards a recognized favourite more distinctly shown than when Miss Marie Wilton first stepped on the stage on Saturday.'[20] Marie Wilton's singing and dancing and Byron's new play did not disappoint. She was at the peak of her performance in burlesque.[21] Wilton was ably supported by the 'grotesquely engaging' portrayal of the village beauty, Amina, by the cross-dressing John Clarke. Clarke suffered from lameness and possessed a harsh, unpleasing voice, which perhaps contributed to his considerable success in 'grotesque' roles and eccentric dancing. *La Sonnambula* required singers to begin with the first few notes of Bellini's opera melody and then abruptly dash off into a popular tune of the day. At the conclusion of the second piece, the actors and the author were repeatedly called to receive the warm applause of an appreciative audience. No less successful was the splendid scenery by C.S. James, mostly consisting of Swiss views and a grand transformation.[22] The evening concluded with A.C. Thoughton's *Van Dyke Brown* (16). The first night had gone well:

> On Saturday evening … the theatre was filled with an audience comprising a very significant assemblage of those moving in the best circles of society – it can at once be recorded as an event already recognized by the neighbourhood as marking an important period in local history. No one on Saturday night could have traversed any of the thoroughfares leading toward the street in which the Prince of Wales's Theatre is situated without observing signs of popular commotion in the vicinity. Approaching the great centre of attraction, the curious investigator into the cause would have seen a singularly dense crowd, and heard a remarkable loud chorus, in which a popular street tune and the most fervent expressions of loyal enthusiasm on the part of the juvenile inhabitants of the district were curiously allied. This vast concourse, evidently remaining under a general impression that the members of the Royal Family were distributed among the various vehicles arriving at the doors in rapid succession, lined the roadway on each side to see the carriages pass, and exhibited an interest in the unusual sight which of itself indicated how great a change had taken place in the thoroughfare. Even the humblest shopkeeper seemed to have made some little effort to bring his establishment into increased harmony with the increased dignity of a building henceforth likely to be associated with brighter prospects for the dwellers around.[23]

---

20 *The Times*, 17 April 1865.

21 Thomas William Robertson described the 'burlesque actress' as follows in the *Illustrated Times* (1860): 'She can waltz, polka, dance a *pas seul* or a sailor's hornpipe, La Sylphide, or Genu-ine Transatlantic Cape Cod Skedaddle, with equal grace and spirit; and as for acting she can declaim à la Phelps or Fechter; is serious, droll; and must play farce, tragedy, opera, comedy, melodrama, pantomime, ballet, change her costume, fight a combat, make love, poison herself, die, and take one encore for a song and another for a dance, in the short space of ten minutes.'

22 *The Times*, 17 April 1865.

23 *The Era*, 17 April 1865.

30 *War to the Knife*, 1865:
Fanny Josephs as Mrs Harcourt,
Marie Wilton as Mrs Delacour,
Fred Dewar as John Blunt and
Sydney Bancroft as Captain
Thistleton. © Victoria and
Albert Museum, London

H.J. Byron's domestic comedy *War to the Knife* (53) replaced *La Sonnambula!* on 10 June and continued until 5 August, the close of the first season. In *War to the Knife* Marie Wilton initiated her plan to perform roles other than the burlesque boy. She took the minor part of a matronly widow, Mrs Delacour, and appeared in women's attire (Fig. 30). The play was regarded as slight, giving the impression that it was hastily constructed, but Byron's efforts were generally praised and critics appreciated his bright, careful style and his true spirit of comedy.[24] The actors were also lauded for their efforts:

Miss Marie Wilton plays the charming widow with ease and point, assuming an air of somewhat matronly wisdom that almost takes the audience by surprise, their propensity to wonder being increased when they perceive how well the vocal Miss Fanny Josephs, so often the heroine or hero of burlesque, can play an afflicted wife. As the wicked 'swell' with nefarious gentility stamped in every line of his face, Mr Sidney Bancroft did himself great credit and for the first time took a decided position.[25]

24   *The Times*, 12 June 1865.
25   *Ibid.*

In addition, *The Times* approved of the production standards: 'The scenes, painted by Mr C.J. James [*they were actually the work of his son, C.S. James*], are in excellent taste and altogether the piece itself and the manner in which it is acted and put upon the stage lead to the hope that the newly-resuscitated theatre will be a home for light comedy as well as for burlesque.'

Actors with experience, and who were receptive to becoming part of a company that embraced an ensemble approach to performance, were the highest priority of the new management. There would be leading actors, of course, but the 'star' system would not prevail. In addition, the managers were determined to produce plays that were demonstrably different from the dramatic fare offered by competing London theatres. Finally, it was imperative that in mounting their productions, they must aspire to the highest standards for both scenery and costuming. It was an ambitious set of objectives.

Among the many promising actors/artists engaged was one who became a significant influence at the theatre and in the life of Marie Wilton. Sydney Butterfield (who legally changed his name to Bancroft in 1861) was born at Rotherhithe in 1841.[26] At the age of twenty he went on the stage at the Theatre Royal, Birmingham. Four years prior to joining the Prince of Wales's Company in London, he performed exclusively in the provinces and claimed to have attempted 346 parts – an average of more than 80 new parts a year. He accepted Marie Wilton's invitation to join the Prince of Wales's. They had appeared in *Court Favour* together in Liverpool and were appreciative of each other's talents. Bancroft's extensive apprenticeship in provincial theatres had prepared him well, and his natural charm and appeal endeared him not only to audiences but also to Marie Wilton. According to Squire Bancroft it was 'love at first sight'.[27]

After the first brief season concluded on 5 August 1865, Wilton and Byron began planning for the next season. Wilton was introduced to Thomas William Robertson (1829–71), Byron's friend, and soon reached an agreement to produce his new play *Society* at the Prince of Wales's.

The Marie Wilton and Squire Bancroft partnership with T.W. Robertson

The 1865–6 season opened on 25 September 1865 with two premieres and a revival. First on the bill was Charles Dance's popular farce *Navel Engagements* (30), in which Sophie Larkin (1833–1903)[28] as Mrs Pontifex and John Hare (1844–

---

26 Bancroft and Bancroft, *Recollections*, 25–54. See also George Taylor, 'Squire Bancroft (1841–1926)', *ODNB*, accessed 19 November 2013. Squire Bancroft was born Sydney White Butterfield. He played all types of role in touring companies and appeared with Marie Wilton in Liverpool in burlesque. After successfully managing the Haymarket for five years, he retired in 1885. He was knighted in 1897. Bancroft joined the Academy of Dramatic Art Council (later RADA) in 1906.

27 Bancroft and Bancroft, *On and Off the Stage*, vol. 1, 165.

28 'Larkin, Sophie', in Pascoe, *Actors and Actresses*, 243–4. Sophie Larkin played two seasons at the Prince of Wales's. She was the original Lady Ptarmigant in *Society* (1865), Lady Shendryn in *Ours* (1866) and the Marquise de Saint-Maur in *Caste* (1867). The following year she was at the St James's and the Holborn Theatre with Fanny Josephs.

1921) [29] as Short made their London debuts. Hare quickly became a leading actor in the company. He had the capacity to play both young as well as doddering old men with equal degrees of success. He performed for nine seasons at the Prince of Wales's, and his range was admired by critics, members of the company and audiences. Following the farce was Byron's piece *Lucia di Lammermoor; or, the Lord, the Lady and the Lover* (78). This burlesque drew heavily on Donizetti's libretto and largely ignored Scott's novel: 'a burlesque writer is always more at his ease when he finds the outline of a play readymade to his hands, and may abandon himself to his jokes and his droll situations without being hampered by the task of construction'.[30] The work, according to the same reviewer, 'was performed by a company of aggregate strength for the performance of all kinds of drama to which it is devoted'.[31] John Clarke amused audiences with his sighing, fainting and wails of despair as the ill-starred beauty Lucy Ashton (Fig. 31), and Marie Wilton commanded rapt attention as the young, heroic Edgar (Fig. 32).[32]

Robertson's play *Society* (150) was placed on the bills with *Lucia Di Lammermoor*. *Society*, for which the author was to receive £1 a performance,[33] had previously been successfully performed in Liverpool. It became available to the Prince of Wales's only after J.B. Buckstone had rejected it for the Haymarket.[34] Prior to 1863, when his first novel *David Garrick* was published, T.W. Robertson's success as a writer and occasional actor was limited. His family managed the Lincoln circuit where he made his acting debut at the age of five, becoming a working member of the company at fourteen. Robertson travelled to London in 1848, found little employment there and decided to visit the Continent. Upon his return, he began translating and adapting French plays for Lacy's Acting Editions. In 1864 *David Garrick* was dramatised and produced at the Prince of Wales's, Birmingham. The highly praised 1865 production of *Society* at the Prince of Wales's Theatre marked the beginning of his long-awaited success (Fig. 33). He was thirty-six years old.[35]

---

29   J.P. Wearing, 'Hare, Sir John [*real name* John Joseph Fairs] (1844–1921)', *ODNB*, accessed 19 November 2013. He trained for the stage with Henry Leigh Murray and secured an engagement at the Prince of Wales's, Liverpool. His first appearance was in 1864 with J.L. Toole. Hare met Squire Bancroft there and they become lifelong friends. He moved to the Court Theatre in 1875. With William Kendal he managed the St James's until 1888. He managed the Garrick from 1889 until 1895. He was knighted in 1907.

30   *The Times*, 28 September 1865.

31   *Ibid.*

32   *Ibid.*

33   T. Edgar Pemberton, *The Life and Writings of T.W. Robertson* (London, 1893), 220–1.

34   Maynard Savin, *Thomas William Robertson* (Providence, RI, 1950). Savin provides cast lists for T.W. Robertson productions and revivals at the Prince of Wales's.

35   *The Principal Dramatic Works of Thomas William Robertson with a Memoir by his Son*, 2 vols (London, 1889), xvii–lxxvii. See also Savin, *Robertson*, 20ff. A more recent work by Daniel Barrett, *T.W. Robertson and the Prince of Wales's Theatre* (New York, 1995) is also of value in assessing Robertson's contributions. See also Michael R. Booth, 'Robertson, Thomas William (1829–1871)', *ODNB*, accessed 19 November 2013. Robertson was born in Newark, Nottinghamshire into a theatrical family. He first appeared on stage in 1834. After two years of schooling at Spalding and Whittlesea, he joined the Lincoln Circuit Company, managed by his uncle Thomas, in 1843. He was scene painter, prompter and sometimes an actor. In 1848, when the company disbanded, he went to London.

31 *Lucia di Lammermoor*, 1865:
Johnny Clarke as Lucy Ashton.
© Victoria and Albert Museum, London

32 *Lucia di Lammermoor*,
1865: Fred Dewar as Harry
Ashton, Marie Wilton as Edgar
and W.H. Montgomery as
Dr Raymond. © Victoria and
Albert Museum, London

33 Thomas William Robertson. © National Portrait Gallery, London

34 *Society*, Act III, 1865. Setting by Charles Stanfield James. *Illustrated London Times*, 7 December 1865. Author's collection

Society is the story of the vulgar, nouveau riche Chodds, father and son, who seek to improve their standing by becoming part of 'society'. In the play Robertson examined a broad spectrum of contemporary social mores and conventions. He held the 'mirror up to nature' to expose their folly. Even though Robertson attempted to write in a more realistic style, critics thought the script retained some of the arbitrary resolutions and turns of plot associated with sentimental drama. Yet there were strong indications that Robertson was capable of creating more complex characters and of transcending the stilted language associated with traditional plays. Because the dialogue was more conversational, the characters on stage appeared as recognisable people in lifelike situations. The charming love story of Maud and Sydney appealed to all. However, it was the bohemian world of the 'Owl's Roost' scene in Act III that excited theatregoers: audiences were permitted a glimpse into an inner sanctum of the Victorian literary world to witness an informal brotherhood of writers meeting in a public house (Fig. 34).[36] Robertson was explicit about the scenic effects he required:

Parlour at the 'Owl's Roost' Public-house. Cushioned seats all around the apartment; gas lighted R. and L. over tables; splint boxes, pipes, newspapers, &c., on table; writing materials on R. table (near door); gong bell on L. table; door of entrance C.; clock above

---

36   Clement Scott, *The Wheel of Life* (London, 1897), 20.

door (hands set to half-past nine); hat pegs and hats on walls. In the chair at L. table head is discovered O'Sullivan; also, in the following order, MacUsquebaugh, Author; and Dr Makvicz; also at R. table, Trodnon (at head), Shamheart, Bradley, Scargil; the Reporter of 'Belgravian Banner' is sitting outside smoking a cigar. The Characters are all discovered drinking and smoking, some reading, some with their hats on.[37]

The audience as well as the reviewers responded with enthusiasm: 'The scenes in which the 'Owls' figure are the best in the piece, not only because they are extremely droll, but because they constitute a picture of the rank and file of literature and art, with all their attributes of fun, generosity, and *esprit de corps*, painted in a kindly spirit.'[38] The effort to bring greater realism to the stage was not universally seen as important. Madge Robertson Kendal, T.W. Robertson's sister, recalled that her brother conferred with their father, William Robertson, about his intentions to have real hooks in the walls of the Prince of Wales's setting for *Society*, so that the actors might hang up their coats. The elder Robertson was sceptical about the idea and reportedly said, 'You'd better try something more romantic than hats and coats on pegs in which to interest the public.'[39] But it was precisely this attention to detail that created the illusion of a real parlour room in a public house.

Production values varied considerably in popular London playhouses. With exceptions, most were 'badly prepared' and suffered from the demands of rapidly changing bills and the cost of mounting them. Rehearsals were slapdash, actors often miscast and scenery was drawn from stock and frequently inappropriate. The 'star system' prevailed at the expense of ensemble production.[40]

The Prince of Wales's offered a positive environment for the actor–audience relationship. The proscenium opening at this time was 20 feet wide and the height ranged from 20 feet at the centre to 17 feet at the sides. The stage was slightly more than 35 feet wide and measured 32 feet from the edge of the stage to the back wall of the building. The seating capacity was around 560. The distance from the edge of the stage to the dress circle was only 36 feet. It was 40 feet 6 inches to the gallery.[41] Actors could speak in a conversational manner and be confident that the patrons in the dress circle and gallery would be able to hear them. Gestures could be refined and subtle. Robertson's more natural dialogue established an intimate relationship with the audience: 'All these people are not lay figures; they are flesh and blood. We feel with them and appreciate their motives; the end has been attained without trick or artificiality, and so the curtain falls upon an act of varied motives and

---

37   Robertson, *Dramatic Works*, vol. 2, 700.

38   *The Times*, 14 November 1865.

39   Dame Madge Kendal, *Dramatic Opinions* (Boston, 1890), 46–7.

40   Michael Baker, *The Rise of the Victorian Actor* (London, 1978), 37.

41   Lorenzen, 'View of the Physical Structure'. All the data strongly argue for a seating capacity around 560. See Chapter Six of this book and the architectural plans for the playhouse prepared in 1882 for the Theatre and Music Hall Sub-committee of the Metropolitan Board of Works.

contrasted characters that once seen can never be forgotten.'[42]

The playwright, actors and scenery routinely received very positive notices in the reviews. Robertson's contributions were carefully analysed:

> What is to be admired in this piece is the fresh genial spirit in which it is written. We can fancy as it progresses that we can see the author pleased with the contrivance of his own plot, and chuckling over the jokes as they come spontaneously from his brain. Even his looseness of construction, his frequent change of scene, his deficiency in everything like a Gallic finish, and the inartificiality of some of his motives, far from offending, suggest the pleasant notion of a perfect freedom from conventional trammels.[43]

The acting ensemble in *Society* earned the respect of the press. Sydney Bancroft was singled out for his portrayal of the noble-minded Daryl and Johnny Clarke was lauded for his comic skills. But it was Marie Wilton's charming characterisation of Maud that drew the highest praise:

> the exquisite grace and tenderness and gentle pathos of her delineation brought the heroine into delightful prominence. Few actresses are so strikingly gifted with the power of portraying an emotion by a glance, and her unobtrusive but most expressive facial play, especially in the third act, could not be too warmly praised.[44]

John Hare's Lord Ptarmigant, the dozing nobleman and victim of a domineering wife, was a masterpiece of characterisation and costuming from the twenty-one-year-old actor:

> To the audience, he was a perfect stranger. But when his sleepy old gentleman, dressed to perfection, like one's grandfather or great grandfather, came quietly on the stage dragging a chair behind him, there was a thrill of astonishment, as well there might be, on the part of those who knew how 'old men' were played before John Hare came to 'reform them altogether'. It was a small and insignificant character, but the little actor had made the hit of the evening. When we were told he was a 'mere boy' we laughed; when we were introduced to him afterwards and found that off stage he was a boy indeed, we could scarcely believe our eyes.[45]

T. Edgar Pemberton, Robertson's biographer, wrote: 'The success of the piece was, indeed, instantaneous, and soon became the talk of the town.'[46]

---

42   *Daily Telegraph*, 24 November 1879.
43   *The Times*, 14 November 1865.
44   *The Era*, 19 November 1865.
45   Clement Scott, *The Drama of Yesterday and Today*, 2 vols (London, 1899), vol. 1, 505.
46   Pemberton, *Robertson*, 172–3.

35 *Little Don Giovanni*, 1865. Setting by Charles Stanfield James. Heal
Collection, Camden Local Studies and Archives Centre, London

Appearing on the bills with *Society* after 25 December was Byron's burlesque, *Little
Don Giovanni* (126). Marie Wilton played the young lover, Little Don Giovanni,
to John Hare's peasant girl Zerlina, and this Christmas-time entertainment was
widely advertised (Fig. 35) on illustrated bills. *Little Don Giovanni* and *Society* filled
the house every night. It was Marie Wilton's final appearance as the burlesque boy:
'The actress would have to become unequivocally a woman. She would have to
reject the masculine dress and freedom of cross-dressed roles and aspire to what
was considered "real" femininity...'[47]

On 5 May 1866 Byron's new work *£100,000* (43) replaced *Society*. Although the
play was filled with Byron's usual array of puns and wit, it received less attention
than the actors: 'Suffice it then for the present to say concerning the acting, that it
was of such excellence as to preclude the awarding of especial praise to one, or two,
or three, or four of the actors at the expense of the others.'[48] The settings, designed
and painted by C.S. James, were also appreciated: 'The art of scenic decoration is
one of those by which in default perhaps of loftier accomplishments, the theatrical

47   Kerry Powell, *Women and Victorian Theatre* (Cambridge, 1997), 50.
48   *Illustrated Sporting and Dramatic News*, 12 May 1866.

36 *Ours*, 1866: Roly-Poly pudding scene. Marie Wilton as Maud Hetherington and Johnny Clarke as Hugh Chalcot. © Victoria and Albert Museum, London

world of the present day is honourably distinguished, and it is always sedulously, though not ostentatiously, cultivated by Miss Marie Wilton.[49]

During the summer, T.W. Robertson offered Marie Wilton his new play, entitled *Ours*. Rehearsals began immediately for a production at the Prince of Wales's, Liverpool on 23 August 1866. Robertson was aware that Marie Wilton was disappointed in the role of Mary Netley. She thought the character was underdeveloped. John Hare was also displeased with his part as Prince Perovski, the unscrupulous Russian. Hare agreed to take the role, with all its perceived weaknesses, as a personal favour to his friend Robertson. The author faced additional challenges when the managers asked him to make substantial revisions in the final act.[50] Ultimately, the obstacles were overcome, the production in Liverpool was a success and confidence was instilled in everyone.

Ours (152) was presented on 19 September to open the 1866–7 season in Tottenham Street. For this play, Robertson received £2 a night.[51] (Also on the bill was J.S. Coyne's *Pas de Fascination* (21), a skit based on the Lola Montez affair.) *Ours* was set before and during the Crimean War.[52] 'Our' regiment is deployed and two sets of young lovers are separated. The war rages on and the young women take the courageous initiative to visit their men in the war zone. In the final act, the power of love is contrasted with the brutality of the conflict. In an effort to establish some normality under these adverse circumstances, the passionate youths pursue calming domestic activities: they play skittles and make a 'Roly-Poly pudding' (Fig. 36). Romance, as always in Robertson, provides the greatest sense of optimism for the future. The *Daily Telegraph* critic offered an analysis of the new work:

> Like the author's previous production, the new piece may be said to represent a new school of dramatic art, and one which is likely to exert an important influence on the dramatists of the next generation. The old types of character are according to this new system of nature-printing cast on one side. Instead of evolving groups from the depths of his theatrical recollections, the modern manipulator turns his camera on to the world without, and reproduces with photographic accuracy the figures and features of living people who are among our personal acquaintances ... Mr Robertson had already contrived to show effectively that personages who preserve the habits and manners of every-day life are quite as likely to interest an audience as those creations of a playwright's imagination which have no existence apart from the actor.[53]

---

49 *The Times*, 9 May 1866.

50 Pemberton, *Robertson*, 188–93.

51 *Ibid.*, 220–1. Bancroft recalled sending a cheque to Robertson in an effort to increase the fee for *Ours*. Robertson returned the cheque with a note of appreciation, saying that he had agreed to the fee and it should remain the same. Bancroft also notes that the most he paid Robertson was £5 for each performance.

52 Bancroft and Bancroft, *Recollections*, 87. According to Bancroft, the three acts of *Ours* were inspired by the 1860 John Everett Millais painting, *The Black Brunswicker*, now in the Lady Lever Art Gallery in Liverpool.

53 *Daily Telegraph*, 19 September 1866.

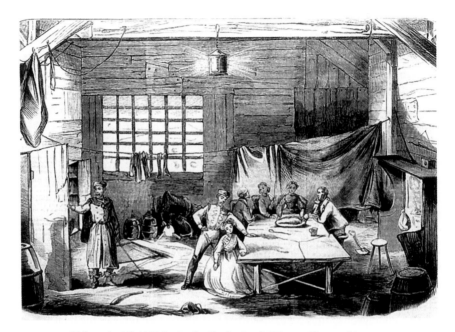

37 *Ours*, Act III, 1866. Setting by Charles Stanfield James. *Illustrated Sporting and Theatrical News*, 22 September 1866. Author's collection

Ours was recognised as a noteworthy achievement and a clear indication that Robertson had made serious strides towards realism in his work. He had refined his character development, language and storytelling.[54]

Marie Wilton's portrayal of Mary Netley, the warm-hearted friend of the heroine, defined her evolving role in the Prince of Wales's company. The character became one of her most acclaimed and repeated roles. Robertson's attention to detail in the staging enhanced the more naturalistic acting style that Wilton and the company sought to achieve. The stirring moment when the brave British troops march off to war touched even the most reserved audience member and repeatedly drew strong applause at its conclusion. For Act III, an engraving (Fig. 37) from *The Illustrated Sporting and Theatrical News* for 22 September 1866 depicts the decrepit little hut near the Crimean battlefront. Robertson's detailed stage directions were specific:

Interior of a hut, built of boulders and mud, the roof built out, showing the snow and sky outside. The walls bare and rude, pistols, swords, guns, maps, newspapers, &c., suspended on them. Door; R.2 E. Window in flat, R.C., showing snow-covered country beyond; rude fireplace, l., wood fire burning; over-hanging chimney and shelf; small stove, R., very rude, with chimney going through roof, which is covered with snow and icicles; straw

---

54   Savin, *Robertson*, 73–81.

and rags stuffed in crevices and littered about floor; a rope stretched across back of hut, with fur rugs and horse-cloths hanging up to divide the beds off; camp and rough make-shift furniture; camp cooking utensils, &c.; armchair, made of tub &c. Cupboards round L., containing properties; hanging lamp, a rude piece of planking before fireplace, stool, tubs, pail, &c. Portmanteau, L. table, L.C., rough chair, broken gun-barrel near fireplace, for poker, and stack of wood. Stage half dark, music, 'Chanson,' distant bugle and answer, as curtain rises.[55]

As characters entered and exited the cabin, snow was made to blow in through the open door.

On 10 October 1866 a new H.J. Byron burlesque, *Der Freischütz; or, the Bill, the Belle, and the Ball* (65), premiered with Lydia Thompson in the burlesque boy role. Lydia Thompson (1838–1908)[56] had been engaged to replace Marie Wilton in burlesque productions. From the beginning of her management, Marie Wilton knew that she must appear in burlesque to maintain the patronage of her loyal followers. She was concerned about her future and eager to better her prospects. She desired to appear in comedy as opposed to just burlesque.[57] Wilton wished to direct her energies to new things, and Byron's work was too limiting. The Wilton–Byron partnership was dissolved amicably two years after it began.

Byron became the manager of the Prince of Wales's, Liverpool that same year. C.J. James replaced Byron as partner (he was still officially the lessee) without investing capital and served in that capacity for the next few years.

In December *Pandora's Box* (67), a burlesque, was Byron's last Christmas piece for the theatre. When *Ours* was withdrawn, *£100,000* (25) was revived on 9 March with Byron's afterpiece *The Maid and the Magpie* (25). Concurrently, rehearsals were underway for T.W. Robertson's most famous play, *Caste*. He dedicated it to Marie Wilton.

Caste (85) was acted for the first time on Saturday 6 April 1867. T.W. Robertson received £3 a night as author.[58] The principal actors in the production were Frederick Younge, Sydney Bancroft, George Honey (1822–80), a colleague from Marie Wilton's days at the Strand Theatre),[59] Lydia Foote (1843–92)[60] and Marie

---

55   Robertson, *Dramatic Works*, vol. 2, 461.

56   W.J. Lawrence, 'Thompson, Lydia (1838–1908)', rev. J. Gilliland, *ODNB*, accessed 19 November 2013. She was a dancer and an actress and first appeared in 1852 at Her Majesty's.

57   Bancroft and Bancroft, *Recollections*, 55.

58   Pemberton, *Robertson*, 220–1.

59   Joseph Knight, 'Honey, George (1822–1880)', rev. Nilanjana Banerji, *ODNB*, accessed 19 November 2013. See also Pascoe, *Actors and Actresses*, 183–4. George Honey became a call-boy at London's Adelphi Theatre in 1843, and subsequently made his debut at the Princess's Theatre in 1848.

60   Joseph Knight, 'Foote, Lydia (1843–1892)', rev. J. Gilliland, *ODNB*, accessed 19 November 2013. See also Pascoe, *Actors and Actresses*, 149–50. Lydia Foote (real name Lydia Alice Legg) made her debut in 1852 as a child at the Lyceum. She appeared at the Olympic in 1863 in Tom Taylor's *The Ticket-of-Leave Man*. She returned for the revival of *Caste* in 1870.

Wilton. In rehearsals for the production, Robertson distinguished himself as a stage manager (director). His approach and techniques were influential, and William S. Gilbert, who frequently attended Robertson's rehearsals, went so far as to say, 'I look upon stage-management, as now understood, as having been absolutely "invented" by him.'[61] John Hare shared Gilbert's enthusiasm for Robertson's ability to work with actors, helping them to translate the printed page into well-developed characterisations and a fully-realised performance:

> My opinion of Robertson as a stage-manager is of the very highest. He had a gift peculiar to himself, which I have never seen in any other author, of conveying by some rapid and almost electrical suggestion to the actor an insight into the character assigned him. As nature was the basis of his own work, so he sought to make actors understand it should be theirs. He thus founded a school of natural acting which completely revolutionized the then existing methods...[62]

The title of the play may have suggested sharp social conflict, but *Caste* was not intended to be inflammatory. Robertson created two parallel stories which illustrated the narrowness of caste: the aristocratic Marquise's refusal to accept the 'common' dancer Esther as her daughter-in-law is juxtaposed with another dancer Polly's reservations about accepting her suitor, Sam, a pipe fitter she believes to be her social inferior. The playwright offers no condemnation of either perspective. On the contrary, he reaffirms that caste 'is a good thing if it is not carried too far'. His optimism prompts him further to observe: 'Let brains break through [caste's] barriers, and what brains can break through, love may leap over.'[63] While there are characters in *Caste* who behave poorly or boorishly, Robertson exposes them without malice. Instead, he advocates hope for, and a belief in, a fair and compassionate world where reason and understanding prevail.

The critics did not view Robertson as a radical or anti-establishment dramatist. Instead they responded positively to Robertson's perspectives and forgave his tendency towards sentimentalism. The *Morning Post* offered its summary of the world Robertson created in his work:

> all these [characters] are ... of the British soil, and thoroughly national in character and feeling. Their sayings and doings awaken in the audience an interest which, so far from waning as the comedy proceeds, increases with each successive scene, and even survives the termination of the play. They look and talk so like the beings of every-day life that we mistake them for such, and have curiosity to know how they are getting on after the fall

---

61   Pemberton, *Robertson*, 200.
62   *Ibid.*, 201.
63   Barrett, *Robertson*, 128–32.

38 *Caste*, Act III, 1867: Marie Wilton as Polly, George Honey as Eccles,
Lydia Foote as Esther and Frederick Younge as George D'Alroy. *Illustrated*
Sporting and Theatrical News, 13 April 1867. Author's collection

of the curtain. Finally, the dialogue, though not effulgently witty or keenly epigrammatic, is singularly neat and easy, and has the rare merit of attributing to each personage the peculiar sort of talk suitable to his or her character and station.[64]

The production of *Caste* was a major theatrical event in 1867.[65] The reviewer in *The Times* concluded that Robertson's success could be attributed to the fact the author was 'scrupulously careful that his audience shall not mistake a sentiment for a principle'.[66] C.S. James' continued the efforts of Madame Vestris, Samuel Phelps and Charles Kean to create scenic realism.[67] A drawing of the setting for Esther's flat was published in the *Illustrated Sporting and Theatrical News* (Fig. 38).

While the audience at the Prince of Wales's had changed since the days when it was known as the Queen's, neighbourhood theatregoers continued to attend performances:

Let it be remembered, too, that the Prince of Wales's Theatre, though it has been fashionable for two years, is by no means in a fashionable neighbourhood, and the gallery must be peopled by many of those working men who patronised it when it was the

---

64 *Morning Post*, 8 April 1867.

65 J.O. Bailey, *British Plays of the Nineteenth Century* (New York, 1966), 373–6.

66 *The Times*, 11 April 1867.

67 Rowell, *Victorian Theatre*, 77–80.

humble 'Queen's'. That such an assembly is pleased with an exhibition which is of a most anti-demagogic kind is a fact worth noting by those who take an interest in the study of the real operative of London.[68]

The fourth season of the Wilton management, 1867–8, began with a resumption of the long run of *Caste* (106). William Suter's farce *Sarah's Young Man* (34) was on the bill when the season commenced on 28 September 1867. By 4 November Marie Wilton and George Honey were appearing in a new W.S. Gilbert farce, *Allow Me to Explain* (25). There were periodic changes to the bills, and on the 18th Buckstone's *Dead Shot* (118) was added. *Caste* was withdrawn on 20 December. On 28 December 1867 Marie Wilton married Sydney Bancroft. He legally adopted the name Bancroft and became Squire Bancroft at this time.[69]

Rehearsals were already underway for the next production, *How She Loves Him* (47), with the author Dion Boucicault in attendance. The play had previously been performed in America. *How She Loves Him* seemed old-fashioned to audiences and critics, compared to recent Prince of Wales's productions. According to *The Times*, the events of the play aroused little interest because Boucicault's newly mounted production had sacrificed the pathos inherent in the text by allowing the actors to indulge in repartee. *The Times* noted, 'Nobody much cared what became of anybody, and this was a sorry condition of affairs in a theatre where the audience had been trained to admire a new species of comedy...'[70] Moreover, the more controlled acting style developed by the company for Robertson's plays appeared to conflict with the presentational style of the Boucicault work. The play failed to attract audiences and it was withdrawn in mid-February of 1868. Boucicault declined to accept any fees.[71]

T.W. Robertson had travelled to Germany during the summer of 1867. His new play was set in a gambling resort in Germany. H.W. Montgomery returned to the theatre for this production, joining newly engaged actors William Blakely and H.J. Montague (1843–78, see Fig. 39).[72] *Play* (109) opened on 15 February 1868. The story was set in and around a casino. Paralleling the gambling at the tables were six characters involved in the game of love.

Hawes Craven (1827–1910), a scenic artist with a growing reputation, replaced C.S. James when he left the theatre to travel on the Continent. Craven designed three major productions at the Prince of Wales's from 1868–70: *Play*, *School* and

---

68   *The Times*, 11 April 1867.
69   George Taylor, 'Squire Bancroft (1841–1926)', *ODNB*, accessed 19 November 2013.
70   *The Times*, 23 December 1867.
71   Bancroft and Bancroft, *Recollections*, 191–5.
72   Joseph Knight, 'Montague [formerly Mann], Henry James (1843–1878)', rev. Nilanjana Banerji, *ODNB*, accessed 19 November 2013. He was born 20 January 1843 in Forebride, Staffordshire. He appeared at Astley's Theatre under Dion Boucicault in 1863. Next he performed at the Adelphi and the Olympic. He opened the Vaudeville Theatre with David James and Thomas Thorne in 1870.

39 *Play*, 1868: H.J. Montague as Frank Price.
© Victoria and Albert Museum, London

M.P.[73] Craven worked closely with Robertson, and his setting for the casino in Act III, scene 2 of *Play* was stunning in its detail and finish; but audiences were subjected to long delays for scene changes.[74]

Most critical responses were tepid and cautioned that little artistic growth could be found in the new production. John Oxenford[75] in *The Times* remarked: 'In the construction of his plot the author has not been as felicitous as in the delineation of his personages. Both these and the incidents hang very loosely together; nor does the atmosphere of gaming, which belongs to the scene of action, and is indicated by the title *Play*, produce much moral concentration. Had the scene in the roulette

73   Anon., 'Craven, Hawes (1837–1910)', rev. Raymond Ingram, *ODNB*, accessed 19 November 2013. Henry Hawes Craven Green attended the Government School of Design in London from 1851–3. He apprenticed to John Gray at the Britannia in 1853 and followed him to the Olympic. He assisted William Roxby Beverly from the late 1850s to the early 1860s. From 1871–1903 Craven was the principal scene painter at the Lyceum under Bateman and Henry Irving. He worked with Gilbert and Sullivan on six operettas at the Savoy.

74   *Morning Post*, 17 February 1868.

75   Klaus Stierstorfer, 'Oxenford, John (1812–1877)', *ODNB*, accessed 19 November 2013. He was born in London and articled to a solicitor. He was a dramatist, critic, translator and song-writer. He was the drama critic for *The Times* for the last twenty years of his life.

saloon been omitted, no important chain would have been broken.'[76] The play held the stage for a respectable run, but it was never revived by the Bancrofts.

The 1868–9 season began on 21 September 1868 with a revival of *Society* (92). The J.M. Morton farce, titled with the sound of a sneeze, *Atchi* (67), was also on the bill. Actors joining the Prince of Wales's company for the season included William Terriss (1847–97),[77] Carlotta Addison (1849–1914),[78] Charles Colette (1842–1924)[79] and Mrs Buckingham White. The managers rearranged the house to create additional stalls and, again, increased their admission prices. In 1867–8, the dress circle had been raised from 3s to 4s. For the 1868–9 season, prices were set at stalls 7s, dress circle 5s, pit 2s. The front row of the gallery was increased by sixpence to 1s 6d. Boxes were now £3 3s, £2 2s and £1 1s.[80] The higher ticket prices did not discourage the theatre's loyal patrons.

On 12 December 1868 *Tame Cats* (11) opened. The managers were unnerved by a chaotic first night when the live macaw, intended to create greater realism, was frightened by the audience, disrupting the evening and overshadowing whatever merits Edmund Yates's (1831–94) play and the performances might have offered. Once the presence of the audience and the glare of the lights frightened the bird, it began shrieking and dragging its stand across the stage. When the final curtain fell, the actors could hear cat-calls from the audience. The production was removed from the bill after only 11 performances.[81] It was the second serious failure for the Bancroft management.

The Bancrofts arranged for T.W. Robertson to read his most recent effort, *School*, and rehearsals were begun immediately. With box office receipts dwindling rapidly, the Bancrofts decided to limit the rehearsal period to three weeks.

School (192) opened on 16 January 1869. Robertson adapted it from the German Roderick Benedix's play *Aschenbrödel* (Cinderella). The play's fairytale-like tone and lifelike characters captivated audiences and critics. John Oxenford in *The Times* acknowledged Robertson's maturation as a dramatist, especially the truthfulness and directness with which the characters were drawn and the brilliance of the dialogue. Oxenford noted: 'The first scene in the wood, the interview between the two pairs of lovers in the grounds of the school, seem pervaded with a spirit which

---

76   *The Times*, 17 February 1868.

77   George Rowell, *William Terriss and Richard Prince: Two Characters in an Adelphi Melodrama* (London, 1987), 7–41. See also Richard Foulkes, 'Terriss, William (1847–1897)', *ODNB*, accessed 19 November 2013. His real name was William Charles James Lewin. He went on the stage in 1867 and became famous in hero roles. He first appeared in London at the Prince of Wales's Theatre in the 1868 revival of *Society*.

78   'Addison, Carlotta', in Pascoe, *Actors and Actresses*, 1–2. Carlotta Addison's real name was Mrs Charles A. La Trobe. She was born in Liverpool in 1849. In 1866 she made her London debut at the St James's Theatre under the management of Miss Herbert.

79   'Collette, Charles', in Pascoe, *Actors and Actresses*, 108. Collette was born in London and was educated for the army and held a commission for several years in the 3rd (Prince of Wales's) Dragoon Guards. He retired in 1866, and in 1868 made his debut on the London stage in *Tame Cats*.

80   V&A: playbill.

81   *The Times*, 14 December 1868. See also Bancroft and Bancroft, *On and Off the Stage*, vol. 1, 265.

40 *School*, Act II, 1869. Setting by Hawes Craven. Courtesy of New York Public Library

suggests a reminiscence of Watteau, though employed not on the conventions of an imaginary Arcadia, but on the manners of the period to which we belong.'[82] The production was distinctive because of 'that polished perfection of realisation that pervades the management of the Prince of Wales's Theatre down to its minutest details'.[83] The schoolroom setting created by Hawes Craven (Fig. 40) was a blending of the real and sentimental worlds. Craven created the mood and atmosphere in his settings. The *Athenaeum* critic was moved to observe: 'The piece is fresh and charming, and stimulates an audience more than any work recently produced. Its complete realism so far as regards the characters, conduces greatly to this result. But its sentiment, especially its tenderness, has a singular charm.'[84] The performances of Marie Wilton as Naomi Tighe and Carlotta Addison as Bella (Fig. 41) made *School* as well acted as any piece on the English stage.[85] *The Times* stated, 'The fact is not to be denied that the production of a new comedy by Mr T.W. Robertson at the

---

82   *The Times*, 18 January 1869.

83   *Ibid.*

84   *Athenaeum*, 23 January 1869.

85   *Ibid.*

41 *School*, 1869: Carlotta
Addison as Bella. © Victoria
and Albert Museum, London

theatre which, once obscure, has become the most fashionable in London, is now
to be regarded as one of the most important events of the dramatic year.'[86]

The Bancrofts recovered completely with the financially and artistically
rewarding production of *School*. Often theatregoers returned to see the production
again during the season. The Bancrofts offered a morning performance of *School*
on 6 March 1869, but the response was insufficient to warrant further pursuit of
the experiment.[87] On the final night of the 1869 season, Charles Dickens was in the
audience. It was to be his last visit to the theatre.[88]

The Bancrofts closed the theatre for two weeks. The audience demand for *School*
remained very strong, but the managers wanted to redecorate, rearrange and
improve the interior of the theatre. To avoid a lengthy interruption, the Bancrofts
asked the workers to clean and paint on a twenty-four-hour schedule. The changes
were described in *The Times*:

All is light, bright and cool. The panels of the boxes, covered with blue quilted satin, are

---

86   *The Times*, 18 January 1869.

87   Bancroft and Bancroft, *Recollections*, 71.

88   Bancroft and Bancroft, *On and Off the Stage*, vol. 1, 281–2.

varied with sculptured medallions of white and gold, and in lieu of the painted imitation of drapery that usually appears on the top of the proscenium, a real drapery of crimson velvet glows upon the eye. The chandelier, generally an obstacle to the sight, rises into a hollow above the ceiling, which is lighted by four lesser chandeliers, shaped like baskets, which perform the office without standing as a medium between the gallery and the stage. Two fountains stand on each side of the stage surmounted by busts of the Prince and Princess of Wales, and the place usually termed the orchestra is filled with mimic rocks, which, rising out of the looking-glass waters, effectively conceal the footlights. The musicians have their post behind the stage, but though they thus seem to interfere with the picture, they are perfectly audible to the audience.[89]

In addition to the improved sightlines, an exit was constructed from the more expensive stalls out to Tottenham Street, providing fashionable patrons with greater ease of egress. In the interest of increasing the number of seats in the stalls, the orchestra was moved behind the scenery at the rear of the stage. The orchestra-pit opening was covered over and decorated with mirrors, rockwork and ferns.[90]

School was resumed on 11 September 1869 to begin the 1869–70 season. The Bancrofts were confident that the public interest in *School* more than justified the continuation of the play. F. Walter's *Quite by Accident* (289) was also on the bill. With the popularity of these two pieces, the Bancrofts mounted only three other plays in the season. For the final performances of *School*, Charles Francis Coghlan (*c.*1842–99)[91] joined the company (Fig. 42), replacing H.J. Montague. Coghlan was to become an important member of the company. On 25 December Walter Gordon's *Dearest Mama* (199) became the curtain-raiser, with *Quite by Accident* continuing as the afterpiece. By this time *School* had been performed a total of 350 times, including the 1868–9 season, and the Bancrofts concluded that it should soon be removed from the bills.

The Bancrofts corresponded with Robertson and he offered them his latest, as yet untitled, script. Robertson's health was poor and he was unable to read the play to the company or to attend rehearsals. The Bancrofts rehearsed the new play for nearly six weeks, an unprecedented length of time for a Robertson script, and they repeatedly travelled to Robertson's home to discuss changes and suggest improvements. From the outset, they sensed that the work was not fully realised, and yet they remained confident. The playwright's health was so poor that the task of naming the play fell to Mrs Bancroft, whose suggestion of *M.P.* (as in Member of Parliament) was eagerly accepted.

---

89   *The Times*, 13 September 1869.

90   Blanchard, *Life and Reminiscences*, vol. 2, 372.

91   Heidi J. Holder, 'Coghlan, Charles Francis (*c.*1842–1899)', *ODNB*, accessed 19 November 2013. He was born in Paris and studied law. He joined the Prince of Wales's company in 1869 and appeared in *School*. He performed at the theatre for seven consecutive seasons.

42 Charles Francis Coghlan. Courtesy of New York Public Library

The first night of *M.P.* (97), 23 April 1870, was filled with apprehension. Robertson was unable to attend the opening. His health had deteriorated further and he was confined to his home. After the conclusion of each act, the Bancrofts sent a messenger to Robertson to report the audience's response. The managers and the company harboured concerns about the strength of the new piece, and they were relieved when the audience and critics reacted positively. While the *Morning Post* praised the production,[92] most reviewers agreed that *M.P.* was less successful than Robertson's previous works.

Tom Taylor, writing for *The Times*, analysed Robertson's relationship with the Prince of Wales's company:

> In the way of light comedy there is nothing in London approaching the pieces and the *troupe* of the Prince of Wales's, taken together ... In a more spacious theatre, and by an audience more largely leavened with the usual pit and gallery public, these light and sparkling pieces would probably be voted slow in movement, slight in texture and weak in interest. But in this pretty little bandbox of a house, with such artists as Marie Wilton, Hare, Bancroft and their associates to interpret them, almost at arm's length of an audience who sit, as in a drawing-room, to hear drawing-room pleasantries, interchanged by drawing-room personages, nothing can be better fitted to amuse. Author, actor, and theatre seem perfectly fitted for each other. It shows rare intelligence in all concerned they have so quickly discovered this, and so consistently acted on the discovery.[93]

In 1870 Marie Wilton became the sole lessee of the theatre.[94] The 1870–1 season opened on 17 September with a revival of *M.P.* (61). Also on the bill were J.P. Wooler's *Locked In* (127) and F. Waller's *Queen Stork* (121) as the opening and closing comic pieces. As the appeal of *M.P.* began to fade, the Bancrofts accepted the reality that Robertson's declining health meant they could not expect another script from him. They decided to revive a success from the past.

On 26 November 1870 *Ours* (247) opened, having been last performed in 1866–7. Critics reviewing the 1870 production were more enthusiastic than they had been about the original one. The Bancrofts offered to increase Robertson's fees, but the author returned their cheque and declined the offer. The highest fees paid to Robertson were at the rate of £5 a performance. Shortly after the beginning of the New Year, the playwright's condition worsened, and on 3 February 1871 Thomas William Robertson died at the age of forty-two. The Bancrofts closed the theatre on the day of his funeral.

---

92   *Morning Post*, 25 April 1870.
93   *The Times*, 25 April 1870.
94   Squire Bancroft was not listed on the playbills as joint lessee or manager until 1878.

Robertson had been held in high esteem by his contemporaries. The *Athenaeum* noted that his plays were

> simple almost to baldness in plot, and altogether free from improbable incident or melodramatic situation. Their hold upon an audience is due to three gifts which Mr Robertson possesses in a remarkable degree, – power of characterisation, smartness of dialogue, and a cleverness in investing with romantic associations commonplace details of life. Mr Robertson's plays are brilliant, epigrammatic, and amusing … He gives us pretty and romantic idylls and then bids us laugh at them. His own laughter is always ready, sometimes it is kindly as the laughter of Thackeray, at others bitter as that of Swift. The great charm of his works is the atmosphere he throws around the scenes of lovemaking, which is entirely his own.[95]

With each successive play, Robertson's characters became more three-dimensional, more complex and more resourceful as they coped with life's complications and challenges. His ideas and themes gave people the impression that they were seeing themselves, or at the least people they knew.[96]

The Bancrofts after T.W. Robertson

Caste (198) was revived to open the 1871–2 season on 18 September. *Cut off Without a Shilling* (198) was continued on the bill. The revival of *Caste*, like that of *Ours* in the previous season, elicited even warmer responses than the initial production and the theatre was full every night. *Caste* was performed until 4 May.

Lord Bulwer-Lytton's 1840 comedy *Money* (73) was on the bills beginning 8 May 1871. *Money* had been a favourite vehicle for William Charles Macready, Helen Faucit and both Edmund and Charles Kean. The play was 'old-fashioned' when compared with Robertson's work, and Bulwer-Lytton's consideration of class conflict and the moral abiguity of money had been explored in a more contemporary manner by Robertson. Friends had advised the Bancrofts against doing the play, which prompted them to rehearse *Money* for more than six weeks in order to feel confident they had done their best. *M.P.* had done well enough, but anything less than a strong positive reception for their production of *Money* would be unacceptable as they planned for the future.[97] Bulwer-Lytton watched approvingly from a box on opening night. Squire and Marie Wilton took relatively minor roles. The audience response was enthusiastic, and the actors were repeatedly summoned before the curtain. The *Athenaeum* offered praise for the disciplined performances in the actors and for the thoroughness of the rehearsal process at the theatre: 'no attempt is made by any

95 *Athenaeum*, 23 January 1869.
96 Booth, *Theatre in the Victorian Age*, 182–4.
97 Bancroft and Bancroft, *Recollections*, 126–30.

one of its members to eclipse his fellows, or to monopolise either the space on the boards, or the attention of the audience. No piece is presented in such a state of unpreparedness that the first dozen performances are no better than rehearsals; no slovenliness in the important accessories of the play is permitted … the performance takes the town with a sort of wonder.'[98]

The 1872–3 season began with *Money* (132) as the principal attraction. *Twenty Minutes with a Tiger* (115) was also on the 21 September first-night bill. Lydia Foote returned to the Prince of Wales's in the role of Clara Douglas. In January the company began rehearsing Wilkie Collins's new play *Man and Wife*, which he had published as a novel in 1870. The first night of the play, 24 February 1873, was a special event. It was the first new, full-length play they had produced since 1869.

The opening-night reviews of *Man and Wife* (136) were generally positive, but there were reservations. Reviewers considered the script antiquated and an odd choice for the Bancroft management. Their adaptation of the novel for the stage drew criticism from some of the press. The Bancrofts were reluctant to show an act of violence on the stage of the Prince of Wales's. In the novel, a murder was the catalyst for all ensuing action. By eliminating the murder from the stage version, the motivation for the action of the play seemed weak. *The Times* reviewer noted: 'everything which gave the book its especial value is absent from the drama.'[99] The well-acted production overcame the criticisms of the press, and audiences, including the Prince of Wales, were fond of the play.[100]

At the beginning of the 1873–4 season, the Bancrofts acquired a second house in Pitt Street to increase storage and dressing-room space. A new royal box was created on the south side of the dress circle by joining two boxes into one. Robertson's *School* (166) opened the new season, and it played from 20 September 1873 until 1 April 1874. The play had not been presented since the 1869–70 season. F. Walter's *Quite by Accident* (112) was also on the bills. Only John Hare, Mr Glover and the Bancrofts remained from the original cast for this production of *School*.

During the more than six-month run of *School*, the managers had ample opportunity to ready Richard Brinsley Sheridan's *The School for Scandal*, which was to be their next production. Squire Bancroft, an amateur antiquarian, relished his numerous trips to the Print and Reading Rooms of the British Museum and to Knole[101] with George Gordon (1839–99),[102] the scenic designer and painter who

---

98 *Athenaeum*, 18 May 1872.

99 *The Times*, 24 February 1873.

100 Bancroft and Bancroft, *Recollections*, 171.

101 One of England's largest homes, the oldest parts dating from the mid-fifteenth century, it was the home of the Sackville family for ten generations. The portraits in the collection are distinctive and the architecture is a mix of Elizabethan and later Stuart design. It was a rich resource for Bancroft and Gordon.

102 George Gordon, with the assistance of Mr Harford, designed the scenery for the Prince of Wales's from 1870 to 1879. Gordon travelled to Australia after leaving the Prince of Wales's in 1879. See Leann Richards, 'The Lost Art of Painting a Scene', *Stage Whispers* (July/August 2010), <http://www.Stagewhispers.com.au>.

43 *The School for Scandal*, 1874: Marie Wilton as Lady Teazle and Squire Bancroft as Joseph Surface. © Victoria and Albert Museum, London

replaced Hawes Craven. He and Gordon pursued every resource to identify and select decorative details. The managers also introduced a minuet in the second act that in time came to be an honoured convention (they believed).

The School for Scandal (108) first night was 4 April 1874. It was a highly anticipated evening. The managers presented the play without the customary farces on the bill. Assessments of the production varied considerably. Clement Scott, reviewing for the *Daily Telegraph*, was dazzled by the scenic design and detail in the staging, the costumes, the use of a black footman for Lady Teazle and the *minuet de la cour*. He praised the performances of Marie Wilton as Lady Teazle and Squire Bancroft as Joseph Surface (Fig. 43), John Hare as Sir Peter Teazle (Fig. 44), Charles Coghlan as Charles Surface, Lin Rayne as Benjamin Backbite and Fanny Josephs as Lady Sneerwell.[103] However, the *Morning Advertiser* believed that the production reeked of mediocrity and that the new interpretation was not successful.[104] The Bancrofts had discarded much of the traditional stage business. *The Times* reported the changes: 'People sit where they used to stand, stand where

---

103   *Daily Telegraph*, 7 April 1874.
104   *Morning Advertiser*, 9 April 1874.

44 *The School for Scandal*, 1874:
John Hare as Sir Peter Teazle.
© Victoria and Albert Museum, London

they used to sit, break into groups where they used to form straight lines; in short, precedent, if it has been regarded at all, has simply been regarded as a thing to avoid.'[105] The acting company was well rehearsed, according to most critics, and the reviewers admired the details in the costumes, settings and stage decoration created by George Gordon. Lady Sneerwell's yellow satin drawing room, used for the first and second acts, was resplendent with harpsichord, china cabinets and tea cups without handles. Sir Peter's house was filled with rich tapestries, oaken tables, cabinets, ancient lamps, candelabra and blue china. One critic observed that the decorations appeared to be on the verge of engulfing the actors and the play.[106]

In the major role of Lady Teazle, Marie Wilton offered a new reading of the character: 'Her ladyship is more of the country hoyden – a squire's daughter fresh from her tambour frame … less of a consummate woman of fashion than she is usually represented to be.'[107] Theatregoers and critics were divided in their responses to this less formal approach to Sheridan's work. Traditionalists thought

---

105   *The Times*, 9 April 1874.
106   *Daily Telegraph*, 7 April 1874.
107   *Pall Mall Gazette*, 14 April 1874.

the production lacked the 'fire and vitality' typically expected in a production of the play. Followers of the Bancrofts were supportive of the more contemporary interpretation.

The Bancrofts selected William Shakespeare's *The Merchant of Venice* as their spring 1875 production. The play offered superior acting roles for the company and was a rich treasure trove for Squire Bancroft's historical interests. As they had done previously, the Bancrofts consciously avoided what they viewed as the pitfalls of conventional productions.

The 1874–5 season began on 19 September with the resumption of *The School for Scandal* (36) until 6 November. On the next night, *Society* (135) was revived and it shared the bill with W.S. Gilbert's *Sweethearts* (135). Gilbert's play was a retitled version of *White Willow*. The play was written for Marie Wilton and John Hare, who were equally adept at portraying both youthful and mature roles. Rehearsals went poorly and Squire Bancroft was aware that Hare was struggling to create the character. Gilbert volunteered to work with Hare in future rehearsals. Finally, Bancroft and Hare mutually agreed that Hare would relinquish the role.[108] Charles Coghlan replaced him. Hare, having negotiated a management opportunity for himself at the Court Theatre, left the Prince of Wales's but continued to be a respected friend and colleague. [109]

Marie Wilton chose to play the role of Jenny Northcott in *Sweethearts* rather than reprise her part in *Society*. It became one of her most memorable characters. She portrayed a young woman of eighteen in Act I and the same character thirty years later in Act II (Fig. 45). Charles Coghlan was Harry Spreadbrow, aged twenty-one in Act I and fifty-one in Act II. As Harry prepares to leave for India, he tells Jenny Northcott that he loves her. She conveys no similar sentiment. Thirty years later, in Act II, Harry returns and encounters Jenny, who also has remained unmarried. He does not recall her last name and casually reveals that he forgot her after a week, but he does remember giving her a camellia. She corrects him and produces the rose that she has kept for thirty years. He kisses her hand and their lives begin anew. *The Times* critic found the production inordinately simple: 'Plot there is literally none. Typical character there is none, the two personages who carry on the action – or rather, the non-action of the piece belong to the mob of lovers who have quarrelled and made it up again.'[110]

While *Society* and *Sweethearts* held the stage, the Bancrofts were working with their actors and design staff to prepare *The Merchant of Venice*. The monumental tasks of editing the text (which Squire Bancroft reserved for himself) and staging the production required Squire Bancroft's full commitment. Some scenes in the

---

108   Jane W. Stedman, *W.S. Gilbert: A Classic Victorian and his Theatre* (Oxford, 1966), 125–7.

109   Hare became manager of the Court Theatre in March of 1875. When he joined the Prince of Wales's Company in 1865 his salary was £2 a week. When he left in 1875, he was receiving £20.

110   *The Times*, 9 November 1874.

45 *Sweethearts*, 1874: Marie Wilton as Jenny Northcott and Charles Coghlan as
Sir Henry Spreadbrow. Setting by George Gordon and William Harford.
Illustrated Sporting and Dramatic News, 21 November 1874. Author's collection

play were rearranged to accommodate problems inherent in scene-shifting on the
small stage and to comply with the decision to construct elaborate settings:

> George Gordon ... with Mr Harford, devoted months of labour to the scenery, which
> was very realistic; elaborate capitals of enormous weight, absolute reproductions of those
> which crown the pillars of the colonnade of the Doge's Palace, were cast in plaster, causing
> part of a wall to be cut away to find room for them to be moved, by means of trucks, on
> and off the tiny stage.[111]

On the playbill for the first night, Mr Gordon acknowledged his debt to Mr E.W.
Godwin, F.S.A., 'for valuable aid in archaeological research'.[112] Squire Bancroft
decided to employ five settings even though Godwin had recommended that there
be no more than three. This decision proved to be a serious error in judgement; the
lengthy delays for scene changes detracted from the rhythm and continuity of the
production. The Bancrofts approached William and Madge Robertson Kendal to

---

111 Bancroft and Bancroft, *On and Off the Stage*, vol. 2, 16–17.
112 HC: playbill, 17 April 1875. To examine Godwin's ideas for the play, see Edward W. Godwin, 'The Architecture
     and Costume of *The Merchant of Venice*', *The Architect*, 13 (27 March 1875), 182–4. Godwin published his article
     prior to the opening of the Prince of Wales's production, and he appears to have been consulted by George
     Gordon.

appear in *The Merchant of Venice*, but they were under contract with J.B. Buckstone at the Haymarket and not available. Marie Wilton decided not to undertake the role of Portia. The Bancrofts offered it to Ellen Terry (1847–1928).[113] She accepted and began rehearsing immediately.

The Merchant of Venice (36) opened on 17 April 1875. Squire Bancroft was aware that the response of the first-night audience was more polite than enthusiastic.[114] In fact, the audience seemed disengaged during the performance. The reviewers, almost without exception, judged the effort to be ill-conceived and considered it a failure. The *Morning Post* observed: 'the painter has well-nigh brushed out the poet and the players. Shakespeare is "nowhere" … the play sinks beneath its load of finery and is killed by the weight of decorations.'[115] The *Morning Advertiser* found the scenery beautiful but overwhelming and the text nearly obliterated. The reorganisation of the scenes obscured the meaning of the play and the evening dragged through four long hours of an episodic and fragmented version of the play.[116] The critics raised doubts about the ability of the Bancroft Company to produce classical drama. They lamented the absence of standard elements and readings of the play. Traditions associated with Shakespearean production were inviolable in the minds of some. The Bancrofts had seriously over-designed the production, but what proved even more perplexing for critics were the misguided performances by the otherwise reliable acting company. They seemed at odds with Shakespeare and each other.

Charles Coghlan was singled out for the harshest criticism. He was accused of abandoning the traditional approach to the role of Shylock. The *Morning Advertiser* asked, 'Is a colloquial rendering of the character a suitable one? … He has brought the Jew down to the commonplace, and the result is that, however much some people may admire the naturalness of his earlier scenes … this pitch was found altogether too low for the latter portion of the play, manifesting its unfitness especially in the last scene.'[117] The *Morning Post*, more adamant about the missing 'points' in the performance, asserted that Coghlan was 'not the Jew that Shakspere [*sic*] drew. Deuce take it, he is not a Jew at all! There is not the slightest tinge of Hebraism in his aspect, air, manner, speech, gait, or gesture. Nothing about him bespeaks the sacred nation … He speaks the text with calm, indifferent fluency, shedding in to it no colour either of poetic fancy or dramatic spirit.'[118]

---

113 Moira Shearer, *Ellen Terry* (New York, 1998). See also Roger Manvell, *Ellen Terry* (New York, 1968); Nina Auerbach, *Ellen Terry: Player in Her Time* (New York, 1987); and Michael R. Booth, 'Terry, Dame Ellen Alice (1847–1928)', *ODNB*, accessed 19 November 2013. Ellen Terry made her first appearance on the stage of the Princess's in *The Winter's Tale* with Charles Kean (1856), with Queen Victoria in attendance. She worked with Henry Irving at the Lyceum for two decades. She was made Dame of the British Empire in 1925.

114 Bancroft and Bancroft, *Recollections*, 206.

115 *Morning Post*, 19 April 1875.

116 *Morning Advertiser*, 19 April 1875.

117 *Ibid.*

118 *Morning Post*, 19 April 1875.

46 *The Merchant of Venice*, 1875:
Ellen Terry as Portia. © Victoria
and Albert Museum, London

The same critic further observed that Ellen Terry (Fig. 46) 'plays the part with charming grace and naiveté and gives the sweetest expression to all the dignified tenderness of her sex'.[119] The *Daily News* believed:

> this is indeed the Portia that Shakespeare drew. The bold innocence, the lively wit and quick intelligence, the grace and elegance of manner, and all the youth and freshness of this exquisite creation can rarely have been depicted in such harmonious combination. Nor is this delightful actress less successful in indicating the tenderness and depth of passion which lie under the frolicsome exterior ... The lady clearly does not belong to the school who imagine that the whole art of acting consists in not acting at all. She is, on the contrary, very inventive in what the players call 'business' – her emphasis is carefully studied, and her action and movements all receive that subtle infusion of colour which raise them into the region of art, and always prevent them from becoming commonplace. But instead of being less natural on this account, sincerity and truth are stamped upon her entire performance.[120]

---

119 *Ibid.*
120 *Daily News*, 19 April 1875.

Ellen Terry recalled her portrayal of Portia as an important milestone in her acting career.[121]

From the earliest rehearsals, the Bancrofts and Ellen Terry observed, with concern, Charles Coghlan's efforts to create his Shylock characterisation. In the opinion of Ellen Terry and many in the press, Coghlan was either ill-prepared or technically unable to master the complexities of the role. Miss Terry harshly described his efforts:

> You could hardly hear a word he said. He spoke as though he had a sponge in his mouth, and moved as if paralyzed. The perspiration poured down his face; yet what he was doing no one could guess ... At rehearsals no one had entirely believed in him, and this, instead of stinging him into a resolution to triumph, had made him take fright and run away.[122]

Coghlan had appeared in several leading roles with success. But in this production he appeared miscast and poorly directed. The critics, in particular Clement Scott and Dutton Cook, found the 'naturalistic' acting style of the Prince of Wales's company to be at odds with Shakespeare. The production suffered further beneath the weight of the elaborate settings and costumes. The audience was alienated by too much spectacle and too little passion in the performances.[123]

The Bancrofts had no recourse but to assume full responsibility for their decisions and accept the failure of the production. Squire Bancroft maintained that 'It may be that it all came a little before the proper time, and that we saw things too far in advance; for the play, in our opinion, only just missed being a great success.'[124] A notice was placed in the newspapers advising the public that *The Merchant of Venice* had not attracted audiences and would be withdrawn after only one month. The production lost £3,000.[125]

Money (60) was the most suitable replacement at hand. It was revived on 29 May 1875 with Ellen Terry in the role of Clara Douglas. Charles Coghlan returned to the Prince of Wales's stage in the principal role of Alfred Evelyn. *Money* was performed until the conclusion of the season on 6 August 1875. It had been a financially difficult year. The managers lost their considerable investment in the scenery and costumes for *The Merchant of Venice*. They had also disappointed their public and the critics. The Bancrofts promptly made arrangements with Charles Reade to produce *Masks and Faces*. In addition, they increased the price of admission in the stalls by 3s to 10s and the dress circle by 1s to 6s; the pit was increased by 6d to 2s 6d.[126]

---

121   Ellen Terry, *The Story of My Life* (New York, 1908), 115–16.

122   *Ibid.*

123   George Taylor, *Players and Performances in the Victorian Theatre* (Manchester, 1989), 188–91.

124   Bancroft and Bancroft, *Recollections*, 206.

125   Barbara Hodgdon and William Worthen, *A Companion to Shakespeare and Performance* (New York, 2008), 234–5.

126   V&A: programme for *Money*, November 1875.

The 1875–6 season opened on 18 September 1875 with a continuation of *Money* (42). On 6 November 1875 Reade's *Masks and Faces* (133) was presented at the Prince of Wales's. The roles of Margaret [Peg] Woffington and Triplet (associated with Mrs Stirling and Benjamin Webster in the original 1852 Haymarket production) were taken by Marie and Squire Bancroft. In keeping with their approach to the 'classics' and their own artistic vision, the Bancrofts made no attempt to reconstruct the 1852 performances. The critics generally endorsed their efforts: Marie Wilton 'is not the Peg Woffington of whom we know by tradition, and she is certainly not the Peg Woffington of Mr Reade's novel, nor is it possible that she should be. She is an actress representing an actress with whom, so far as we can tell, she could have nothing in common save superior talents and a superior knowledge of her art.'[127]

The Bancrofts had produced only two new plays following the death of T.W. Robertson in 1871: *Man and Wife* (1873) and *Sweethearts* (1874). Both plays had been performed for more than 130 nights and were successful, but the managers chose not to revive either play. Instead they commissioned a new work from H.J. Byron. In February of 1876 Byron read his script to an attentive but solemn group of actors. The Bancrofts had already concluded, in private, that they could not ask Ellen Terry to play the part written for her. Charles Coghlan saved the day by refusing to play the role written for him and the Bancrofts then asked Byron to write another play, which they promised to produce in April.[128]

Byron's *Wrinkles, a Tale of Time* (20) replaced *Masks and Faces* on 13 April 1876. The reading of the script by the author concerned the Bancrofts. The first two acts were 'bitterly disappointing' and the third was no better. They resolved to never accept an unwritten play in the future. In rehearsals, their reservations about the script quickly became reality. Nothing seemed to work in the play, and Byron resisted changes suggested by the producers. Even the actors, who had on previous occasions compensated for script weaknesses, could not overcome the shortcomings of the play.[129] The reviews and the opening-night audience confirmed suspicions that the play would have to be removed from the bills immediately: '*Wrinkles* … is not a good play, though, of course, being written by Mr Byron, there are many "good things" in it. But the story is a stale one, and somewhat wearisomely told; nor is it one that in its first freshness could ever have commanded a high degree of interest.'[130]

On 6 May 1876 *Ours* (78) was on the stage. It had last been performed during the 1870–1 season. The Prince of Wales's acting company had changed from that time, but the new members of the company were regarded as equal to the original cast.

---

127   *The Times*, 15 November 1875.
128   Bancroft and Bancroft, *Recollections*, 199.
129   *Ibid.*, 200.
130   *The Times*, 15 April 1876.

As before, the critics found *Ours* to be an appealing production:

> The whole performance was, in short, bright, natural, and agreeable, and marked throughout with that ease and smoothness which can be seen only in those theatres where the interests of the public, and of the author, are not sacrificed to the individual excellence, whether real or fancied, of the actor…[131]

Reviewers observed that Ellen Terry appeared comfortable in a realistic lighter role. *Ours* represented the best of Robertson, and this revival firmly established the play as an invaluable part of the Bancroft repertoire.

At the close of the twelfth season, 4 August 1876, C.J. James retired after more than thirty-five years as lessee, manager and business manager at the theatre in Tottenham Street.

The acting company assembled for the 1876–7 season consisted of experienced performers with established reputations. The Bancrofts recruited Ida Hertz,[132] Arthur Cecil (1843–96),[133] Charles Sugden,[134] Henry Kemble (1848–70), [135] W. Younge, Miss Buckstone, William Kendal (1843–1917)[136] and his wife Madge Robertson Kendal (1848–1935).[137]

The Bancrofts initially planned to stage Wilkie Collins's *The Moonstone* for the new season, but after a final consultation with Collins they all felt that the play was too melodramatic for the company and the theatre.[138] Instead the Bancrofts produced an adaptation of Victorien Sardou's *Nos intimes*. The adapters were Saville and Bolton Rowe, the *noms de plume* for Clement Scott, drama critic and author (1841–1904),[139] and Benjamin Charles Stephenson, dramatist and writer

---

131   *The Times*, 8 May 1876.

132   'Hertz, Ida', in Pascoe, *Actors and Actresses*, 179. Ida Hertz made her stage debut in 1870 at the Standard Theatre.

133   Joseph Knight, 'Cecil, Arthur [*real name* Arthur Cecil Blunt] (1843–1896)', rev. Nilanjana Banerji, *ODNB*, accessed 11 November 2013. He made his professional debut at the Gallery of Illustration in 1869.

134   'Sugden, Charles', in Pascoe, *Actors and Actresses*, 321–2. Sugden began his acting career in 1869 under the name of Charles Neville at the Theatre Royal, Brighton. His first London appearance was in October of 1871 at the Globe.

135   'Kemble, Henry', in Pascoe, *Actors and Actresses*, 234–5. His grandfather was Charles Kemble. After King's College School, London, he entered the Privy Council office and subsequently made his debut at the Theatre Royal, Dublin in 1867.

136   Richard Foulkes, 'Kendal, William Hunter [*real name* William Hunter Grimston] (1843–1917)', *ODNB*, accessed 19 November 2013. He was intended for medicine, but his attraction to the stage led to his first appearance at the Soho Theatre in April of 1861. He was a silent partner with John Hare at the Court Theatre and later, with Hare, shared the management of the St James's from 1879–88.

137   Richard Foulkes, 'Kendal, Dame Madge [*real name* was Margaret Shafto Robertson. She was spouse of William Kendal] (1848–1935)', *ODNB*, accessed 19 November 2013. She was the sister of Thomas William Robertson. Madge's first speaking role was in 1854 at the Marylebone Theatre. She appeared as Ophelia in her adult debut at the Haymarket in London with Walter Montgomery in 1865. She joined J.B. Buckstone's company and continued at the Haymarket. From 1879–88 the Kendals shared in the management of the St James's with John Hare. She became a Dame of the British Empire in 1926.

138   Bancroft and Bancroft, *On and Off the Stage*, vol. 2, 59–63.

139   Victor Emeljanow, 'Scott, Clement William (1841–1904)', *ODNB*, accessed 19 November 2013. He began his career in 1860 as a clerk in the War Office. From 1872 he was the drama critic for the *Daily Telegraph*. He also contributed to the *Sunday Times*, *Weekly Dispatch*, *Figaro in London* and *Observer*.

(1838–1906).[140] The play was reset in England and renamed *Peril*. Squire Bancroft considered the Prince of Wales's production an adaptation of Sardou's play, not a translation.

On 30 September 1876 a fashionable first-night audience gathered to see *Peril* (154). They responded warmly to the play, and the anxious managers were relieved. Some critics were disappointed that the Bancrofts had looked to the French, and not the English, as a source for the new production. But *The Times* critic expressed deeper artistic concerns: 'if the authors have done as well as they have done, and if the acting is so good throughout, how is it that the whole performance is not to be considered as eminently satisfactory and successful?' The writer questioned the decision to reset the play in England, as opposed to the original French locale, and was troubled by the collision of cultures that resulted. In his view, there was too much emphasis on relatively innocent flirtation resulting in an almost tragic consequence.[141] Audiences were unperturbed by these minor concerns. They filled the theatre. Squire Bancroft was proud of the detailed setting (Fig. 47) created by George Gordon and William Harford with the assistance of Mr Phillips and Mr Ballard:

> the old oak hall of Ormond Court took days to erect, and was so elaborately built with its massive staircase and rooms leading from a gallery as to make it impossible to remove it entirely for change of scene. We so arranged the play as to allow the hall to remain almost intact during the three acts, the boudoir being constructed to be 'set' inside the walls of it; in fact, from November to the following April the stage wore the aspect, day and night, of an Elizabethan interior, furnished with a wealth of oak and armour, so mixed with decorative china and modern luxuries as to make it often worth a visit apart from its stage aspect.[142]

The Bancrofts were encouraged by the popularity of the production to offer three matinee performances on alternate Saturdays beginning 20 January.

On 31 March 1877, the Bancrofts replaced *Peril* with two very different productions: Clement Scott's short play *The Vicarage* (73) and Dion Boucicault's *London Assurance* (108). *The Vicarage* was a one-act piece, written under Scott's *nom de plume*, Saville Row. It was described as a 'fireside story'. It was adapted and anglicised from the French original, *Le Village* by Octave Feuillet. George Clarke (William Kendal) visits his old friend Mr Noël Haygarth, the Vicar (Arthur Cecil). The Vicar lives a staid and duty-bound existence with his wife (Marie Wilton). Clarke entices the Vicar with glorious tales of travel and good living, nearly

---

140 'Stephenson, Benjamin Charles', in Kurt Ganzl, *Encyclopedia of Musical Theatre* (Oxford, 1987). His first professional success was *Charity Begins at Home* at the Gallery of Illustration in 1872.

141 *The Times*, 3 October 1876.

142 Bancroft and Bancroft, *On and Off the Stage*, vol. 2, 75.

47 *Peril*, 1876. Settings by George Gordon and William Harford. *Illustrated London News*, 25 November 1876. Author's collection

48 *The Vicarage*, 1877: William Kendal as George Clarke, Marie Bancroft as Mrs Haygarth and Arthur Cecil as Rev. Noël Haygarth. © Victoria and Albert Museum, London

convincing him to abandon his home and wife. In the end, it is the traveller who is converted to domesticity (Fig. 48). The play was charming, but it was the ensemble performance of the three actors that most beguiled audiences. Marie Bancroft – beginning with this production, Marie Wilton was identified in the playbills as Mrs Bancroft – played a matronly woman to great effect. She revealed how she used her personal life to create her character:

> When I played the Vicar's wife I had to deliver a particular speech which always affected me deeply – 'God gave me a little child; but then, when all was bright and beautiful, God took His gift away,' etc. The remembrance of the death of my own child was revived in these words. My mind was full of his image, and my tears came in tribute to his memory. I could not have stopped them if I had tried. The effect upon my audience was that not a heart amongst them did not feel with me. Their silence spoke volumes, and their tears told me of their sympathy.[143]

The second piece on the bills was the 1841 comedy *London Assurance*. Dion Boucicault approved Squire Bancroft's request to reduce the play to four acts instead of the original five. At the conclusion of the first performance, an ominous silence filled the playhouse. The actors retired from the stage assuming that the audience disapproved. The *Morning Post* offered an explanation:

> In itself a strained and artificial piece, *London Assurance* has owed the success it has enjoyed to the number of effective characters it supplies and to the wit of a portion of its dialogue … This piece Mr and Mrs Bancroft have mounted in the superb fashion we have come to expect at their theatre, and have cast with the care they never fail to exhibit. If the result is less of a success than might have been expected from the pains bestowed, the principal measure of the blame must fall upon the inherent faults of the comedy…[144]

The Times critic had doubts about the practice of 'modernising' old plays and applying realistic scenery and acting approaches to them: 'Had the period to which it is supposed to belong been preserved in all its outward and visible signs, the many faults and absurdities of the piece, its grave sins against both social and literary propriety, might have been, at least, less conspicuous.'[145]

The Bancrofts began the 1877–8 season on 28 September 1877. They selected Tom Taylor's *An Unequal Match* (83) to be the first production of the year. It had been licensed for the Haymarket in 1857 and was an old favourite of audiences. It was offered with Taylor's farce *To Parents and Guardians* (77). Once again the

---

143   Bancroft and Bancroft, *On and Off*, vol. 2, 96.

144   *Morning Post*, 2 April 1877.

145   *The Times*, 2 April 1877.

49 *Diplomacy*, 1878: Madge Kendal as Dora. © Victoria and Albert Museum, London

Bancrofts applied their more naturalistic production approach to an older play. The response illustrated how changes in production style created unease among some critics and theatregoers:

> They are so terribly slow, and quiet, and gentle that the blacksmith's fatherly emotion at greeting his daughter in her own house seems almost hysterical, and Hester's shriek on finding, as she supposes, her jealous suspicions verified, startles like the explosion of a torpedo. The acting at this house has always been predominantly free from the extravagance and noise that so often disfigure the stage, but here surely there is a danger of falling into the opposite extreme. This is more like a company of lotos-eaters than a company of clever actors, as these are, playing in a bright and amusing comedy.[146]

Early in 1877 Squire Bancroft learned that Victorien Sardou was about to produce his new play *Dora* at the Théâtre du Vaudeville in Paris. The Bancrofts' earlier success with *Peril* encouraged him to visit Paris to see the new piece. Before the performance concluded, Bancroft wrote a cheque for £1,500 to purchase Sardou's play. Clement Scott and B.C. Stephenson (Saville and Bolton Rowe) were entrusted with the task of producing an adaptation. The Bancrofts picked a name from a hat to select the play's title: *Diplomacy*. John Clayton (1843–88)[147] was engaged to play the role of Henry Beauclerc, and Roma Guillon Le Thière (d. 1903)[148] took the role of the Marquise de Rio-Zares.

Diplomacy (309) opened on 12 January 1878 and over the next year it more than returned the investment made to acquire the property. *Diplomacy* became one of the Bancrofts' most appreciated long-running plays. Audience demand for tickets was so high that the managers kept the production running through the summer holidays. In the adaptation of Sardou's play a young English officer, Julian Beauclerc (William Kendal), makes the acquaintance of the Marquise de Rio-Zares (Miss Le Thière) and her daughter Dora (Madge Kendal) (Fig. 49) while visiting Monte Carlo. He falls in love with Dora, and marries her, mindful of his brother Henry Beauclerc's (John Clayton) objections. Following the wedding, he learns that his bride is a suspected spy. His brother Henry, through diplomacy, proceeds to unravel the mystery. The conflict is resolved when the Countess Zicka, played by Marie Bancroft (Fig. 50), is unmasked, exposed by the unmistakeable scent of her distinctive Japanese perfume. William Kendal's newfound prowess as a serious actor surprised the critics. Others in the company were praised for their refined and forceful performances. The *Daily Telegraph* reviewer appreciated Madge

---

146 *The Times*, 2 October 1877.

147 Joseph Knight, 'Clayton, John [*real name* John Alfred Calthrop] (1843–1888)', rev. Nilanjana Banerji, *ODNB*, accessed 19 November 2013. After abandoning his plan to join the Indian Civil Service, he joined Miss Herbert's company at the St James's in 1866.

148 'Le Thière, Roma Guillon', in Pascoe, *Actors and Actresses*, 250. See the *Athenaeum*, 17 July 1903. She was born in France. Her first appearance was at the Royalty in 1865 as Emilia in *Othello*.

50 *Diplomacy*, 1878: Roma
Le Thière as Marquise de
Rio-Zares and Marie Bancroft
as Zicka. © Victoria and
Albert Museum, London

Kendal's artistic achievements:

> It may be emphatically observed that a performance so thoroughly complete and
> satisfactory in all respects has not been seen in London for very many years. Mrs Kendal,
> as the heroine Dora, charmingly delineates the various phases of feeling by which she is
> actuated: playful and pathetic in the earlier scenes, earnest in her emotion when accused
> so unjustly of wronging the man she loves so devotedly, and stirring the deepest depths of
> the heart when, with wild frenzy, she beats with her hands the closed door through which
> her agonized husband has passed and locked behind him.[149]

The popularity of the production prompted the Prince of Wales to view the play
from the dress circle rather than wait for a box.[150]

The Bancrofts and the Kendals gave up their roles when they left for the summer
holidays. They were replaced by Johnston Forbes-Robertson (1853–1937)[151] as

---

149 *Daily Telegraph*, 21 January 1878.
150 Bancroft and Bancroft, *Recollections*, 224.
151 Ralph Berry, 'Robertson, Sir Johnston Forbes (1853–1937)', *ODNB*, accessed 19 November 2013. He made his
     first London appearance in 1874. His first success was in *Dan'l Druce, Blacksmith* at the Haymarket in 1876.
     He worked with Henry Irving at the Lyceum and toured both England and America. He managed the Lyceum
     beginning in 1895. He was knighted in 1913.

Count Orloff, Sophie Young as Countess Zicka, Amy Roselle[152] as Dora and H.B. Conway[153] as Julian. The Kendals arranged with Squire and Marie Bancroft to take *Diplomacy* on tour to provincial theatres. After nearly a year, *Diplomacy* closed on 10 January 1879.

More than a few critics likened *Diplomacy* to T.W. Robertson's *Caste*, and this comparison may have encouraged the Bancrofts to revive *Caste* (120) on 11 January 1879. It had been eight years since the company last played it. Matinee performances were offered from 18 January to 1 March. *Caste* closed in May, and three different works were performed from 31 May 1879: Palgrave Simpson's *Heads or Tails* (54), W.S. Gilbert's *Sweethearts* (54) from the 1874 season and J.B. Buckstone's *Good for Nothing* with Mrs Bancroft as Nan (54). The season ended on 1 August 1879.

The Bancrofts announced that they were concluding their management of the Prince of Wales's. They had leased the Haymarket and would continue at the Tottenham Street playhouse only until 29 December 1879. The lure of the Haymarket with its larger seating capacity of more than 1,100, modern amenities and prestige could not be resisted. The limitations of the old Prince of Wales's were increasingly evident.

Duty (28), adapted by James Albery from Victorien Sardou's *Les Bourgeois de Pont-Arcy*, opened the abbreviated 1879–80 season on 27 September 1879. The subject of the play was considered more sensational than *Diplomacy*. A son's effort to restore his father's reputation following an accusation of adultery was more titillating than diplomatic intrigue. The son places duty to his family above his own marriage, happiness and future. The acting assignments were Mrs Herman [Jane Elizabeth] Vezin (1827–1902)[154] as Lady Dean, Marion Terry (Ellen Terry's sister) as Mabel Holne, Augusta Wilton (Mrs Bancroft's sister) as Zoe Smith, Linda Dietz[155] as Marcelle Aubry, H.B. Conway as Sir Geoffrey Dean, Arthur Cecil as John Hamond and Johnston Forbes-Robertson as Dick Fanshawe. Neither Squire nor Marie Bancroft acted in the production. The managers and the press generally agreed that the play was not successful. Indeed, *The Times* critic thought the Bancrofts had a production 'not far removed from a failure'. He also found it difficult to conceal a 'distaste for these illegitimate English-French pieces that are neither one thing nor the other, and when they fail to succeed under such conditions as they receive at the Prince of Wales's Theatre there is some hope that

---

152 'Roselle, Amy', in Pascoe, *Actors and Actresses*, 288–9. She first appeared at the Theatre Royal, Exeter and made her London debut in 1871 at the Haymarket.

153 'Conway, H.B.', *Illustrated Sporting and Dramatic News*, 27 April 1878. (Real name H.B. Coulson.) He first appeared on the London stage in 1872 at the Olympic and moved to the Lyceum under Irving.

154 J. Parker, 'Vezin [née Thomson; *other married name* Young], Jane Elizabeth [Eliza] (1827–1902)', rev. J. Gilliland, *ODNB*, accessed 19 November 2013. By 1845 she was performing at the Victoria Theatre in Melbourne. She first appeared in London with Samuel Phelps at Sadler's Wells in 1857.

155 'Dietz, Linda', in Pascoe, *Actors and Actresses*, 119. She first appeared in London in 1873 at the Haymarket.

they may come in time to disappear altogether from our stage'.[156]

The Bancrofts turned to the dependable *Ours* (61) to conclude their management of the Prince of Wales's. The company that gathered for the 22 November 1879 restaging featured Squire and Marie Bancroft in their original roles as Hugh Chalcot and Mary Netley. The revival of *Ours* stirred emotions. It was the play and production that epitomised the Bancrofts' artistic accomplishments at the Prince of Wales's.

The Bancroft–Robertson partnership was a mutually rewarding one, and they brought out the best in each other. At the Prince of Wales's Theatre, the Bancrofts presented Robertson's plays more than 2,240 times.[157] They also revived his works at the Haymarket in later years. The most popular Robertson play was *School* with 551 performances, followed by *Ours* (538), *Caste* (509), *Society* (377), *M.P.* (158) and *Play* (109). The other major productions for the Bancrofts were Sardou's *Diplomacy* (309), Lytton's *Money* (234), W.S. Gilbert's *Sweethearts* (189), Sardou's *Peril* (156), Sheridan's *The School for Scandal* (144), Collins's *Man and Wife* (137) and Reade's *Masks and Faces* (133).[158] The long run was the basis of the success enjoyed by the Bancrofts. On their last night at the theatre, 29 January 1880, the Bancrofts were repeatedly summoned before the curtain to receive the warm and appreciative applause of their friends. Finally, the emotional audience of well-wishers quieted, and Squire Bancroft spoke nostalgically about the playhouse but quickly turned to their Saturday evening performance at the Haymarket. He wished Edgar Bruce, the new manager of the Prince of Wales's, success and bid the audience *au revoir*, not goodbye. There was little sadness in Squire Bancroft's speech. The Bancrofts had attained great popularity and artistic success at the Prince of Wales's, but they were ready for new challenges and the prospects of the Haymarket. The Haymarket was not a venture without risk. On average, the nightly expenses of the Prince of Wales's never exceeded £70; at the Haymarket they would begin at £100 a night and increase to £120 in five years. The initial cost of renovation at the Haymarket was £20,000, while the decorating and improvements at the Prince of Wales's totalled only £10,000 over a decade and a half.

The fifteen years the Bancrofts invested in the Prince of Wales's were acknowledged and honour was bestowed on them by theatregoers and the press. They surrounded themselves with talented actors and created an ensemble that was the talk of the city. The little theatre in Tottenham Street was a near-perfect

---

156 *The Times*, 10 November 1879.

157 My total number of performances does not match W. Craven Mackie's in 'The Bancroft and Bancroft Repertory, 1865 to 1885', *Educational Theatre Journal*, 27/1 (1975), 98–110. I have included all revivals, including those of less than one hundred performances, to arrive at the total number of performances. I have not included matinee or provincial performances in these totals.

158 The repetition and revival of several opening and afterpieces attests to their popularity and their durability: F. Waller's *Quite by Accident* (501), S.T. Smith's *Cut Off With a Shilling* (306), J.P. Wooler's *A Winning Hazard* (198) and C.J. Mathews's *Twenty Minutes With a Tiger* (190).

environment for the pursuit of their artistic visions. Many successful actors and artists of the day were fortunate to have appeared at the theatre and benefited from the encouragement and direction they received from the Bancrofts. Ellen Terry reflected on how her career was shaped by her experiences:

> I learned a great deal at the Prince of Wales's, notably that the art of playing modern plays in a tiny theatre was quite different from the art of playing in the classics in a big theatre. The methods for big and little theatres are alike, yet quite unlike … At the Prince of Wales's, I had to adopt a more delicate, more subtle, more intimate style. But the breadth had to be there just the same – as seen through the wrong end of the microscope.[159]

The Marie Wilton–Squire Bancroft partnership succeeded as a result of their deliberate play selections, the long runs of their productions, the reduction of costs by shortening the bill, meticulous mounting of plays, regularly raising ticket prices and rewarding their actors with good salaries to create a stable company.[160] Marie Wilton had 'learnt from her predecessors [in particular Madame Vestris], and moved onwards through her own career with great good sense'.[161] The Bancrofts became a production team and their work displayed a strong commitment to the theatre as both a performing and visual art. The balanced ensemble production at the Prince of Wales's became the trademark of the Bancroft artistry.

Finally, the Bancrofts were dedicated practitioners of their art. They reaffirmed the respectability of the theatrical profession and set high standards for those who would follow them. They consciously attempted to make their audiences feel as if they were at home, and they painstakingly prepared quality productions.[162] The Prince of Wales's Theatre had served them well in the pursuit of their careers on the London stage, and their departure from Tottenham Street was, indeed, the end of an era for the little playhouse. It would be nearly impossible for any successor to equal the stature and reputation the Bancrofts carried with them to the Haymarket.

---

159 Terry, *Story of My Life*, 148–9.
160 Davis, *Economics of the British Stage*, 283.
161 Bratton, *Making of the West End Stage*, 205.
162 Powell, *Women and Victorian Theatre*, 47–8.

Chapter Six

Edgar Bruce: The Colonel *and the closure, 1880–1882*

The playhouse was closed for approximately three weeks while the new manager conducted rehearsals for his 1880 season. Edgar Bruce (*c.*1845–1901) was an actor and manager. He began his career in 1868 at the Prince of Wales's, Liverpool. After an initial appearance in London at the Strand in 1869, Bruce gained further experience in both London and the provinces before joining the Wyndham Comedy Company and travelling to the United States and Canada. He appeared in productions of *Caste*, *Ours* and *School* during that time. In 1873, when he returned to London, he joined the Court Theatre. While there, he began to focus his energies on management, and took the Haymarket in June of 1875 for a short season. He managed the Globe in 1876 and the Royalty in 1879.[1] The press welcomed him to the Prince of Wales's Theatre: 'Bruce has got together an excellent company, and as he has already shown that with adequate experience he combines sound judgment and good taste, there is reason to hope that he will be enabled to conduct the establishment in a manner not unworthy of its honourable traditions.'[2]

The Prince of Wales's season opened on Saturday 21 February 1880 with two pieces, Sidney Grundy's farce *Little Change* (118) and *Forget-Me-Not* (132) by Herman C. Merivale (1839–1906)[3] and Florence Crauford Grove (1838–1902).[4] Bruce had chosen well and the public responded immediately. The acting company consisted of Edgar Bruce, Edwin Bayley, Arthur Brewett, Fanny Mary Bernard-

---

1   'Bruce, Edgar', in Adams, *A Dictionary of the Drama*. See also the Tonie Edgar Bruce Collection in the Victoria and Albert Museum Theatre Collection. Obituary in the *Sheffield Daily Telegraph*, 12 April 1901.

2   *Morning Post*, 23 February 1880.

3   Elizabeth Lee, 'Merivale, Herman Charles (1839–1906)', rev. William Baker, *ODNB*, accessed 18 November 2013. He also wrote under the name of Felix Dale. He was a barrister, author and civil servant. In 1874 he left the law and devoted his career to literature and the theatre.

4   Florence Crauford Grove was a mountaineer and author.

Beere (1856–1915),[5] Ada Gordon, John Clayton,[6] J.G. Shore, Charles P. Flockton,[7] Ian Robertson, F.V. Walter, Geneviève Ward (1837–1922),[8] Kate Pattison, Mrs Leigh Murray,[9] Annie Layton, Miss Pattison, Herbert Beerbohm Tree (1852–1917)[10] and Mrs Vere.

Forget-Me-Not had been licensed and performed previously at the Lyceum in August of 1879. The conflict of the play is the struggle between English propriety and a social-climbing French interloper. *The Times* critic and others found the plot of the play contrived, but very well performed.[11] Geneviève Ward portrayed a blackmailing adventuress with consummate skill (Fig. 51). She was a powerful villainess and the character became an integral part of her repertoire which she performed frequently throughout her career.[12] Reviewers felt that Bruce's company had promise and that *Forget-Me-Not* was a sound choice for the first offering: 'both as a work of stagecraft and as a literary work, this play is unquestionably superior to anything that has been given to our theatre for some little time. It is cleverly managed and cleverly written, in parts very cleverly written.'[13] However, the production did require some attention: 'The piece was there; Miss Ward was there; Mr Clayton, Mr Flockton, Mrs Murray and Miss Pattison were there, to give their experienced help. But where, oh where, were the appointments for which the Bancrofts had made the house so celebrated.'[14] The manager was also chided for presenting an old-fashioned tableau at the end of the play that detracted from the realism created in the verbal duel between the two principal characters 'in accordance, as we can only suppose, with that ridiculous tradition of the theatre which bids the central figure of the play to be still the central figure on which the curtain must fall … three clever acts are

---

5   Fanny Mary Bernard-Beere, née Whitehead. Obituary in *New York Times*, 27 March 1915. Mrs Bernard-Beere was born in Norwich and was the goddaughter of William Makepeace Thackery. Her dramatic debut was at the Opéra Comique in Paris in 1877.

6   John Clayton had previously appeared at the Prince of Wales's for three seasons: 1869–70, 1877–8 and 1878–9.

7   'Flockton, Charles, P.', in Pascoe, *Actors and Actresses*, 148. Flockton made his first appearance on the London stage in 1868.

8   'Ward, Geneviève Teresa', in Pascoe, *Actors and Actresses*, 368–70. Victor Emeljanow, 'Ward, Dame (Lucy) Geneviève Teresa (1837–1922)', *ODNB*, accessed 18 November 2013. She was born in New York and trained as a singer in Florence. She began her operatic career in London in George Macfarren's *Robin Hood* (1861) at Covent Garden. She took the Lyceum in 1879 and performed in Herman Merivale and F.C. Grove's *Forget-Me-Not*. From 1893–9, she appeared at the Lyceum under Henry Irving. In 1921 Geneviève Ward was made Dame of the British Empire.

9   Mrs Leigh Murray appeared at the Prince of Wales's in the following seasons, 1867–8, 1871–2, 1872–3, 1873–4 and 1876–7. See the brief biography in the *Theatrical Times*, 2 September 1848.

10   B.A. Kachur, 'Tree, Sir Herbert Beerbohm [*real name* Herbert Draper Beerbohm] (1852–1917)', *ODNB*, accessed 18 November 2013. He began his professional career in 1878 with the Bijou Comedy Company in a provincial tour. His London debut was at the Olympic Theatre under Henry Neville in 1878. In 1887 he undertook the management of the Comedy and the Haymarket, where he continued for ten years. He was manager of Her Majesty's from 1897–1917 and was knighted in 1909.

11   *The Times*, 4 March 1880.

12   Geneviève Ward and Richard Whiteing, *Both Sides of the Curtain* (London, 1918), 81–100.

13   *The Times*, 4 March 1880.

14   *The Theatre*, 1 April 1880.

51 *Forget-Me Not*, 1880: Geneviève
Ward as Marquise de Mohrivart and
John Clayton as Sir Horace Welby. ©
Victoria and Albert Museum, London

disfigured by a device which would seem clumsy in the boldest melodrama
that ever woke the echoes on the Surrey side'.[15] In *The Times* review of 1 April,
the critic concluded that a minor unevenness in the acting company appeared
to have been addressed, but the comparison with the scene decorations of the
Bancrofts persisted: 'The scene now is better, Mr Bruce having awoke out of his
nap; but it is still coarse and vulgar, entirely devoid of taste and originality which
so distinguished the appointments of his predecessors.'[16]

On 11 May 1880 Bruce offered a matinee performance of Émile Augier's
L'Aventurière, in French, with the American-born Geneviève Ward in the role
of Clorinde. In 1877 Geneviève Ward had travelled to Paris and studied the
classic and contemporary repertoire with M. Regnier at the Comédie-Française.
She supervised the rehearsals of the production with the able assistance of her
personal stage manager Horace Wigan (1815/16–85).[17] Actors engaged for this

---

15   *The Times*, 4 March 1880.

16   *The Times*, 1 April 1880.

17   Joseph Knight, 'Wigan, Horace (1815/16–1885)', rev. Klaus Stierstorfer, *ODNB*, accessed 18 November 2013. He
      first appeared in Dublin in 1853 using the name Danvers. He made his London debut in 1854. He was an actor
      and author and managed the Holborn Theatre in 1875.

special performance were: H. St Maur, M. Marius, Horace Wigan, George Power (by permission of D'Oyly Carte), Miss Herbert and Herbert Beerbohm Tree. The Prince of Wales was in the audience. The performance was a pleasant surprise for audiences and the critics:

> Miss Ward's … proficiency in the French tongue is certainly remarkable, less perhaps on account of the purity of her accent than because her knowledge of the language is such as to enable her to act as well as to recite, to give her attention not only to the character she is herself engaged with, but also to those who divide the scene with her. The same praise, though not, perhaps, in quite the same degree, is due to Mr Beerbohm Tree, who plays the part of Monte-Prade, and plays it really very cleverly in the circumstances.[18]

In a subsequent review, the courage of the actors was acknowledged:

> Still it was, doubtless, looked on as not only a daring experiment, but also almost a hallucination, to expect that any English actors could be got together with sufficient knowledge of the French language, and the requisite power, if they possessed the facility of speaking, to support their accomplishments with suitable delivery and tolerable histrionic capabilities … All this she satisfactorily accomplished.[19]

The first Bruce season concluded on 23 July 1880.

Forget-Me-Not (31) was revived on 25 September 1880. Sydney Grundy's comedy *In Honour Bound* (146) was also on the bill. Bruce next produced an adaptation of a Dutch play by Rosier Fassan entitled *Annie-Mie*. Previously it had been performed in Dutch at the Imperial Theatre. Audiences were provided with a detailed plot synopsis to help them follow the action. One reviewer found the performance 'unintelligible'. Bruce invited Clement Scott to translate, adapt and rework the original script. The opening night for *Annie-Mie* (35) was 1 November 1880. The reception was tepid. The play was exceedingly long; the melancholy script drifted into sentimentality; and the action was often incomprehensible. Writing for *The Theatre*, Ernest A. Bendall reported that the play failed to elicit much of a response from the audience even though the story 'leads through seduction and attempted murder to the elaborated suffering of an unwedded mother and the remorse of a hasty paternal avenger'.[20] Bendall concluded that performances by Geneviève Ward, Mr Flockton, Johnston Forbes-Robertson, Charles Cecil, Mrs Leigh Murray and James Fernandez could not compensate for the mediocrity of the adaptation. The production lasted only a month.

---

18   *The Times*, 12 May 1880.
19   *The Theatre*, 1 June 1880.
20   *The Theatre*, 1 December 1880.

Edgar Bruce engaged Charles Coghlan, who had previously appeared at the Prince of Wales's during the Bancroft management. Coghlan had acquired an adaptation of an Italian play by Paolo Giacometti (1816–82) entitled *La morte civile*. It was considered by the press to be a polemic supporting divorce. The original play was a favourite acting vehicle for the Italian star Tommaso Salvini. Coghlan retitled the play *A New Trial* (29) and it opened on 18 December 1880. The central character of the play, Corrado (Coghlan), has escaped from prison after serving thirteen years for the murder of his wife's brother. He finds shelter in a small Calabrian town where he unexpectedly discovers his wife Rosalia (Amy Roselle) living with another man. Corrado pleads for reconciliation with his wife, but when he is rejected he chooses suicide in order to be released from his misery. He swallows poison as his daughter enters the room. She is told that Corrado is her father, and he dies 'in ghastly convulsions'[21] at the child's feet. Coghlan's acting performance was restrained and presented in a 'plain, downright, unvarnished style, which is certainly effective, but no less certainly deepens the repulsive nature of the work'.[22] Murder and suicide were difficult topics for audiences during the Christmas season.

On 2 February 1881 Bruce produced a new comedy entitled *The Colonel* (550). The immediate popularity of this piece exceeded even his most optimistic expectations. The author of *The Colonel*, Francis Cowley Burnand (1836–1917), was a prolific writer of more than 100 farces, burlesques and extravaganzas. Among his many plays was the parody *Diplunacy*, based on the 1878–9 Prince of Wales's success *Diplomacy*, which satirised not only the play but also the actors in the Bancroft Company.[23] *The Colonel* was based on Messrs Bayard and de Wailly's *Le Mari à la campagne*. In 1849 Morris Barnett had written a play based on *Le Mari à la campagne* for the Haymarket entitled *The Serious Family*. While Barnett's play had focused on religious fraud and hypocrisy, Burnand chose to satirise the affectations and excesses of Aestheticism. The three acts of Burnand's play were titled Severity, Laxity and Liberty.

The *Observer* and the *Illustrated London News*, among others, found the play to be amusing and entertaining. While noting that the Aesthetes were lampooned without mercy, the *Theatre* critic urged readers to be compassionate and accept eccentricity as part of embracing change:

> Mr Burnand shows how by [Aestheticism's] influence and practice men become unfaithful to their wives, its professors are gluttons and winebibbers, selfish rascals and intolerable impostors, and that society will not be satisfied until the love of the beautiful or aim at the

---

21   *The Times*, 20 December 1880.

22   *Ibid*.

23   Jane W. Stedman, 'Burnand, Sir Francis Cowley (1836–1917)', *ODNB*, accessed 18 November 2013. He was educated at Eton and Cambridge (where he was instrumental in the creation of the Cambridge Amateur Dramatic Society) and became a prolific writer of burlesques and farces. He began writing for *Punch* in 1862 and became editor in 1880. Burnand was knighted in 1902.

ideal is supported by the culture of the coarse. Perhaps it is like breaking a butterfly on a wheel to be serious with such a subject, but for my own part, I would rather endure the crudities and childishness of all the Maulbys and Postlethwaites [well-known Aesthetes] in existence than I would have society reconverted to the tastelessness of fifteen years ago.[24]

The *Punch* writer found the evening to be satisfying on several levels, judging the acting 'admirable' and Mr Bruce Smith's aesthetic settings 'consummately precious'.[25] He noted the effective performances by individual actors:

Mrs Leigh Murray, Myra Holme and Amy Roselle … have caught the posture and trick of speech of the School to the life; while Miss Amy Roselle's Mrs Blyth and Miss Grahame's Nellie were bright and pleasant performances. Mr Coghlan's Colonel is a masterly performance, he shows us an American gentlemen, not a vulgar caricature of a soldier in the U.S. Army … Mr Fernandez created a Streyke out of his own inner consciousness, which made Maude wild. Mr Roland Buckstone was amusing as Basil Giorgione while Mr Herbert was a fresh manly representative of Mr Forrester.[26]

The Times observed that 'Mr Burnand laughs in three acts at the languid graces of the Grosvenor Gallery'.[27] Moreover, he 'pitilessly denounces all his surroundings, and tears his way among the neo-aesthetic school like an elephant raging through a rice plantation'.[28]

The scenic design for *The Colonel* required Bruce Smith to create a room in a home that was decorated in an outlandish manner. George du Maurier (1834–96), the author and cartoonist for *Punch*,[29] offered Burnand and Smith explicit suggestions for creating the appropriate visual context for the play:

Try & have a room papered with Morris' green Daisy, with a dado six feet high of green-blue serge in folds and a matting with rugs for floor (Indian red matting if possible), spider-legged black tables & sideboard, black rush-bottomed chairs and arm chairs; blue china plates on the wall with plenty of space between – here and there a blue china vase with an enormous hawthorn or almond blossom sprig also on mantelpiece pots with lilies & peacock feathers – plain dull yellow curtains lined with dull blue for windows if wanted. Japanese sixpenny fans now & then on the walls in picturesque unexpectedness.[30]

---

24 *The Theatre*, 1 March 1881.

25 *Punch*, 19 February 1881.

26 *Ibid*.

27 The Grosvenor Gallery was an art gallery established in 1877 by Sir Coutts Lindsay and his wife Blanche. The gallery provided a venue for the artists of the Aesthetic Movement who were not exhibited by the Royal Academy.

28 *The Times*, 4 February 1881.

29 Leonée Ormond, 'Du Maurier, George Louis Palmella Busson (1834–1896)', *ODNB*, accessed 18 November 2013. He was a cartoonist for *Punch* from 1865.

30 Lionel Lambourne, *The Aesthetic Movement* (Oxford, 1996), 121.

52 *The Colonel*, Acts I and III, 1881. Setting by W. Bruce Smith. *Illustrated Sporting and Dramatic News*, 19 February 1881. Author's collection

An engraving in the *Illustrated Sporting and Dramatic News* (Fig. 52) provides an impression of the setting created for Acts I and III of *The Colonel*.

The *Illustrated London News* noted that even 'select' artistic audiences were quite prepared to laugh at their own enthusiasms, 'delighted by the subtle education of the Philistines who came all unsuspecting to enjoy a gay evening in the theatre little thinking that they were absorbing the philosophy at which they were laughing.'[31] The popularity of *The Colonel* ensured a long and financially rewarding run.[32] F.C. Burnand's play had anticipated by some two months the William S. Gilbert and Arthur Sullivan production of *Patience*, which also satirised the Aesthetic Movement.

The Royal Highnesses, the Prince and Princess of Wales, requested that Edgar Bruce's company perform *The Colonel* at Abergeldie Castle on 4 October 1881. Queen Victoria was persuaded to attend the performance and she noted in her diary:

The piece given was *The Colonel* in three acts, a very clever play, written to quiz and ridicule the foolish aesthetic people who dress in such an absurd manner, with loose garments, large puffed sleeves, great hats and carrying peacock's feathers, sunflowers and lilies. It was very

---

31   *Illustrated London News*, 26 March 1881. Anne Anderson, *The Colonel*, July 2004, section on Costumes and Settings, <http://www.xix-e.pierre-marteau.com>. Aesthetic décor was a commercial success in the 1880s. Shops soon offered art, furniture, pottery and Oriental goods.

32   F.C. Burnand, *Records and Reminiscences, Personal and General*, 2 vols (London, 1904), vol. 2, 151–66. Burnand lamented the fact that Squire Bancroft had 'chucked' the idea of doing *The Colonel* at the Theatre Royal, Haymarket. In 1884 the profits from *The Colonel* enabled Bruce to fund the construction of the Prince's Theatre in Coventry Street. It was renamed the Prince of Wales in 1886.

well acted … It was the first time I had seen professionals act a regular play since March '61. We got home shortly before twelve, having been very much amused.[33]

The Colonel continued at the Prince of Wales's in the New Year, 1882. Bruce's good fortune, however, was short-lived. On 29 July 1882 he received notice from the Theatre and Music Hall Sub-Committee of the Metropolitan Board of Works that the Prince of Wales's was to be closed. For several months the playhouse had been under close inspection. E.A.E. Woodrow (1860–1937), an architect acting on orders from the Superintending Architect of Metropolitan Buildings, George Vulliamy, had conducted a thorough examination of the building. New laws regarding the structural soundness of buildings inhabited by the public and the prevention of fire were the basis for the study.[34]

Woodrow submitted his preliminary report to the Theatre and Music Hall Sub-Committee of the Metropolitan Board of Works at a meeting on 23 March 1882. The building was described in detail and Woodrow concluded that the entire structure appeared to be in a seriously unsatisfactory condition. The interior of the playhouse would have to be completely reconstructed to correct the defects. Woodrow provided suggestions for alterations considered necessary to meet safety standards for the 560-seat theatre:

1. The construction of a proscenium wall to divide the stage from the audience carried up above the roof and covered down below the stage. Any openings in this wall should be closed by iron doors.
2. The re-instatement of the brick arches over the cellar, which have been cut-away, so as to provide a fireproof division between the cellar and the ground floor.
3. Stone steps should be provided from the cellar floor into Tottenham Street, the only means of escape for the persons employed under the theatre.
4. The gallery staircase should be entirely reconstructed to be of stone 4 feet wide built at both ends.
5. The roof over the upper part of the gallery should be raised, the height of the storey at the upper part being only 6 feet.
6. The stairs from the Dress Circle level to the Upper Circle should be rearranged so as to avoid winders.
7. A new Stall exit should be provided on the South side through the house No.7 Pitt Street and the floor and ceiling over should be plugged with Portland Cement Concrete.
8. The present Stall exit on the north side should be enlarged in width to 4' 6" and the doors should be bolted only on the inside.

---

33   Lambourne, *The Aesthetic Movement*, 119.
34   In the following pages I have quoted and summarised the minutes of the Theatre and Music Hall Sub-Committee of the Metropolitan Board of Works. Passages cited are from 23 March, 4 April, 14 June, 20 June, 1 August and 8 August 1882.

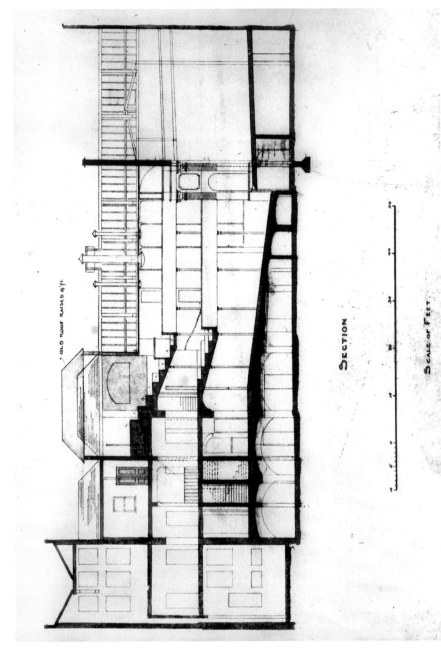

OLD ROOF RAISED 4 ft.

SECTION

SCALE OF FEET

53 Sectional plan of the Prince of Wales's Theatre, 1882 by E.A.E. Woodrow. By permission of the London Metropolitan Archive

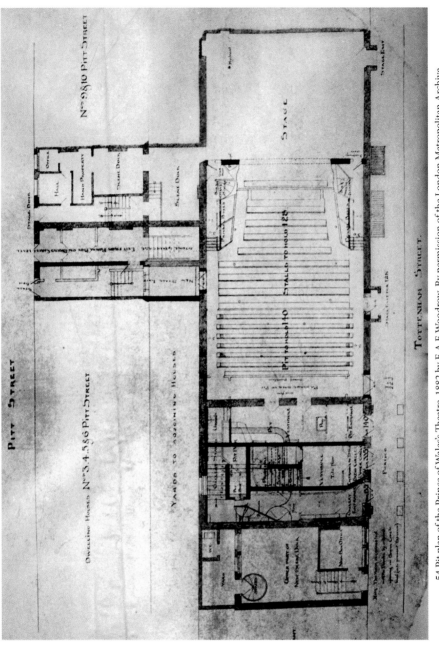

54 Pit plan of the Prince of Wales's Theatre, 1882 by E.A.E Woodrow. By permission of the London Metropolitan Archive

9. An exit from the pit with doors 4' 6" wide should be provided on the north side of the house leading into Tottenham Street.
10. All doors should be made to open outward.

The Sub-Committee adopted the recommended improvements list and was prepared to visit the theatre as soon as plans showing the necessary improvements were completed. Copies were to be served on the owner. The revised plans were submitted at the 4 April meeting of the Sub-Committee and approved. The sectional plan (Fig. 53) and the pit plan (Fig. 54) show the required changes in wide, dark lines. At the suggestion of the architect, the Sub-Committee made five additional demands:

1. The entrances to the three principal divisions of the house to be separated by brick walls.
2. A new stone staircase built to the box level.
3. An enlargement of the space in the rear of the dress circle.
4. A new brick wall in the rear of the gallery to separate the audience area from the storeroom.
5. A general widening of the corridors and gangways to three feet in width.

On 14 June the Sub-Committee inspected the building. They compiled a lengthy list of observations and concerns. The south-side external wall had been braced in and appeared weakened; the roof over the theatre, with the weight of slates, tiles and glass supported by only a wooden frame, was a potential threat to audience safety. The space between the roof and the auditorium ceiling served as a storage area for old props and was found to be very dusty and dirty. In general the building was an obvious fire hazard. The quantity of stock (scenery and properties) kept in the theatre was also considered excessively large. The paint shop in the basement and the carpenters' workshop at the back of the gallery were both dirty and in a dilapidated condition. The entrance and exit arrangements barely served the needs of a calm audience, let alone one panicked by an emergency. The exit-time calculations were considered too long:

Gallery – 4 ½ minutes
Upper boxes – 8 minutes
Dress circle – 7 ½ minutes
Pit – 5 minutes
Stalls – 7 ½ minutes

There were fireplaces in the green room, the dressing rooms and the carpenters' workshops. None of them had guards. The auditorium itself was not heated. The gas meters located under the stage would have to be moved to a vault under the street for safety purposes. Finally, the water supply to the building was inadequate. Only two tanks with 250 gallons of water each were available in the event of an emergency. Under perfect conditions, fire-fighting equipment could not be expected to arrive at the site in less than eight minutes. In addition, the proscenium would have to be rebuilt in brick or stone in place of the current lathe and plaster. Finally, a curtain or screen of metal or possibly canvas blanketing or baize that could be filled with water would have to be installed.

Six days later on 20 June 1882, the Sub-Committee reconvened:

> After discussion it was resolved on the motion of Mr Selway that it be reported to the Building Act Committee that the Sub-Committee, having viewed the Prince of Wales's Theatre, Tottenham Street, Tottenham Court Road and considered the drawings and reports prepared by the Superintending Architect on the subject, are of opinion that the structural defects of the building cannot be remedied at a moderate expenditure and that it be recommended to the Building Act Committee that a communication be made to the Lord Chamberlain in accordance with this opinion.

This action effectively rescinded Edgar Bruce's licence issued by the Lord Chamberlain. The press reported, 'it is estimated that the alterations thought necessary for the safety of frequenters of the Prince of Wales's Theatre would prove almost as costly as the demolition of the old house and the erection of a brand new one upon the same site'.[35] Saturday 29 July 1882 was to be the final performance of *The Colonel* and the end of Bruce's management of the Prince of Wales's Theatre.

Bruce consulted with his solicitor, Mr Bolton, and asked to appear before the Sub-Committee. On 1 August 1882, shortly after his licence expired, the meeting was held. Bruce's legal advisor stated 'that his client was desirous that the Board withdraw their objections to the renewal of the present licence of the Theatre for the period of one year from 29 September next on condition certain structural improvements were made to their satisfaction'. This unexpected proposal precipitated an abrupt adjournment so that the Sub-Committee might consider the matter. Bruce submitted a proposal to alter the exits of the theatre and reduce the audience capacity from 560 to 535. The Sub-Committee upheld their previous decision and considered the matter closed. There would be no licence and no exception for Bruce.

While there was speculation that Squire Bancroft and Edgar Bruce had reached an impasse over who would finance any renovations, the closure resulted from the enforcement of public safety regulations and the overall condition of the old building. Razing the old and decrepit structure, in the judgement of the Sub-Committee, was the only realistic course of action.

---

35   *Daily News*, 24 July 1882.

Many people mourned the passing of the Prince of Wales's from the list of active London theatres, but the *Illustrated Sporting and Dramatic News* provided a pragmatic assessment of the situation:

> So the Prince of Wales's theatre is to come down at last. It seems rather hard on Mr Bruce, who had just added to his premises a new foyer, and had arranged for a play by Mr Albery. But the interests of the public must be looked to, and for our own part, we must confess to having always felt it a dangerous experiment to pass an evening in a stall here, or at the Strand, or the Royalty, or, indeed, any of the older theatres built on a 'pokey' scale as regards passages and stairs.[36]

The Prince of Wales's interior space had been remodelled and refurbished from time to time over the nearly one hundred years of its history, but the performance and audience spaces remained largely unchanged throughout most of its history.[37] In the Sub-Committee report, the seating capacity for the theatre is established as 560. While it may have held a few more people at one time in the history of the building, any number beyond 600 would seem highly unlikely.[38] In the sectional view of the house (Fig. 53), it is evident that there was no fly gallery for scenery, hence the ongoing references to scenic display being limited on the little stage. The façade of the stage was never updated in any extensive way, and vestiges of the old forestage and proscenium were still in evidence in 1882.

The Tottenham Street playhouse, under its various names, was a place of entertainment for Londoners from 1775 to 1882. It was also in use as a meeting hall until at least 1896. The building was neither an architectural masterpiece nor particularly commodious for audiences or actors. On the contrary, it was a modest, functional structure and one of the smallest playhouses in the city. For nearly 100 years, the theatre was a destination for a cross-section of the city of London populace. When the final curtain dropped, there were many saddened to see the little house vacant, derelict and awaiting demolition. But there was one final scene to be played in Tottenham Street.

---

36   *Illustrated Sporting and Dramatic News*, 29 July 1882.

37   For a review of the physical structure data, see Lorenzen, 'View of the Physical Sructure'.

38   While there is some disagreement about the seating capacity of the theatre, I have elected to adopt the Theatre and Music Hall Sub-Committee count of 560 seats. It is similar to the capacity numbers found in Brayley's *Historical and Descriptive Accounts of the Theatres of London* (1826), James Winston's account book for the Queen's in 1831 found in the Heal Collection, and Grant's *The Great Metropolis* (1836). All of these writers are then supported by the 1882 plans prepared for the Metropolitan Board of Works. There is no evidence to suggest that the playhouse was ever expanded beyond its original size. It was certainly remodelled and renovated, but the seating capacity was always limited. Bruce's offer to reduce the seating to 535 provides additional evidence for the seating capacity of the building.

Epilogue

General Booth, but no salvation, 1885–1903

Left to spiders and rats for over two years, the theatre in Tottenham Street was in a state of decay when the Salvation Army expressed interest in the building. The Salvation Army had rented the Grecian Theatre on the City Road, Shoreditch, after it closed in August of 1882 and converted it into a meeting hall.[1] The Army's solicitor wrote to the Superintending Architect of Metropolitan Buildings, George Vulliamy, on 28 November 1884 to inquire about the possibility of using the Tottenham Street theatre building for 'evangelical purposes'. The architect replied that he was uncertain as to the full implications of using the building in that manner, but he assumed that since the building would be used for public events, all the suggested alterations that ended Edgar Bruce's management would be required. In spite of these obstacles, the *War Cry* soon reported that General Booth would become the lessee and manager of the old playhouse. A writer for the *Pall Mall Gazette*, with the Bancrofts clearly in mind, envisioned the new tenants in action: 'The devil will soon find out that the theatre is *Ours*. The Salvation Army will welcome to its meetings there all classes of *Society*, quite irrespective of *Caste*, and will be pleased to receive all the *Money* that the congregations like to put in the collections.'[2]

Another writer was indignant about the obvious political manoeuvres that afforded the Army special consideration:

> The Prince of Wales's Theatre had to be closed because the authorities declared it to be unsafe. How comes it, then, that the Salvation Army has been allowed to take possession and to cram it to overflowing at prices ranging from three pence upwards? In fire and panics there is no respecting of persons, and the howlers and tambourine-thumpers and banner-wavers and concertina-players who pretend to have all the righteousness on their side would stand as little chance of salvation in an ugly rush as the most ungodly of playgoers.[3]

---

1   Blanchard, *Life and Reminiscences*, vol. 2, 537.
2   *Pall Mall Gazette*, 24 February 1885.
3   HC: clipping, 1885.

55 View of the interior of the Prince of Wales's, *c*.1900. Commemorative booklet published by Dr Edward Distin-Maddick for the opening of Scala Theatre, 1905. Author's collection

According to a report in *Reynolds's Newspaper* of 22 March, some modest improvements were undertaken for either safety or cosmetic purposes:

> The Prince of Wales's Theatre has undergone a considerable change. The external appearance has been much improved, and the building inside has been thoroughly cleaned. The elevated gallery in which the 'gods' were wont to look down upon the performances on the stage has been swept away; and the stage itself has undergone a complete transformation.[4]

The Salvation Army conducted its meetings at the theatre from March 1885 for at least the next decade. It was not until 25 January 1896 that a notice appeared in the *Builder* that the building had been returned to its theatrical ghosts.[5]

In 1901, the property was advertised as part of Benjamin Lisle's estate sale. On the day of the sale, 14 October 1901, bidding reached £9,600 before the theatre was withdrawn from sale.

---

4   *Reynolds's Newspaper*, 22 March 1885.
5   W.F.D., *Builder*, 25 January 1896.

56 View of theatre exterior, c.1903. By permission of the London Metropolitan Archive

By June of 1902, Messrs Phillips, Phillips and Beard controlled the building, but they in turn passed the property to Dr Edmund Distin-Maddick[6] (1857–1939). Finally, the *Daily Chronicle* sounded the death knell for the old playhouse on 7 September 1903 (Fig. 55):

> It is not often that an old building survives to quite such an advanced stage of decrepitude as did the old Prince of Wales's Theatre in Tottenham-street, Tottenham Court-road. It is now being carted away in small pieces. The present frontage of the theatre (if any of it is left) dates from 1780. Behind it a strange dynasty of assemblies has exhausted itself. An earlier crowbar had brought a cleaner end to a house where more than one British monarch has been entertained.[7]

A photograph of the old building in its last days provides one last look before all but the old portico was demolished (Fig. 56). The new owner of the property planned to incorporate it as the stage door entrance for a new theatre.

Dr Distin-Maddick commissioned Frank T. Verity (1864–1937)[8] to design a theatre for the site. Distin-Maddick purchased additional land nearby and constructed the Scala Theatre. The playhouse opened on 23 September 1905 and was razed in 1969. Today the site is occupied by a development of apartments and offices. Photographs of the old Prince of Wales's Theatre are displayed in the foyer.

---

6   Obituary, *The Times*, 8 July 1939. Dr Edmund Distin-Maddick became the manager of the Scala Theatre, the flagship for the Charles Urban Kinemacolor show, from 1910–14. He was a doctor, a surgeon in the Royal Navy, and became Admiral Surgeon of the Fleet.

7   *Daily Chronicle*, 7 September 1903.

8   Francis Thomas Verity was a prominent cinema architect and also designed the Criterion Theatre in Piccadilly Circus which opened in 1874. He subsequently received commissions to design other London theatres, including the Royal Comedy in Panton Street, the Pandora in Leicester Square, the Novelty in Great Queen Street and the Royalty, Soho. The firm Verity & Beverley remains active today.

Bibliography

Secondary works

A'Beckett, Arthur William, *The A'Becketts of 'Punch'* (New York, 1903).

Ackerman, Robert, *The Microcosm of London; or London in Miniature*, 3 vols (London, 1904).

Adams, W. Davenport, *A Dictionary of the Drama* (London, 1904).

Allen, Shirley S., *Samuel Phelps and Sadler's Wells Theatre* (Middletown, CT), 1971.

Angelo, Henry, *The Reminiscences of Henry Angelo*, 2 vols (New York and London, 1969).

Aretz, Gertrude, *Die Frauen um Napoleon* (Graz, 1932).

Armstrong, William, 'The Art of the Minor Theatre', *Theatre Notebook*, 10 (1955–6), 89–94.

——'The Nineteenth-Century Matinee', *Theatre Notebook*, 14 (1959), 56–9.

Arundell, Dennis, *The Story of Sadler's Wells, 1683–1964* (New York, 1965).

Ashton, John, *The Dawn of the XIXth Century in England: A Social Sketch of the Times*, 2 vols (London, 1886).

Auerbach, Nina, *Ellen Terry: Player in Her Time* (New York, 1987).

Avery, Emmett L. (ed.), 'The London Stage, 1700–1729', in Avery et al. (eds), *The London Stage, 1660–1800*, vol. 2.

Avery, Emmett L., Scouten, Arthur H., Hogan, Charles Beecher, Stone, George Winchester, Jr and Van Lennep, William (eds), *The London Stage, 1660–1800*, 11 vols (Carbondale, IL, 1960–8).

Axton, William F., *Circle of Fire* (Lexington, KY, 1966).

Bailey, J.O., *British Plays of the Nineteenth Century* (New York, 1966).

Baker, H. Barton, *History of the London Stage: And its Famous Players (1576–1903)*, 2nd edn (London, 1904).

Baker, Michael, *The Rise of the Victorian Actor* (London, 1978).

Baker, Theodore, *Biographical Dictionary of Musicians* (New York, 1900).

Baldick, Robert, *The Life and Times of Frédérick Lemaître* (London, 1959).

Bancroft, Squire and Bancroft, Marie, *Mr. and Mrs. Bancroft: On and Off the Stage*, 2 vols (London, 1888).

——*The Bancrofts: Recollections of Sixty Years* (London, 1909).

Barrett, Daniel, *T.W. Robertson and the Prince of Wales's Theatre* (New York, 1995).

Bennett, Susan, *Theatre Audiences: A Theory of Production and Reception* (London, 1997).

Bernard, John, *Recollections of the Stage* (Boston, 1832).

Besant, Sir Walter, *London in the Eighteenth Century* (London, 1903).

——*London in the Nineteenth Century* (London, 1909).

Bingham, Frederick, *A Celebrated Old Playhouse: The History of Richmond Theatre, from 1765 to 1884* (London, 1886).

Biography of the British Stage (London, 1824).

Blanchard, E.L. 'History of the Prince of Wales's Theatre', *Era Almanack* (London, 1874).

——*The Life and Reminiscences of E.L. Blanchard*, ed. Clement Scott and Cecil Howard, 2 vols (London, 1891).

Boase, Frederic, *Modern English Biography*, 6 vols (Truro, 1897).

Booth, Michael, *English Melodrama* (London, 1965).

——*English Plays of the Nineteenth Century*, 5 vols (Oxford, 1969–76).

——*Prefaces to English Nineteenth-Century Theatre* (Manchester, 1980).

——*Victorian Spectacular Theatre, 1850–1910* (London, 1981).

——*Theatre in the Victorian Age* (Cambridge, 1991).

Boulton, William B., *The Amusements of Old London*, 2 vols (London, 1901).

Bratton, J.S., *Acts of Supremacy: The British Empire and the Stage, 1790–1930* (Manchester and New York, 1991).

——*The Victorian Clown* (Cambridge, 2006).

—— *The Making of the West End Stage: Marriage, Management and the Mapping of Gender in London, 1830–1870* (Cambridge, 2011).

Brayley, Edward Wedlake, *Historical and Descriptive Accounts of the Theatres of London* (London, 1826).

Broadbent, R.J., *Annals of the Liverpool Stage*, 2 vols (Liverpool, 1908).

——*A History of Pantomime* (New York, 1964; 1st edn 1901).

Burke, Thomas, *English Night-Life* (London, 1941).

Burnand, F.C., 'Something About a Little Theatre off of Tottenham Court Road', *Era Almanack* (1879).

——*Records and Reminiscences, Personal and General*, 2 vols (London, 1904).

Butterworth, Philip, *Theatre of Fire* (London, 1998).

Carlyle, Carol Jones, *Helen Faucit: Fire and Ice on the Victorian Stage* (London, 2000).

Chancellor, E. Beresford, *London's Old Latin Quarter* (London, 1930).

Clinton-Baddeley, V.C., *All Right on the Night* (London, 1954).

Coleman, John, *Players and Playwrights I have Known*, 2 vols (Philadelphia, 1890).

Colligan, Mimi, *Canvas Documentaries: Panoramic Entertainments in Nineteenth-Century Australia and New Zealand* (Melbourne, 2002).

Colvin, H.M., *A Biographical Dictionary of English Architects, 1660–1840* (London, 1954).

Cook, Dutton, *Nights at the Play* (London, 1881).

Cowan, Anita, 'Popular Entertainment in London 1800–1840: The Relationship between Theatre Repertoire and Theatre Location', PhD thesis (University of Washington, 1978).

Crozier, Alice C., *The Novels of Harriet Beecher Stowe* (New York, 1969).

Davidge, William, *Footlight Flashes* (New York, 1866).

Davis, Jim, 'Presence, Personality and Physicality: Actors and Their Repertories, 1776–1895', in Donohue (ed.), *Cambridge History of British Theatre*, vol. 2.

——*John Liston, Comedian* (London, 1985).

——(ed.), *Victorian Pantomime* (Basingstoke, 2010).

Davis, Jim and Emeljanow, Victor, *Reflecting the Audience: London Theatregoing, 1840–1880* (Iowa City, 2001).

Davis, Tracy, *Actresses as Working Women* (London, 1991).

——*The Economics of the British Stage, 1800–1914* (Cambridge, 2000).

Davis, Tracy C. and Donkin, Ellen (eds), *Women and Playwriting in Nineteenth-Century Britain* (Cambridge, 1999).

Dibdin, Thomas, *Reminiscences of Thomas Dibdin* (London, 1837).

Dickens, Charles, *Sketches by Boz*, 2 vols (London, n.d.).

——*Memories of Joseph Grimaldi* (New York, 1968).

Disher, M. Willson, *Greatest Show on Earth* (London, 1937).

——*Blood and Thunder* (London, 1949).

Donaldson, Frances, *The Actor Managers* (London, 1970).

Donohue, Joseph, *Theatre in the Age of Kean* (Totowa, NJ, 1975).

——(ed.), *The Cambridge History of the British Theatre*, 3 vols (Cambridge, 2004).

Doran, John, *Their Majesties Servants; or, Annals of the English Stage* (London, 1897).

Downer, Alan S., 'Players and the Painted Stage', *Modern Language Association of America*, 46 (1946), 522–76.

Duncan, Barry, *The St. James's Theatre, 1835–1957* (London, 1964).

Elkin, Robert, *The Old Concert Rooms of London* (London, 1955).

Emsley, Clive, Hitchcock, Tim and Shoemaker, Robert, 'London History – A Population History of London', Old Bailey Proceedings Online <http://www.oldbaileyonline.org>, version 7.0, accessed 27 November 2013.

Erle, Thomas William, *Letters from a Theatrical Scene-Painter* (London, 1880).

Everynight Book for 1826 (London, 1826).

Ferris, Lesley (ed.), *Crossing the Stage: Controversies on Cross-Dressing* (London, 1993).

Filon, Augustin, *The English Stage* (London, 1897).

Fisher, Judith L. and Watt, Stephen, *When They Weren't Doing Shakespeare* (Athens, GA and London, 1989).

Fitzball, Edward, *Thirty-Five Years of a Dramatic Author's Life*, 2 vols (London, 1859).

Fitzgerald, Percy, *The World Behind the Scene* (London, 1881).

——*A New History of the English Stage*, 2 vols (London, 1882).

Foote, Horace, *A Companion to the Theatre and Manual of the British Drama* (London, 1829).

Fumaroli, Marc, *When the World Spoke French*, tr. Richard Howard (New York, 2001).

Galt, John, *The Lives of the Players*, 2 vols (Boston, 1831).

Gamble, William Burt, *The Development of Scenic Art and Stage Machinery* (New York, 1920).

Ganzl, Kurt, *Encyclopedia of Musical Theatre* (Oxford, 1987).

Garber, Marjorie, *Vested Interests: Cross-Dressing and Cultural Anxiety* (New York, 1997).

Gayle, Maggie B. and Stokes, John (eds), *The Cambridge Companion to the Actress* (Cambridge, 2007).

Gilliland, Thomas, *The Dramatic Mirror* (London, 1808).

Godwin, Edward W., 'The Architecture and Costume of *The Merchant of Venice*', *The Architect*, 13 (27 March 1875).

Grant, James, *The Great Metropolis* (London, 1836).

Grove's Dictionary of Music and Musicians, ed. J.A. Fuller Maitland, 2nd edn, 5 vols (London, 1904–10).

Gustafson, Zadel, *Genevieve Ward* (London, n.d.).

Hamilton, Cicely and Baylis, Lilian, *The Old Vic* (New York, n.d.).

Hartnoll, Phyllis (ed.), *The Oxford Companion to the Theatre* (Oxford, 1967).

Hemming, F.W.J., *Theatre and State in France, 1760–1905* (Cambridge, 1994).

Highfill, Philip H., Jr, Burnim, Kalman A. and Langhans, Edward A. (eds), *A Biographical Dictionary of Actors, Actresses, Musicians, Dancers, Managers and other Stage Personnel in London, 1660–1800*, 16 vols (Carbondale, IL, 1973–93).

Hodgdon, Barbara and Worthen, William, *A Companion to Shakespeare and Performance* (New York, 2008).

House of Commons, *Report from the Select Committee on Dramatic Literature, with the Minutes of Evidence* (London, 1832).

Howard, Diana, *London Theatres and Music Halls, 1850–1950* (London, 1970).

Hughson, David, *Walks through London* (London, 1817).

Innes, Arthur D., *A History of the British Nation* (London, 1912).

Jackson, Allan S., *The Standard Theatre of Victorian England* (New Jersey, 1992).

Jackson, Russell (ed.), *Victorian Theatre* (London, 1989).

Kelly, Michael, *The Reminiscences of Michael Kelly*, 2 vols (London, 1826).

Kendal, Dame Madge, *Dramatic Opinions* (Boston, 1890).

——*Dame Madge Kendal by Herself* (London, 1933).

Knight, Charles, *Knight's Cyclopaedia of London* (London, 1851).

Knight, William G., *A Major London 'Minor': The Surrey Theatre, 1805–1865* (London, 1997).

Lambourne, Lionel, *The Aesthetic Movement* (Oxford, 1996).

Leacroft, Richard, *The Development of the English Playhouse* (London, 1973).

Leacroft, Richard and Leacroft, Helen, *Theatre and Playhouse* (London, 1984).

Lewes, George Henry, *On Actors and the Art of Acting* (London, 1875).

Lorenzen, Richard. 'Managers of the Old Prince of Wales's Theatre', *Theatre Notebook*, 24 (1969), 32–6.

——'The Old Prince of Wales's Theatre: A View of the Physical Structure', *Theatre Notebook*, 25 (1971), 132–45.

Macgeorge, A., *William Leighton Leitch, Landscape Painter. A Memoir* (London, 1844).

Mackie, W. Craven, 'The Bancrofts and Bancroft Repertory, 1865 to 1885', *Educational Theatre Journal*, 27/1 (1975), 98–110.

Macqueen-Pope, W.J., *Theatre Royal Drury Lane* (London, 1945).

——*Haymarket: Theatre of Perfection* (London, 1948).

Malcom, James Peller, *Anecdotes of the Manners and Customs of London* (London, 1808).

Mander, Raymond and Mitchenson, Joe, *The Lost Theatres of London* (London, 1968).

Manvell, Roger, *Ellen Terry* (New York, 1968).

Marsh, John, *The John Marsh Journals: Life and Times of a Gentleman Composer: 1752–1828*, ed. Brian Robins (Stuyvesant, NY, 1998).

Marshall, Thomas, *Lives of the Most Celebrated Actors and Actresses* (London, n.d.).

Marston, Westland, *Our Recent Actors*, 2 vols (London, 1888).

Maude, Cyril, *The Haymarket Theatre* (London, 1903).

Mayer, David, *Harlequin in His Element* (Cambridge, 1969).

Mayhew, Henry, *London Labour and the London Poor*, 3 vols (London, 1851).

Meer, Sarah, *Uncle Tom Mania: Slavery, Minstrelsy, and Transatlantic Culture in the 1850s* (Athens, GA, 2005).

Mekeel, Joyce, 'Social Influences on Changing Audience Behavior in the London Theatre, 1830–1880', PhD thesis (Boston University, 1983).

Merchant, W. Moelwyn, *Shakespeare and the Artist* (London, 1959).

Moody, Jane, 'Illusions of Authorship', in Davis and Donkin (eds), *Women and Playwriting in Nineteenth-Century Britain*.

——*Illegitimate Theatre in London, 1770–1840* (Cambridge, 2000).

Morley, Henry, *Journal of a London Playgoer* (London, 1866).

Morley, Malcom, *The Old Marylebone Theatre* (London, 1960).

Murray, Christopher, *Robert William Elliston, Manager* (London, 1975).

Nalbach, Daniel, *The King's Theatre, 1704–1867* (London, 1972).

Nicholson, Watson, *The Struggle for a Free Stage in London* (London, 1906).

Nicoll, Allardyce, *A History of the English Drama, 1660–1900*, 6 vols (Cambridge, 1965).

Oxberry, William, *Oxberry's Dramatic Biography and Historic Anecdotes* (London, 1826).

Oxford Dictionary of National Biography (*ODNB*) online (Oxford, 2004) <http://www.oxforddnb.com>.

Pascoe, Charles E., *Our Actors and Actresses: The Dramatic List*, rev. and enlarged edn (London, 1880).

Pemberton, T. Edgar, *The Life and Writings of T.W. Robertson* (London, 1893).

——*The Kendals: A Biography* (London, 1900).

Penley, Belville S., *The Bath Stage* (London, 1892).

Perkins, Jocelyn, *Westminster Abbey* (London, 1937).

Pindar, Peter [Dr John Wolcott], *The Works of Peter Pindar, Esq.*, 3 vols (London, 1794).

Playfair, Giles, *The Prodigy: A Study of the Strange Life of Master Betty* (London, 1967).

Porter, Jane and Porter, Anna Maria, *Coming Out; and the Field of Forty Footsteps*, 3 vols (London, 1828).

Powell, David, *William West and the Regency Toy Theatre* (London, 2004).

Powell, Kerry, *Women and Victorian Theatre* (Cambridge, 1997).

——(ed.), *The Cambridge Companion to the Victorian and Edwardian Theatre* (Cambridge, 2004).

'Prince of Wales's Theatre (c. 1870)', *Windsor*, 35 (1911).

Ranger, Paul, *'Terror and Pity reign in every Breast': Gothic Drama in the London Patent Theatres, 1750–1820* (London, 1991).

Rees, Abraham, *The Cyclopaedia; or Universal Dictionary*, 9 vols (London, 1819).

Reid, Erskine and Compton, Herbert, *The Dramatic Peerage, 1891–1892*, 2 vols (London, 1892).

Reynolds, Ernest, *Early Victorian Drama* (New York, 1965).

Rice, Charles, *The London Theatre in the Eighteen-Thirties*, ed. Arthur Colby Sprague and Bertram Shuttleworth (London, 1950).

Richards, Kenneth and Thomson, Peter, *Nineteenth-Century British Theatre* (London, 1971).

Richards, Leann, 'The Lost Art of Painting a Scene', *Stage Whispers* (July/August 2010), <http://www.Stagewhispers.com.au>.

Roberts, J.R. Howard and Godfrey, Walter H. (gen. eds), *Survey of London*, vol. 21: *Tottenham Court Road and Neighbourhood* (London, 1949).

Robertson, Thomas William Shafto, *The Principal Dramatic Works of T.W. Robertson with a Memoir by his Son*, 2 vols (London, 1889).

Robinson, Henry Crabb, *The London Theatre 1811–1866: Selections from the Diary of Henry Crabb Robinson*, ed. Eluned Brown (London, 1966).

Rosenfeld, Sybil, *The Theatre of the London Fairs in the 18th Century* (Cambridge, 1960).

Rowell, George, *Queen Victoria Goes to the Theatre* (London, 1978).

—— *The Victorian Theatre, 1792–1914: A Survey*, 2nd edn (Cambridge, 1978).

—— *William Terriss and Richard Prince: Two Characters in an Adelphi Melodrama* (London, 1987).

Russell, Gillian, *The Theatres of War, 1793–1815* (Oxford, 1995).

Savin, Maynard, *Thomas William Robertson* (Providence, RI, 1950).

Scott, Clement, *The Wheel of Life* (London, 1897).

—— *The Drama of Yesterday and Today*, 2 vols (London, 1899).

Scott, Walter (ed.), *The Monthly Chronicle of North-Country Lore and Legend* (London, 1889).

Senelick, Laurence, *The Changing Room* (London, 2000).

Shearer, Moira, *Ellen Terry* (New York, 1998).

Sheppard, F.H.W. (gen. ed.), *Survey of London*, vol. 35: *Theatre Royal, Drury Lane and The Royal Opera House, Covent Garden* (London, 1970).

Sherson, Erroll, *London's Lost Theatres of the Nineteenth Century* (London, 1925).

Slonimsky, Nicolas (ed.), *Baker's Biographical Dictionary of Musicians* (New York, 1958).

Southern, Richard, *Changeable Scenery* (London, 1948).

—— 'The Problem of A.B.'s Theatrical Drawings', *Theatre Notebook*, 4 (1949–50), 49–72.

—— *The Victorian Theatre* (London, 1970).

Speaight, George, *The History of the English Toy Theatre*, rev. edn (London, 1969).

Stedman, Jane W., *W.S. Gilbert: A Classic Victorian and his Theatre* (Oxford, 1966).

—— *W.S. Gilbert's Theatrical Cricitism* (London, 2000).

Stephens, John Russell, *The Censorship of English Drama, 1824–1901* (Cambridge, 1980).

—— *The Profession of the Playwright: British Theatre 1800–1900* (Cambridge, 1991).

Stirling, Edward, *Old Drury Lane* (London, 1881).

St Pancras Notes and Queries, Contributed by Various Hands to the St Pancras-Guardian (London 1903).

Taylor, George, *Players and Performances in the Victorian Theatre* (Manchester, 1989).

Terry, Ellen, *The Story of My Life* (New York, 1908).

The Thespian Dictionary; or Dramatic Biography of the Present Age, 2nd edn (London, 1805).

Timbs, John, *Curiosities of London*, new edn (London, 1868).

Toll, Robert C., *Blacking Up: The Minstrel Show in Nineteenth-Century America* (New York, 1974).

Tolles, Winton, *Tom Taylor and the Victorian Drama* (New York, 1940).

Vivian-Neal, Henry, *Their Exits* (London, 2012).

Vlock, Deborah, *Dickens, Novel Reading and the Victorian Popular Theatre* (Cambridge, 1988).

Ward, Geneviève and Whiteing, Richard, *Both Sides of the Curtain* (London, 1918).

Waters, Hazel, *Racism on the Victorian Stage* (Cambridge, 2007).

Watson, Ernest Bradlee, *Sheridan to Robertson: A Study of the Nineteenth-Century London Stage*, 2nd edn (New York, 1963).

West, E.J., 'From a Player's to a Playwright's Theatre: The London Stage, 1870–90', *Quarterly Journal of Speech*, 27 (1942), 430–6.

Wewitzer, R., *A Brief Dramatic Chronology of Actors on the London Stage* (London, 1817).

White, Henry A., *Sir Walter Scott's Novels on the Stage* (New Haven, CT, 1927).

Wilkinson, Robert, *Londina Illustrata* (London, 1819).

Williams, Clifford John, *Madame Vestris: A Theatrical Biography* (London, 1973).

Williamson, Jane, *Charles Kemble: Man of the Theatre* (Lincoln, NE, 1964).

Wilson, A.E., *The Lyceum* (London, 1952).

Wilton, Frederick C., *The Britannia Diaries, 1863–1875: Selections from the Diaries of Frederick C. Wilton*, ed. Jim Davis (London, 1992).

Winston, James, *Drury Lane Journal: Selections from James Winston's Diaries, 1819–1827*, ed. Alfred L. Nelson and Gilbert B. Cross (London, 1974).

Winter, James, *London's Teeming Streets, 1830–1914* (London, 1993).

Wright, Thomas, *The Works of James Gillray, the Caricaturist with the Story of his Life and Times* (London, 1873).

Wright, Thomas and Evans, R.H., *Historical and Descriptive Account of the Caricature of James Gillray* (London, 1851).

Wyndham, Henry Saxe, *The Annals of Covent Garden Theatre*, 2 vols (London, 1906).

Newspapers and periodicals

The Age
Athenaeum
British Stage and Literary Cabinet
Builder
Daily Chronicle
Daily Courant
Daily News
Daily Telegraph
The Drama; or, Theatrical Pocket Magazine
Dramatic Magazine
The Era
Examiner

Figaro in London
Gentleman's Magazine
Illustrated London News
Illustrated Sporting and Dramatic News
Illustrated Sporting and Theatrical News
Illustrated Times
Literary Beacon
Lloyd's Weekly Newspaper
London Magazine
London Standard
Mirror of the Stage; or, New Dramatic Censor
Morning Advertiser
Morning Chronicle and London Advertiser
Morning Post
New Monthly Magazine
The News
Pall Mall Gazette
Punch
Reynolds's Newspaper
Sheffield Daily Telegraph
The Stage; or Theatrical Inquisitor
Tallis's Dramatic Magazine
The Theatre
Theatrical Examiner
Theatrical Journal, and Stranger's Guide
Theatrical Observer and Daily Bills of the Play
Theatrical Repertory; or, Weekly Rosciad
Theatrical Times
The Times
The Town
Walker's Quarterly

Special collections
Bristol: University of Bristol Theatre Collection: The Mander and Mitchinson Theatre Collection
British Library Theatre Cuttings: 8–11, 60–2, 64 and 66–74.
Cambridge, MA: Houghton Library, Harvard University: Harvard Theatre Collection
Columbus: Ohio State University: The Lawrence and Lee Theatre Collection
London: British Library: 17th and 18th Century Burney Collection Database
London: Holborn Public Library: Camden Local Studies and Archives Centre:

Heal Collection (abbreviated HC)
St Pancras Rate Books
London: London Metropolitan Archive: British National Newspaper Archive
London: Metropolitan Board of Works: minutes of meetings of the Theatre and Music Hall Sub-Committee
London: Victoria and Albert Museum: Theatre and Performance Collection (abbreviated V&A)
New York: New York Public Library Digital Gallery: Billy Rose Theatre Collection

Index